W9-BCZ-919

POPULAR ETHICS
IN ANCIENT GREECE

BY THE SAME AUTHOR

Early Ionian Historians
The Local Historians of Attica
The Lost Histories of Alexander the Great

POPULAR ETHICS IN ANCIENT GREECE

Lionel Pearson

STANFORD UNIVERSITY PRESS

STANFORD, CALIFORNIA

1962

Stanford University Press
Stanford, California

Library of Congress Catalog Card Number: 61-16885

Printed in the United States of America

ACKNOWLEDGMENT

A year's leave of absence from my teaching duties made it possible for me to start serious work on this book in the academic year 1957–58. I am deeply indebted to Stanford University for this privilege of a sabbatical year and to the John Simon Guggenheim Foundation which granted me a fellowship for this period. It is also a pleasure to acknowledge my gratitude to the Institute for Advanced Study at Princeton, which made me a member of its company of scholars for the first term of that year, and to the American School of Classical Studies at Athens, which extended hospitality to me in late winter and spring. The Stanford University Press has given me constant encouragement at all stages of my work, and I am most happy to express my appreciation to all its staff members whose good will and skilful co-operation have contributed so much to this book.

L. P.

ACKNOWLEDGMENTS

[illegible]

CONTENTS

POPULAR ETHICS
IN ANCIENT GREECE

INTRODUCTION

This book is a study of Greek ethical thought; it is an attempt to discover how the Greeks who were not philosophers reasoned with themselves and argued with others over ethical issues. It is not a study of Greek society or an attempt to describe Greek attitudes towards particular questions or obligations within the family or the community; it is not, therefore, directly concerned with such matters as sexual morality or business ethics or the practice of law or diplomacy, except in so far as particular instances may be valid to establish general principles or standards in judging conduct and character. Nor is it a history of Greek ethics. It is concerned mainly with the Athenians of the fifth century, for the obvious reason that we know much more about them than about the members of any other ancient Greek community, earlier or later. Periclean Athens is, in very many ways, the central point of all Greek civilization. If we did not possess the histories of Herodotus and Thucydides and the plays of the great Athenian dramatists, it is hard to see how we could begin to understand what it was like to live in an ancient city-state; we would not even know what the subjects were that Greeks liked to discuss among themselves, or on what questions they agreed or agreed to differ, far less the manner in which they argued or the terms they used.

The fifth century in Athens was a period of exceptional literary activity and artistic brilliance, and its achievements in art and literature give us an insight into its intellectual and emotional life such as is scarcely possible in any other period of history in any country before the seventeenth century. At other moments of history we know as much or more about the intellectual ferment in particular groups or particular classes of the community, but the history of fifth-century Athens shows an apparent sharing of intellectual and artistic interests among all branches of the population. There is no question of a division of interest between one kind or quality of art and another. It is not like ancient Rome, where the rabble that was enthusiastic about the circus and the gladiatorial contests was oblivious to the interests of Seneca and Lucan. On the contrary, as we learn from Aristophanes—a writer of successful and popular comedies, and a fine artist besides—the politics and poetry and thought of the age were discussed by everyone alike; politicians and poets and thinkers were not unsuitable characters for the comedies that were presented at the great dramatic festivals. Unlike the scholars of Alexandria in the third century, the poets of fifth-century Athens wrote for the general public of their city; they were not writing for a court circle or a learned coterie or a discontented minority. It is for this reason that modern scholars feel themselves justified in reconstructing the current opinions and the prevailing intellectual atmosphere of Periclean Athens.

There is no other city or epoch in the ancient world for which a similar claim can be made. Athenian writers—notably Thucydides and Euripides—warn us that the intellectual climate was different in Sparta; and the variation in political and social sentiment is well illustrated, for example, by the Old Oligarch in the pseudo-Xenophontic *Constitution of Athens*. But other cities do not speak for themselves as Athens does; where literary activity is less intense than in Athens, it is scarcely possible to make even a useful conjecture about current opinion.[1]

The half-century that ends with the collapse of the Athenian empire in 404 B.C. is a magnificent and terrifying period of his-

[1] Superscript numbers refer to the Notes, pp. 207–54.

tory. Thucydides shows us the heights and depths of which it was capable, from the splendid pride and confident righteousness of the Funeral Oration of Pericles to the mean and degrading heartlessness of the Melian Dialogue, in which the Athenian spokesmen are made to admit that they care nothing for any principle of morality; they warn the unfortunate Melians that it will be waste of time for them to make any appeals to pity or idealism. Athens was a democracy in which no citizen was allowed to shirk his civic responsibility; all had to take their turn at making decisions and upholding or rejecting principles, whether in the assembly, the council, or the law courts. One could hardly expect an artificial or antiquated system of ethics to survive under such severe strain. Tradition alone would not be enough to keep it alive, and there was no authority either of the state or of religion to prolong its life in the face of public opinion; one might expect something like an ethical revolution as part of the consequences of the political crisis.

Yet despite the terrible upheaval of the Peloponnesian War, there was no radical change in the religious customs or the system of education in the century that followed. Sacrifice was still offered to the same gods, and wealthy men were still found to maintain their temples. Boys were still expected to study the poems of Homer and learn the same lessons from them. The sanctity of the gods' holy places, the respect for oaths sworn in their name, the admiration for the old heroes, still continued; the great crisis of the fifth century did not cause an open breach with the religious traditions of the past, and any suggestion of such a breach would have been opposed just as fiercely in the fourth century as in the fifth.

There were irregularities, of course. Many an Athenian parent must have found it hard to explain to his son why the Athenians gave active support to the Phocians, who financed their war against Thebes by plundering Apollo's treasure in Delphi.[2] In due time, however, the Phocians were defeated and suffered a terrible and humiliating punishment, when Philip of Macedon, the interloper from the north, turned against them. They were obliged to repay in instalments the money they had stolen; but eventually they were allowed to redeem themselves, to make atonement and recover their self-respect and their position in the Greek world. And even though Athens did support the Phocians, we shall search Greek literature and Greek documents in vain for any explicit approval of the Phocian sacrilegious behaviour. There is no permanent disregard for the sanctity of Apollo's temple. Despite the growth of philosophic schools, despite new developments in religion, despite the keen intellectual life and vigour of the Greek world, the old traditions do not die. Perhaps a man, if asked to explain why he made sacrifice to Apollo or why he consulted the oracle, might not give the same answer as his grandfather; but it would be just as serious a breach of good manners to ask him the question in the later fourth century as a hundred years before. It may be impossible at any period of Greek history to determine the exact quality or the dogmatic detail of religious faith. But of its reality and vitality and its ability to survive temporary lapses and outbreaks of impiety we have abundant evidence.

We have to rely on the philosophers and the orators for our understanding of the intellectual life of the fourth century. Unluckily for us, the numerous histories and tragedies written in this century have largely disappeared; the works of Xenophon and the fragments of Menander (which are happily increasing in number) do not offer evidence comparable in quantity or quality to what we find in the historians and dramatists of the fifth century. It is, therefore, hardly possible to speak of popular thought as distinctly as can be done in the time of Herodotus and Sophocles. Indeed, Plato and Aristotle take us into what is almost a different world, the world of the philosophers, a curious society in which we never know how many members there may be at any one time; we are often left wondering whether Plato is speaking only for himself and a handful of fellow philosophers or for a substantial section of his fellow Athenians. The Ionian philosophers, it is scarcely necessary to say, so far as they discussed ethics at all, discussed it in quite different terms from those used by the historians and dramatists. And the professional philosophers who attracted attention in Periclean Athens—the sophists as they were called—used methods of argument and even styles of writing that can be generally distinguished from the more popular style of their non-philosophical contemporaries. In the fifth century we can claim to know a good deal about current ideas on ethics; we can distinguish the new from the traditional, the heterodox from the orthodox. It would be rash to make a similar claim for the fourth century.

This is the best apology that I can offer to a reader who is disappointed that this book does not go beyond the fifth century. Aristotle, in a famous sentence in the *Poetics,* speaks of tragedy "realizing itself" or "reaching its natural fulfilment" in the fifth century. Perhaps this means not that tragedy exhausted its possibilities with Sophocles and Euripides or that nothing was left for their successors to add, but that these successors, so far as Aristotle knew them, did not in fact make any significant additions.

Something similar might be said about popular ethics. Xenophon and the orators of the fourth century, on whom we must depend for non-philosophic thought in their time, often corroborate what we can learn from fifth-century writers but add very little that is new. The critical initiative seems to have passed to the philosophers; even Menander's occasional new contributions can usually be traced to a philosophic source. With the foundations of the famous schools of philosophy at Athens—the Garden and the Stoa as well as the Academy—philosophy comes to be part of the intellectual equipment of the ordinary educated man; two centuries later, Polybius, the next historian whose work has been preserved in bulk, not only has a knowledge of philosophy but takes for granted that it is shared by his readers. Thucydides and Euripides, certainly, are aware of what the sophists were saying in their time, but they do not parade their knowledge; and orators like Lysias and Demosthenes carefully avoid doing so, since it was considered imprudent to let the jury think that one's client had "new-fangled ideas."

Although the main emphasis in the chapters that follow is on the fifth century and no formal attempt will be made to describe the history of Greek ethics as an orderly and logical development, some discussion of Homer and Hesiod and other early Greek poets is necessary, in order to show the traditional background of later thought and the heritage that later ages received, whether by way of family teaching handed on from one generation to another or by the study of literature. The evidence for ethical ideas in earlier centuries is by no means as full or as clear as it is for the fifth century, and it cannot be said that the earlier poets present plentiful evidence of the kind of moral uncertainty and scepticism that the Attic drama reveals.

Some modern writers have therefore drawn the conclusion that earlier ages did not question traditional teachings and were scarcely aware that such things as moral problems existed. They have tried to present the history of thought in ancient times as an orderly evolution, divided into definite stages by great discoveries; and they have seized upon the fifth century as the first period of moral awakening, when man became conscious of his freedom to make decisions and first recognized the possibility of a conflict of obligations. They have maintained that only then did he start to seek answers to problems of conduct in himself and his own reason rather than in the authority of religion and tradition.[3] This hypothesis may appeal to those students of antiquity who conceive of ancient history mainly as a conflict between the individual and a higher authority, and who take it for granted that intellectual development in ancient Greece followed a similar pattern to the intellectual evolution of Europe since the seventeenth century. These are very considerable assumptions and not to be taken lightly. An even more serious weakness in this theory than its acceptance of the historical analogy is its confusion of the history of thought with the history of literature. The early poets are not historians, they are limited in their selection of themes by literary tradition and convention; no one expects them to offer a complete record of the life and thought of their times.

Early Greek poetry does not, in fact, offer the best starting point for a discussion of Greek ethics. It has seemed preferable to begin with the doubts and uncertainties of the fifth century, which are presented to us in the most concentrated form by Plato in the first two books of the *Republic.* This should prepare the way for an examination of the type of thinking that is found in Homer and the other early Greek poets, where (naturally enough) the terminology is different and demands a fairly detailed study. In the *Republic,* as in Thucydides, ethical argument is centred upon justice and the just man's recognition of his duty. Homer's characters use a different language; they recognize man's separate obligations—to excel, to observe due moderation, and to respect his fellow men—but they are not concerned to reconcile obligations when they appear to be in conflict with one another. With Hesiod, Solon, and Theognis, justice gradually takes its place in the centre of the argument, and in the fifth century all other issues are dwarfed by the one great question: "What is justice?"—except for people who evade answering it by saying it does not exist or is too simple to need an answer or that man is making a mistake to bother himself with such matters.

ONE. Greek Popular Ethics—A Sketch

What common characteristics did the Greeks share which set them apart from barbarians, as they called their neighbours, and despite their lack of political unity, gave them the right to be considered a people—the Hellenic *ethnos,* formally divided into three branches, Ionian, Dorian, and Aeolian? The question is old and familiar, and so are the answers. The Greeks had a common language for one thing; their separate dialects did not develop into separate languages, so that there was no linguistic barrier between one city-state and another and little incentive to learn a foreign language. With their common language they developed and fostered a common literature, distinct and separate from anything that other languages had to offer. They also developed a common artistic tradition, not insulated from outside influences, but never dominated by them. They worshipped, or at least recognized, the same gods. This statement deserves qualification, particularly when early times are concerned, since individual gods and goddesses took on different aspects in different cities. The Artemis of Ephesus, for example, with her famous temple, is very different from the huntress Artemis, the virgin goddess of the forests who is familiar in both Greek and Latin poetry; and the martial Aphrodite of Corinth seems more like Athena than the Aphrodite that we know from Homer and the tragic poets.[1] But just as the different dialects never became different languages, so the different aspects or local variations of a divinity never developed into different gods or goddesses; and as the city-states grew and came to know one another better, they tended to give a similar outward form to the expression of their religion. Recognition of a common religion did not prevent the Greeks from fighting with one another, even on religious grounds in defence of the dignity or the property of a god or goddess; but it made agreements and treaties more possible when they respected oaths sworn in the name of a recognized god,[2] and when they feared the anger of that god if they damaged his property in the territory of an enemy. They also had numerous customs in common, a Greek way of life which they treasured, common social traditions and conventions; and despite obvious differences in political arrangements between one city and another, they shared as their special political treasure their belief in the institution of the independent, self-governing city-state.

All these answers to the old question are familiar enough. But another answer, which is sometimes added as an afterthought, is that the Greeks had a common ethical heritage, a common basis of morality and moral values.[3] This is easy to say and difficult to contradict, but it is not so easy to say readily in what this common basis of morality consisted. It is not an adequate explanation to say that acts considered immoral or unjust in one city would be considered equally reprehensible in another, because that kind of practical agreement can be explained in terms of social tradition without recourse to ethics at all. A common ethical tradition should mean that with respect to important moral issues the Greeks thought alike as well as acted alike. Is it fair to say this, within limits and with due regard for the influence of exceptional circumstances?

One might well hesitate before agreeing. Any statement beginning "the Greeks thought" is likely to be little better than a half-truth if it is based on the word of a single Greek author. And although Greek literature abounds in proverbs and aphorisms which are not the property of any single author or century or city, an attempt to construct a system of thought from them is unlikely to have much value. It is naïve to suppose that aphorisms are anything but the vaguest of counsels.[4] It might be said that Greek literature shows us clearly enough what qualities the Greeks admired, and one can point to these qualities, using the Greek words and attempting to explain their meaning by a careful series of alternate translations: *arete,* the true excellence of man, distinction, virtue, the bravery of a fighting man; *sophrosyne,* sound-mindedness, prudence, self-control; *dikaiosyne,* justice—whatever exactly that means. But since these are qualities that everyone admires, though often without being able to define them, a mere list of this sort will not teach us very much about the Greeks. We are no better off for knowing that they respected moral platitudes which are still current in our own time; and we cannot be satisfied to believe that they failed to distinguish between moral platitudes and serious thought.

On the other hand, it might be argued that an analysis of classical Greek literature will not really show what current thought was, but will merely reveal the ethical conventions of a literary tradition. Perhaps the best way to meet this objection is to make a comparison with Latin literature. The Romans are often represented as more easily satisfied with moral platitudes than the Greeks; and some people are content to regard the conventional Roman as pompous and self-satisfied with his *gravitas* and *humanitas* and *magnitudo animi.* The fact is that many Latin writers were taught a kind of mechanical morality and psychology in the rhetorical schools, which was useful as a resource for the public speaker, but it does not follow that the public utterances of the Romans always bore a close resemblance to what they thought as individuals.[5] And writings of professional rhetoricians, like the *Suasoriae* of the elder Seneca, may be very treacherous guides. Furthermore, Latin writers laboured under the difficulty of reconciling their conventional ideas with the teachings of Greek philosophy. It is amusing to speculate what happened when a conventional young Roman, who was sent to study philosophy at Athens, tried to explain, in Greek, what he meant by qualities like *gravitas.* Or did Greek teachers of philosophy pay no attention to the current ways of Latin speech and oblige their Roman pupils to put aside their native ways of thinking and adopt the Greek pattern?

Greek literature, however, unlike Latin, is a purely native growth, and until the fifth century there is no influence of philosophical or rhetorical training to be expected. Even in Euripides the links with earlier literature are stronger than with the sophists of his own day. The extraneous and artificial elements which might mislead an unwary reader of Latin literature are absent in classical Greek prose and poetry. Isocrates insisted that a Greek was a Greek not by virtue of his birth, but because of his *paideia,* his upbringing and education. And this education was overwhelmingly literary. Whether by their intention or not, the poets were the teachers of Greece until the sophists and philosophers took over their task. It was from his reading of Homer that the young Athenian in the Periclean age was first made to think about the why and wherefore of human conduct; and it was his reading of Homer and the poets of archaic Greece that fitted him to understand the moral issues which were presented by the great tragedians of the fifth century.[6]

Again the objection will perhaps be made that this literary background is extraneous to real life, that the common man who has not enjoyed the benefit of a literary education will not think along the same lines as the educated man, and that even the educated man may not think along these lines except when he is concerned with literature. But an unanswerable reply to this objection is provided by the tremendous popularity of the Attic drama, as shown, for example, by the constant references to it in the Old Comedy, which certainly sought the attention of the common man. Such popularity is not intelligible unless there were very large numbers who were interested in the plays and who must have understood something of the issues involved in them. It does not follow that tragic characters are always represented as thinking in the same terms as the average Athenian; the Ajax of Sophocles is an example of a character who would be absurdly out of place in Periclean Athens. But it was said of Euripides, whether in praise or criticism, that his characters were like ordinary men,[7] and some of them, such as Electra's rustic husband in the *Electra* or the Nurse in the *Hippolytus,* are intended as ordinary uneducated men and women. Does their mode of thinking differ greatly from that of the characters in Sophocles and Aeschylus? If it does not, if they are concerned with the same issues and argue in the same terms, we are then entitled to believe that we can learn something about popular ethics from any Greek tragedy. And if the same type of argument is to be found in the historians, particularly in speeches assigned to historical characters on issues that must have concerned the historian's contemporaries, then there is some hope of establishing valid conclusions about the ethical thought current in fifth-century Athens.

Despite the wealth of material that historians and dramatists have to offer, the most natural starting point for a discussion of Greek popular ethics is in the first two books of Plato's *Republic*. The main purpose of the *Republic,* in terms of ethics, is to show how justice can be realized in a state and in an individual; and, before the main constructive task of designing the ideal state is attempted, it is considered necessary to show that the ordinary, unphilosophic individual is incapable of the task, that he lacks the necessary knowledge, since real justice is unattainable without a knowledge of reality. It might be doubted whether any such conclusion is actually established in the first two books, and hence there has been some uncertainty among scholars about Plato's precise purpose in writing them. If they are taken by themselves, it must be admitted that they do not show very clearly in what respect the ordinary man lacks the necessary knowledge; indeed, the precise nature of his ignorance cannot be recognized until the difference between appearance and reality and between knowledge and opinion has been explained—that is, until the Platonic theory of ideas has been set forth in full detail. It is arguable, perhaps, that Plato might have set forth his epistemological theories first and then proceeded to show that the ordinary man was incapable of knowledge.

Such an arrangement would certainly be less effective and provide a less satisfactory dramatic structure for the dialogue, but to the purely philosophic reader the discussion in the first two books, before Socrates himself begins to develop the principal theme, appears a scarcely necessary part of the *Republic*. It contains too many logical flaws, and it merely leads to a conclusion which the philosopher would be prepared to grant without much hesitation—that popular thinking is imprecise and confused. But its historical value is very great indeed. It reinforces the lessons to be learnt from the dramatists and historians of the fifth century; it shows even more clearly than they do the methods and patterns of Greek ethical thought in the second part of the fifth century. The dramatic date of the *Republic* is deliberately chosen; the discussion is supposed to take place in the closing years of the Peloponnesian War, at a time when traditional ethics was struggling to maintain itself in the face of many difficulties. It was a time when men often thought they knew, in general terms, what was right, but found themselves unwilling or unable to make their behaviour conform to a traditional pattern, and when attempts to argue either for or against the tradition seemed to satisfy no one.

Without evidence from other sources it would be hardly fair to draw this conclusion from the *Republic* alone or from Plato alone. The earlier dialogues, in which we find puzzled young men becoming more and more puzzled and receiving very little enlightenment, might be interpreted simply as evidence of Plato's own uncertainties. But we have only to turn to Thucydides to see that Plato (or perhaps we may say Socrates) was not alone in his uncertainty. When the Athenians first decided to massacre the people of Mytilene in punishment for their rebellion and then changed their mind, the historian evidently thought that some kind of ethical thinking must have motivated both the first and the second decision; but he succeeds only in making the merciful decision appear just as discreditable as the savage one. And when, a few years later, the savage decision is taken to massacre the Melians, he shows the Athenians quite unable to justify their action. So also the behaviour of Alcibiades and the behaviour of the Athenians towards Alcibiades present apparently insoluble problems. The belligerent parties in the war, as time goes on, seem to understand less and less clearly their reasons for behaving as they do.

Nevertheless, when they are shown making a serious attempt to explain their behaviour, they do so either in traditional terms or else by denying and perverting traditional terms. The ethics of revolution, as described by Thucydides in his famous chapters inspired by the revolution in Corcyra (iii.82–83), offers nothing new; the terms are old, though their application may be different. The Athenians at Melos simply refuse to listen to any arguments based on general principles (v.87). Diodotus, who proposes to spare the Mytilenians (iii.42–48), abandons any attempt to prove that justice is on his side and is content with arguments from expediency. In other speeches the old familiar arguments occur over and over again: that the behaviour of one state towards another must be guided by its sense of obligation to an ally or its right to take vengeance—to do good to its friends and harm its enemies, as Polemarchus argues in the first book of the *Republic*.[8]

Plato grew up during the Peloponnesian War, and he chooses the ethical atmosphere of his youth as the background for most of his dialogues. Thus, he gives us the kind of survey that none of the fifth-century writers can provide; he offers a particularly good introduction to the study of popular ethics because he tells us what to look for.

In the opening scene of the *Republic*, Polemarchus, the son of Cephalus, detains Socrates and his companions in the Piraeus and insists that they come to his father's house for entertainment and conversation. The elderly Cephalus makes only a brief appearance before leaving the company of younger men to their own devices; but the few remarks that he makes are supposed to be typical of the traditional attitude of the older generation. Plato shows quite clearly that Cephalus is intended to represent conservative and traditional opinion. He is preparing to offer a sacrifice to the gods, and when he leaves the company he goes to carry out the sacrifice (331d); the others show no interest in or concern for his religious duties. He quotes Pindar, the poet of an older generation, rather than Euripides or Sophocles. He does not regret his career as an honest businessman, and now that the end of his life is not far off, he is happy to think that he has cheated no one and has met his obligations to men and gods. He takes it for granted that such behaviour is properly described as just; but when invited to say whether justice may actually be defined as "telling the truth and giving back what one has received," he is content to leave further discussion to the younger men.

Cephalus has nothing to say about the positive contributions and special obligations of a superior and privileged citizen, which Socrates will attempt to describe and explain in the later discussion. Socrates asks him what he considers the chief advantage he has gained by being a wealthy man, and instead of describing any services he has rendered to the state by virtue of his position, he is content to point out the happiness of a clear conscience. His conception of justice is extremely limited in comparison with the ideal that Socrates will expound in the later books. He thinks of it in mainly negative terms; and it appears that his son, Polemarchus, has inherited his attitude, for when asked if he agrees with the definition of justice which his father has found acceptable, he says: "Yes, if we can believe Simonides," substituting another of the older poets in place of Pindar. "He says that it is just to return to each man what is due to him; and I think that he is quite right to say so" (331e).

When pressed for interpretation and explanation of what Simonides means by "due," Polemarchus soon comes out with another traditional definition of justice: "doing good to one's friends and harming one's enemies." But he is helpless in face of the cross-examination to which Socrates subjects him (which will not be described here), and has apparently not considered previously that justice should serve any general purpose beyond meeting particular situations. A more skilful dialectician than Polemarchus might have questioned the analogy with the arts and sciences that Socrates invites him to accept.[9] But it is apparent that he is not prepared to answer the fundamental question: What is the real object of justice? What benefit can the just man render to the community as a whole? This does not mean he rejects the idea that a just man improves his fellow men and confers a moral benefit on them. Believing as he does that poets are teachers of justice and consequently just men themselves in a high degree, Polemarchus grants very readily the assumption that just men are moral teachers, and that their prime obligation is the moral improvement of the community. Faced, then, with the suggestion that the just man should not harm anyone, he is forced to admit that the traditional definition of justice is untenable. He is not imaginative enough to recognize that what Socrates means by justice is something quite different from the limited conception of it which he has been taught by his father. He will not even say (as he should) that the traditional definition has some value as a practical guide to conduct, or that it has in fact guided the conduct of many unimaginative and unambitious people, who are content to think in terms of particular circumstances, not in terms of ideals.

We are not concerned here with the logical validity of the argument with which Socrates claims to refute Polemarchus. It could perhaps be maintained that the refutation is deliberately brief and inadequate, indeed almost frivolous, because the readers for whom the *Republic* was intended had long recognized the weakness of the traditional definition, "helping one's friends and harming one's enemies." It was not necessary for Plato to remind readers how widely held this definition was and how commonly people referred to it in justification of their conduct. The historians and dramatists explain conduct so constantly by reference to this definition of justice that its popularity as an accepted guide to behaviour in the fifth century cannot be questioned.

In treaties of alliance it was usual for the parties concerned to swear that they would have the same friends and enemies. In this way a definite relation was established between states; and the obligation resulted to help or refuse help if any one of the new friends or enemies should stand in need of it.[10] A relation of friendship or enmity could equally well be established by an initial friendly or unfriendly act. One could make a friend by doing or receiving a favour, and whoever received the favour was bound to return it;[11] if either party denied or evaded the obligation, the act of neglect was considered an injustice and a reasonable ground for dissolving the friendship. Herodotus supplies numerous examples of this point of view in international relations. It is taken for granted that a favour must be returned, and ingratitude is the commonest kind of injustice that changes a friendly relationship into a hostile one. In the *Prometheus* Aeschylus shows Prometheus complaining bitterly that his punishment at the hands of Zeus is unjust; he has conferred a great benefit on Zeus, and Zeus, in his opinion, is grossly ungrateful and treacherous to him. In Thucydides, when the people of Mytilene revolt from Athens (which is supposed to be a friendly state, since they are both members of the Delian League and should share common friends and enemies), the Mytilenian speaker justifies their behaviour on the ground that the Athenians have not treated them like friends; thus, they argue, their apparent treachery and ingratitude to Athens is not really an unjust act. In Euripides, to take only one example, Hecuba complains bitterly of Odysseus that he is like a demagogue who is prepared without scruple to harm his friends, sacrificing them if he can please the multitude (*Hecuba* 256–57).

It will be shown in greater detail in subsequent chapters how well aware people in Athens were of the weakness of this traditional definition of justice, but that they nonetheless claimed to respect it as a guide to conduct. Popular ethics does not abandon a traditional precept simply because it is found to be not universally applicable. But for Plato a definition is worthless unless it is absolutely and universally valid. Furthermore, popular ethics regards a man as just if his motivation is good, if he does what he thinks will benefit the man whom he thinks to be his friend (unless, of course, his opinion appears quite untenable to others). Plato would not agree, since he would refuse to recognize as justice any action that was not based on knowledge; justice in the Platonic sense is therefore a rare virtue. In the *Gorgias* Plato refuses to admit that rhetoricians are truly powerful with the community, on the ground that the recommendations they urge on the assembly are only what they think to be best either for themselves or for the people. They convince their hearers that a certain course of action will benefit them and contrive to make them happy with their decision. Plato calls this a form of flattery. So also he might have argued in the *Republic* that a man who ostensibly helps a friend is generally only pleasing or flattering him, not really helping him at all. For Plato motivation is a matter of small importance compared with real knowledge and finality; for popular judgment it matters almost more than anything else.

The importance of intention and motivation is equally clear in the definition of justice which Thrasymachus, the "angry young man," has to offer. He is irritated by the argument between Socrates and Polemarchus and the apparent unwillingness of Socrates to reveal any positive opinions of his own. The argument seems quite worthless to him, because he has abandoned the idea that justice has anything to do with friendship. In his first definition he represents justice as entirely a matter of the law; and since, in his view, the laws in any state are established by the governing class in such a way as to serve its own interest, he considers that justice or obedience to the law can be defined as serving the interest of the stronger; that it is fear, not good will, which makes people comply with the law when it is against their interest to do so.[12]

When Polemarchus began his discussion with Socrates, he

thought of a just man wanting to help anyone whom he thought to be his friend. But Socrates talked him out of this by reminding him that an apparent friend may in reality be an enemy, and finally persuaded him to admit that he meant not an apparent friend, but a real friend and a good man. Once this change was made in the definition, the original meaning and point of it—the stress on motivation—was lost, and Polemarchus was no longer sure of himself or able to maintain his argument. Socrates tries to break down the resistance of Thrasymachus by following the same procedure with him. As conceived by Thrasymachus, the helpless citizen, who obeys the law, supposes that he is doing what the ruling classes want. He has to obey whether the law is in fact advantageous to the rulers or not, but he does what he thinks will benefit them, in the same way as the original just man of Polemarchus does what he thinks will benefit his friend. Socrates points out that rulers may make mistakes and pass laws which are not in fact in their interest, and asks if it is still a just act to obey such laws. Thrasymachus falls into the trap. He pretends that he saw the difficulty himself; he says that when he speaks of "the stronger" or "the ruler" he means the perfectly expert ruler who knows his business. But once he has shifted his ground in this way, the whole point of his original definition is lost. He, too, has abandoned the emphasis on motivation.

The argument that follows is inconclusive, because the "perfectly expert ruler" means for Thrasymachus the ruler who works in his own interest, while for Socrates it means the ruler who considers the interest of his subjects. Thrasymachus ridicules Socrates for not accepting facts as they are; actual rulers, he says, are not altruistic, but (like shepherds) are concerned only that their flock shall serve them; they seek their own advantage, and so long as they have their own way, their behaviour must be called unjust. It is only the subjects, compelled to seek the advantage of others, who act justly. Justice means loss; injustice means gain. He is sure of his opinion, and has no wish to discuss the matter further (344d).

It is only after the violent outburst of Thrasymachus, when he would have left if the others had not compelled him to remain, that Socrates agrees (outwardly, at least) to argue with him on his own terms. He questions the validity of his attitude towards justice as a practical guide to conduct. The outburst of Thrasymachus showed that his definition of justice was not greatly different from the original definition of Polemarchus; he agreed that it consisted in benefitting those who expected or claimed the right to be benefitted. Although he offers the formal definition of justice as "the good of somebody else," he does not equate justice with kindness or universal good will any more than Polemarchus does. The difference between them is that Thrasymachus does not recognize any valid obligation to benefit anyone, whether friends or rulers or anyone else, because in his opinion the intelligent man will always consult his own interest. The contrast between "the just" (τὸ δίκαιον) and "the expedient" (τὸ συμφέρον) is a recognized commonplace in all discussions of conduct in the fifth century. Socrates intends to show that the contrast is a false one, but this object is not immediately recognized by the others, who assume that the subject of discussion has changed and that the question at issue now is not the nature of justice, but the relative importance, for practical purposes, of "the just" and "the expedient" (which Thrasymachus identified with "the unjust"). It was not necessary for Polemarchus to say that his preference was for "the just" when there was any question of choice between justice and expediency; Socrates takes it for granted that this would be his choice, and that Thrasymachus is the only person present who would consistently prefer expediency to justice.

The attitude of Thrasymachus is far more extreme than that of the ordinary worldly cynic who insists a man should be guided by considerations of expediency rather than justice. He will not admit even that justice is a virtue or an excellence; and though he does not go so far as to call it a vice, he calls it a kind of stupidity or simple-mindedness (εὐήθεια) and identifies injustice with prudence or wise counsel (εὐβουλία). Rather unexpectedly, however, he accepts the analogy with the arts and sciences that Socrates proposes, and by admitting that injustice has neither method nor consistency nor stability puts himself in an untenable position. And since injustice involves deceit and mutual distrust and provides no basis for collaboration, it is shown to be impossible as a rule of government. Glaucon, however, when Thrasymachus withdraws, quite rightly reminds Socrates that he has not really dealt with the more generally current cynical view of justice, namely that it is not a desirable end in itself, but acceptable as a means because of the results which follow from it; that since crime in the long run does not pay, men generally accept justice as a compromise between a successful life of perfect injustice (which they cannot hope to pursue) and an unsuccessful life as helpless victims of other people's injustice. As the argument proceeds, it becomes evident that most people are more concerned with appearing just or acquiring a reputation for justice than with real justice.[13] And so the way is gradually prepared for the central argument of the whole dialogue—the difference between appearance and reality and the relative importance and value of each.

The extreme immoralist attitude of Thrasymachus need hardly be considered as having much relevance for popular ethics. His attempt to construct injustice into a system (however unfairly or inadequately it may be presented by Plato) would have met with little favour outside sophistic circles. There is no need to believe that the sophists were sincere and ardent immoralists or that they seriously advocated adopting injustice as a rival principle to justice or a logical guide for practical living (though it is quite likely that such views of the sophists were entertained by people of strict old-fashioned opinions and that Plato exploited their prejudices).[14] It is, indeed, by no means a simple matter to establish precisely what views were held by the sophists, who are often regarded as representative of the immoralist school. Even the views of Antiphon are not altogether clear, though we have some remarkable extracts from his work in papyrus fragments.[15]

But our interest is not so much in the arguments used by Socrates to counter the immoralist view as in the views expressed by Thrasymachus before he is led on by Socrates to explain and elaborate what he means. It is because he claims to be expounding a single consistent philosophy of justice and injustice that Socrates finds it so easy to refute him; what renders him so vulnerable is that he has tried to combine three quite separate and distinct notions, each one opposed in a different way to traditional ideas of ethics. In the first place he claims that justice is not properly a virtue or excellence and that the current vocabulary of ethics is therefore wrong; in the second place, he thinks justice is to be measured according as it benefits the stronger man, that the term is properly applied only to someone who obeys an order, whether from fear or hope of immediate gain (so that, if it is a virtue at all, it is a virtue of the weak, not of the strong); in the third place, he thinks that in all instances, when faced with the alternative of justice and expediency, a man must be a fool if he does not choose expediency (so that if justice as a form of unselfishness is a virtue at all, it is still a foolish virtue). The literature of the fifth century shows us individual historical and tragic characters expressing one or another of these opinions; but no one except Thrasymachus attempts to combine all three of them. Such an attempt at combination is perhaps to be explained as a sophistic *tour de force*, but it is not to be expected from popular ethics, which is content to isolate particular examples of justice and injustice and use different definitions for different occasions. Thrasymachus has evidently passed beyond this stage; but he has not advanced far enough to recognize that a combination of different qualities and definitions is no substitute for a universal definition. Polemarchus, at least, was prepared to stand by his opinion that justice was some form of unselfishness; and, once Thrasymachus withdraws from the discussion, it is the third opinion, which sets up justice and expediency as opposites, that comes in for more detailed examination in Book II.

The first opinion of Thrasymachus, which demands a reversal or distortion of ethical terms, is described by Thucydides as part of the ethics of revolution, the corrupt morality which became increasingly prevalent during the course of the Peloponnesian War. He emphasizes that its prevalence was due to the pressure of war, that "violent teacher" which "assimilates men's emotions to the situations that they have to meet" (iii.82.2). "They changed the customary meaning of terms as they changed their values with respect to particular situations," he says (82.4), and he describes how gross foolhardiness could pass for courage and intelligent hesitation for cowardice, and how a man who plotted someone's death was considered to be taking fair precaution. He asserts that in so far as people trusted one another at all, it was only because they were all criminals together, with the result that rogues were proud to be called clever and (though less frequently) good men were called stupid and were ashamed of it.[16]

In such an atmosphere it is understandable that speakers on public occasions should avoid or even deprecate the use of any conventional ethical terms. Thucydides tries to show an extreme example of this tendency in the Melian Dialogue. The Athenians, who are determined to subdue Melos by force if it does not surrender, invite the influential citizens of the island to discuss matters with them in an informal conversation. The Melian spokesman begins by complaining that the actual situation is hardly consistent with an offer of frank discussion, because "if we win by proving the justice of our case, the outcome for us is war, and if we give in the result is slavery" (v.86). The reference to justice merely annoys the Athenians, whose spokesman replies that any reference to "hypothetical notions about the future" is a waste of breath; the Athenians are not concerned with "fine words" or prepared to claim that they come with justice on their side, because any appeal to justice is out of place when a more powerful party is determined to use its power against a weaker opponent. The Melians attempt, rather feebly, to argue in terms that the Athenians may understand, by suggesting that what the Athenians propose to do will not in fact bring them "security" (ἀσφάλεια, v.98), the favourite watchword of aggressors as explained by Thucydides in his account of the ethics of revolution. But when their efforts in this direction fail, they return to ethical considerations of honour (the shame of accepting slavery) and piety, for which the Athenians show very little respect.

It is not usual to regard the Melian Dialogue as a faithful record of an actual discussion. The fact remains, however, that in such a situation the Athenians would not be disposed to argue in terms of justice; here was a perfect example of war "assimilating the emotions of men to a situation." The situation presented by the rebellion of Mytilene was perhaps less exacting. The Athenians had no justification except "security" for their attack on Melos; but against Mytilene they had a clear and definite grievance. The revolt of an ally, bound to loyalty and friendship by solemn oaths, was an offence against justice, and they were fully entitled to appeal to justice in explaining whatever steps they took against such a rebel. Thucydides does not describe the speeches at the assembly in Athens when the drastic decision was taken to kill all the adult male citizens and enslave the women and children; he merely says that it was an emotional decision, made in anger (ὑπὸ ὀργῆς), and that the change of mind on the following day came from reflection, when the Athenians considered the savagery of their verdict (iii.36.2–4). After this warning, the reader might expect that a speaker who wanted the verdict changed would dwell on the savagery of wholesale massacre and plead for moderation in the name of mercy and justice. But Diodotus, in the speech assigned to him by Thucydides, does nothing of the kind. He concentrates on the virtue of prudence or wise counsel (εὐβουλία), the very word that Thrasymachus used to characterize injustice, and the dangers of thoughtless, foolish, overhasty action. He directs the attention of his listeners exclusively to the interests of Athens; the guilt of the Mytilenians or any claim that they might have to mercy he dismisses as irrelevant to the issue.

Indeed, so far as justice is relevant at all, Diodotus admits that it is on the side of severity; it is on that side that the opportunity for "fine words" lies, and he asks his audience not to be unduly influenced by them. In the language of the sophists, familiar from the *Clouds* of Aristophanes, his is the Unjust Argument, since he deprecates any appeal to justice, and his opponent Cleon has been using the Just Argument.[17] Indeed, he says, although in all cities punishments are established for crimes, to suppose that deterrents will ever actually stop crime is stupidity or simple-mindedness (εὐήθεια, iii.45.7)—the word that Thrasymachus used to characterize justice. Only towards the end of his speech does Diodotus permit himself to hint that wholesale massacre is unjust: "If you destroy the common people of Mytilene, who had no part in the revolt and, of their own accord, surrendered the city to us when they gained control by arms, you will commit an injustice by killing your benefactors" (iii.47.3). But even so, in his final paragraph, he cautions his audience once again not to be influenced too much by feelings of pity.

If we turn from the speech of Diodotus to the speech of Cleon, who is in favour of upholding the original savage verdict, we find that his view of justice corresponds to the second opinion of Thrasymachus. He regards the Athenian empire as a tyranny, maintained with difficulty over unwilling subjects who are constantly plotting against it. It does not matter whether the laws are perfect or imperfect, they must be obeyed and enforced; clever men, therefore, who are too often disposed to think for themselves and set themselves up as "cleverer than the law," are less competent administrators, less desirable citizens than ordinary men with less education. And so far as Mytilene is concerned, justice is taken to be identical with serving the interests of Athens; the idea that injustice on its part could fail to harm Athens is dismissed as ridiculous (iii.38.1).

Like Thrasymachus, Cleon expects to find justice more readily in a dull-witted man than a clever one; but unlike Thrasymachus, instead of despising or decrying stupidity, he appears to commend it. It is this aspect of his speech which gives it an ethical character (and there is an ethical element in all Thucydidean speeches); it is more than a conventional plea for the enforcement of law and the punishment of illegal behaviour. The point of view that Cleon expresses is comparable to the attitude of the Spartan king Archidamus in his speech at the Congress of Sparta when he extols Spartan moral character, which emphasizes self-control and wise counsel (*euboulia*) without too much learning (i.84.3). The vocabulary of ethics is not perverted here, as it is by Diodotus and Thrasymachus, who associate *euboulia* with injustice, not with justice. On the contrary, there is a strong element of philistinism in Archidamus, as there is in Cleon too, who is said to have hated and feared new fashions (Aristophanes makes him know only one musical mode—the Dorian[18]). The hint that education and independent thought may break down morals is vigorously denied by Pericles in the Funeral Oration, in his vindication of intellectual freedom at Athens and his insistence that Athenians excel not because of obedience to law or discipline but because of their character and intelligence (ii.39.4). Thucydides leaves us in no doubt that he himself dislikes Cleon just as intensely as Aristophanes did, and that he regards his philistinism as totally at variance with the best Athenian traditions.

The opinion that justice can be defined simply as obedience to the law or serving the interests of authority means that it is a virtue of weaker characters. A dramatist who held this point of view would give us a very different version of the Oedipus legend and the Oresteia from those made familiar by the great tragedians. Not only would he make Creon, the dogmatic authoritarian, the hero of the *Antigone,* but the weakness and "wise counsel" of Ismene, in the *Antigone,* and Chrysothemis, in the *Electra,* who dissuade their more adventurous sisters from defying authority, would be not merely condoned but commended. As they are characterized by Sophocles, though they think that "yielding to the stronger" is the wiser course, they do not think it the more admirable. Ismene admires the true loyalty of Antigone to her brother, "ill-counselled" though it may be, when she tells her at the close of the opening scene:

Of this be sure:
Unwise thou art, but true friend to thy friends.
(*Antigone* 98–99)*

Chrysothemis is more explicit:

Justice lies not in the way I tell thee,
But as thou art deciding.
(*Electra* 338–39)

She will not, or dares not, urge the "just" action, because its consequences are too terrible:

If I would live in freedom,
I must obey the stronger in all ways.
(339–40)

The chorus, in the usual manner of a tragic chorus, would like to suggest a compromise:

Before the gods,
Act not in anger; good there is in both
Your arguments; if only thou couldst learn
To act by hers, and she in turn by thine.
(369–71)

Not even the Odysseus of the *Philoctetes,* who is a craftier character in every way, attempts to persuade Neoptolemus that obedience to authority and serving the national cause is the same thing as justice; but he comes near to persuading the younger man that he is faced with a situation in which he must, temporarily, forget the demands of justice, because

If this thou wilt not do,
Great sorrow thou wilt bring on all the Greeks.
(*Phil.* 66–67)

The notion that justice is in conflict with wise counsel and that the just man is not intelligent is what really perturbs Glaucon, and he wants Socrates to prove to him that this is a false notion. But it is the third opinion of Thrasymachus, which assumes a conflict between justice and expediency, that appears more constantly in Greek classical literature than the others.

* All line references are to the Greek editions of the texts.

Neither Antigone nor Electra, in Sophocles, gives much thought to this conflict, and their sisters know better than to attempt any appeal to selfish motives. "What gain can there be," Electra asks, "in giving in?" (352–53). Odysseus is less scrupulous in arguing with Neoptolemus: "When action leads to gain, thou shouldst not hesitate" (*Phil.* 111). But Neoptolemus cannot see that the gain for him, personally, is very great: "What gain for me that he should go to Troy?" (112). Creon, in the *Antigone,* is quick to suspect that desire for gain is the reason for any breach of the law (which is what he means by an unjust action). The ugly word "gain" (*kerdos*) appears at the end of his first scene with the chorus, after he has set forth his views on honest statesmanship (221–22), and after the Guard has reported that his edict has been disobeyed, he delivers a violent tirade against the evil influence of money, which

> Sacks cities and thrusts men from their homes,
> Teaches and misleads men's honest minds
> To turn to deeds of evil.
>
> (*Antigone* 296–99)

One might think it would be a strange world in which the possible conflict between justice and self-interest was not recognized. But conflicts occur only with reference to particular situations, when the claims of justice are acknowledged in terms of some particular obligation, the obligation to help one's friends, keep a contract, or obey authority. Socrates had no great difficulty in showing Polemarchus that particular obligations of this kind can be in conflict with one another; we can, in fact, do a friend harm by keeping a contract (for example, by returning a weapon that we have agreed to return, if the friend in the meantime has lost his sanity). But, though conflicts of this kind could occur, a conflict between one or another of these obligations and the claims of expediency was more common and often of more practical difficulty. Hence it was natural to think of justice as a form of unselfishness that was manifested when one acted in a way contrary to one's own interests. When there was no apparent conflict between interest and obligation, the nature of justice, in that particular situation, might be difficult to define. But such a situation posed no practical problem of behaviour; and when there is no practical problem, the curiosity of the ordinary man is not aroused. The problem becomes an academic one, a matter for the professional philosopher.

A most instructive illustration of attitudes prevalent in the fifth century towards conflicts of justice and expediency is offered by the account in Thucydides of the quarrel between Corcyra, Epidamnus, and Corinth, by the arguments used by the different parties in negotiations between themselves and in the subsequent appeal of the Corcyraeans to Athens. Thucydides presumably intends to show the standard of international ethics that was generally recognized before the special circumstances of war altered the scale of values. The Peloponnesian War has not yet broken out; this is an account of peacetime diplomacy. In an appeal for assistance from an old ally or a request for a new alliance, the petitioner is in a strong position if he can show that he is offering a course of action which is both just and expedient. But more often he will be compelled to stress the claims of either justice or expediency at the expense of the other.

Corcyra (the island of Corfu) was a colony of Corinth, and Epidamnus (Durazzo) was a colony of Corcyra. The relation between colony and mother-city was supposed to be a relation of friendship, and the obligation of one to help the other was recognized. The party in power at Epidamnus was having difficulty in maintaining itself against the attacks of its rivals, who had been driven into exile; it appealed to Corcyra for help in effecting a reconciliation and restoring peace, but its appeal was rejected. Consequently it went over the head of Corcyra and appealed to the more powerful city of Corinth, after first obtaining the Delphic oracle's approval. Corinth agreed to help for two reasons, according to Thucydides: first, on the score of justice, since Epidamnus was after all a Corinthian colony even though settled from Corcyra; and second, because the Corinthians welcomed the opportunity to humble Corcyra, whose behaviour towards its mother-city had not been satisfactory. The claims of justice and expediency appeared to coincide. The Corcyraeans resented Corinthian interference, and since they favoured the Epidamnian party in exile and were prepared to support them with armed force, a war was soon in preparation; but the Corcyraeans acted in proper diplomatic fashion by offering to submit the matter to arbitration. Such obedience to authority—an authority recognized by all parties, whether the Delphic oracle or a group of acceptable cities—would be a form of just behaviour. But if Corinth would not agree to it, then Corcyra would have to help itself; in the interests of its own safety it would have to seek friends elsewhere, a necessary but unjust course (although the Corcyraeans avoid saying so explicitly), because it involved breaking the bond of friendship that bound them to the mother-city. Corinth rejected their appeal, hostilities began, and the Corcyraeans carried out their threat by seeking assistance from Athens (i.24–31).

Thucydides gives us the speeches of both the Corcyraean and the Corinthian emissaries before the Athenian assembly. The Corcyraeans are concerned, in the first place, to show that the Athenians will gain by accepting them as allies, that is by accepting an immediate obligation to help which will be returned by Corcyraean assistance when war on a large scale breaks out, as is considered inevitable before long. The issue of justice arises for the Athenians only because they are bound by the terms of the Thirty Years Peace not to make alliances with states that are already tied to the Peloponnesian group, as Corcyra was tied to Corinth. The Corcyraeans, therefore, argue that Corinth, by her behaviour, has broken the bond of friendship with them, so that Athens will not be going against the treaty by making Corcyra her ally. These are the arguments that the Corinthians have to counter. Their conclusion is exactly the opposite: if the Athenians refuse the Corcyraean request, "you will be doing what is proper (keeping your contract) and making the decision that is best for yourselves" (i.43.4). The Athenians, after due consideration, decide to maintain technical correctness by making only a limited form of alliance with Corcyra, agreeing only to help them if they are attacked; but Thucydides makes it quite clear that their decision is determined solely by what they think will be useful to them in case war breaks out.[19]

Neither the arguments invoked nor the motives of the Athenian decision will surprise a modern reader. It is worth noticing, however, that the speakers are more concerned with putting their opponents in the wrong than with efforts to maintain peace; nothing is said about the good of the Greek states or of either group of allies as a whole; such an appeal to the cause of international peace might be considered the equivalent, in political terms, to the general claims of absolute justice apart from any considerations of expediency for the individual. The approach to diplomacy is indeed just as limited and as negative as the attitude towards justice of the elderly Cephalus, described in the opening scene of the *Republic*. When Thrasymachus challenges Socrates to say what he thinks justice is, he warns him that he will not be satisfied with phrases like "what we must do" or "what is useful" or "what is expedient" (336d). The tendency to seek the more general definition was not common in popular thought; the search was for something more particular, if the speeches of Thucydides are a trustworthy guide. Plato's protest against this tendency shows the real ground of his dissatisfaction with popular ethics.

The *Euthyphro* shows us that Plato was equally dissatisfied with popular religion and for very similar reasons. Euthyphro can describe some of the acts of a pious man, but he is even less competent to explain the essence of piety than Polemarchus was to explain the essence of justice. His attempts to answer the questions of Socrates and his apparent belief that piety consists in pleasing the gods and serving them, without knowing what it is that makes certain acts pleasing to them, are closely parallel to the first attempts of Polemarchus in the *Republic.* In the *Euthyphro* Socrates makes no secret of his own opinion that piety is a part or aspect of justice (12a). To please the gods, who in the cosmic sphere are the equivalent of the perfectly expert rulers in a state, is certainly an act of a pious man; but just as Socrates in the *Republic* will not admit that anyone knows justice who is ignorant of the principles that guide perfectly expert rulers, so, if Plato had written a *Respublica Divina,* he could not have admitted that anyone understood piety unless he shared the knowledge that the gods possessed. Plato's explicit criticism of popular religion does not go as far as this; but he did complain that the life of the gods on Olympus, as represented in literature, showed them without a true knowledge of either justice or piety. Homer's gods were no more perfectly expert rulers and had no better claim to man's unquestioned obedience than the rulers of any existing state.

There is no suggestion, either in Plato or elsewhere, that there was a tendency among Athenians to explain justice in terms of piety, to fall back on a religious explanation of ethics. Euthyphro shows no hesitation in agreeing that piety is a part of justice, but he does not regard justice as a part of piety (*Euth.* 12d). It follows that justice and piety cannot be considered as being in conflict with one another; it is a mistake to suppose that the theme of the *Antigone* is a conflict between the claims of law and religion, of church and state.[20] It is true, however, that popular religion, as a guide to conduct, may fail for the same reasons that popular ethics fails when it appears to make a demand that is inconsistent with self-interest or "wise counsel" or even "the interest of the stronger."[21]

Plato also found fault with popular ethics because of its indebtedness to the literary tradition, because it believed that there were valuable lessons to be learnt from Homer and other poets of the past. In his opinion they were most inadequate teachers. We may be repelled by his apparent hostility to literature and his decision to banish poets, especially tragic poets, from his ideal republic. But the strength of his convictions is the surest proof that literary tradition had an overwhelming influence on popular ethics and in the ethical training of the young. It should not surprise us to find that the patterns of Greek ethical thought are already outlined in the *Iliad* and the *Odyssey*, in Hesiod and the gnomic poets of archaic Greece. It is in the tragic poets, however, that the theme of conflict between obligations is most vigorously pursued and the shortcomings and inconsistencies of popular thinking most clearly revealed.

Even though the patterns of thought may be found in the earlier literature, it does not follow that the vocabulary will always be the same. It is not until the fifth century that justice comes to predominate as the key word in any discussion of man's virtues or duty, and it is an appropriate word to use when man's relations with his fellow men are set in the established surroundings of a civic community. The choice of this word might be taken as an indication that fifth-century Athens thought of ethics in exclusively political terms, that man's relation to the state and the law overshadowed his relation to fellow individuals. An attempt will be made in the following chapters to show that this is a misunderstanding; only the perversion or corruption of popular ethics, as seen in the views of immoralists and authoritarians, minimizes the importance of the relation between individual and individual. It was always important for a citizen to earn the respect of his fellow citizens and to pay attention to what they thought, just as it was not only necessary but right, in most circumstances, to obey the laws of the state; and in the *Crito* Plato makes Socrates remind Crito that his obligation towards his own city is real and strong. But neither in Homer nor in the literature of Periclean Athens is popular approval or the voice of the state the ultimate criterion of what is right or just or best.

TWO. Homer

"The men of olden times were better men than we are, and you should study their behaviour and try to imitate it. And the world in which they lived was a better world than ours; the good man was rewarded and the evil man was always overtaken by inevitable punishment." It is difficult to believe that anyone has ever grown up without hearing such words from his elders. Aristophanes and Plato heard them often enough in the mouths of their teachers when they were boys; and the moral lessons to be learnt from Homer were considered not the least of the reasons for studying the *Iliad* and the *Odyssey* in classical Athens. The courage of Hector, the steadfastness of Odysseus and his faith in the gods, the constancy of Penelope, and the mature wisdom of Nestor were all held up as models for imitation. If Achilles and Agamemnon could hardly be commended for their stubborn pride, at least they finally recognized their error and did their best to redeem it, while Aegisthus and the suitors, whose crimes were beyond atonement, were surely and inevitably punished.

Plato, as he grew older, found much to criticize in the attitude of his teachers towards Homer. He found fault with the manner in which both gods and men were depicted in the poems, and considered their behaviour by no means a suitable model for the young. Indeed, the traditional attitude towards Homer was one of the signs which led him to believe that his contemporaries were neither clear nor consistent in their ethical teaching. But even Plato would have agreed without hesitation that the common religious and ethical heritage, which they shared or claimed to share, was best exemplified by their unanimous respect for the poems of Homer. They knew that their beliefs were first given form and meaning in these poems; they would have thought Greek civilization was at an end if their children were no longer taught to read them carefully and if their childish ideas of piety and good behaviour were no longer formed in this way. It made little difference whether adult Greeks believed literally in the story as Homer told it; it was the vitality of his poetry, its irresistible appeal to imaginative and sensitive minds, that kept for Homer his undisputed place as the great teacher.

It follows, then, that Greek popular ethics—the traditional part of ethics that survives political changes and literary and artistic revolutions—cannot be understood unless we examine the source to which Greeks looked back and to which they directed the attention of their children in their formative years, telling them that "the men of olden times were better men than we are, and the world in which they lived was a better world than ours."[1]

Whether better or worse, the world depicted in the Homeric poems is certainly very different from the world of democratic Athens. Plato might have elaborated his reasons for rejecting Homer as a schoolbook by pointing out that the lessons of the *Iliad* and the *Odyssey,* when they were not objectionable, were utterly out of date in his day and age. But he might also have been forced to admit that the Homeric society was in some ways closer to his own ideal state than to the democratic society of Athens. In Athens every citizen was a potential leader; but in Homer's world, as in Plato's ideal republic, the obligation to excel was confined to a privileged few. The opinions of the common herd are scarcely considered in Homer; their task is to obey and serve the needs of their rulers; their attitudes and their motives are of no importance. When Thersites speaks out in the assembly, there is no suggestion that he is defending the rights of the rank and file; he is merely behaving in an unseemly fashion and his humiliation pleases everyone.

It is a mistake to draw the further conclusion that the actual world for which the Homeric poems were composed was exactly like this. The author or authors of the *Iliad* and the *Odyssey* were not themselves aristocrats expounding their traditional code. If the poets who developed and perfected the epic style were themselves members of the noble families, it would be expected that they would take their place as social equals among them. But the poets who appear in the *Odyssey,* at Ithaca and at the court of king Alcinous, are not men of high birth; their families are of no consequence, and the position of respect that they hold is earned by their artistry, not granted them as their birthright. They hold an intermediate position between the servants of the palace and the members of the family. Other types of professional skill or devoted service might earn a similar position of respect; a priest, a seer like Calchas, a swine-herd like Eumaeus who has spent his life in the service of the family, or a "venerable housedame" who keeps the keys of the storeroom may be considered as belonging to this intermediate class, and it is not difficult to imagine the existence of other representatives, who arose from humble beginnings and whom the poet does not care to introduce into his story, perhaps out of a fear that his noble masters may not be interested in their deeds or thoughts. A poet of noble birth might have had fewer scruples about introducing us to a wider range of society.

We hear hardly anything of the deeds of the rank and file in the battles of the *Iliad,* and the battle itself is represented as a series of duels between champions. There is, in fact, no attempt to describe battle realistically, and for a good reason; the poets themselves were not soldiers and possibly had no first-hand experience of fighting. If so, their knowledge of the code of courage and the conventions of the battlefield may have been acquired at second hand, and their interpretations of the feelings of warriors when threatened by danger and death may be based on their own imagination.

These considerations may weaken our faith in the historical accuracy of the *Iliad* and the *Odyssey* in matters of aristocratic psychology as well as in external details. But their importance should not be exaggerated. The main thing is that they absolve us from the necessity of trying to reconcile apparent contradictions. For example, in the famous scene in which Diomede and Glaucus exchange their armour in token of friendship, the poet remarks that "Zeus took away the wits of Glaucus, who exchanged golden armour for the brazen armour of Diomede—something worth a hundred oxen for something worth nine oxen" (*Il.* vi.234–36). This should not force us to believe that the aristocratic code was undermined by an ungenerous mercenary spirit, but only that the poet himself—a poor man for whom such magnificent gestures were unthinkable—is allowing his own sense of values to intrude. The poet cannot imagine how a sane man could give away a precious possession which would cost most men a lifetime's work to acquire.

It is true, nevertheless, that one has no right to speak of Homeric society as though any aspect of it ever existed exactly as described in any part of either the *Iliad* or the *Odyssey*. One may speak of Homeric man only in so far as one means the characters who speak and whose acts and thoughts are described in the language of the epic. This statement, which would have been a truism a century ago, can and should still be made despite all the archaeological discovery of the intervening years. We can now talk confidently of Cnossos, Troy, Mycenae, and Pylos as actual centres of power in which real kings, whatever their actual names, had their palaces; and we have learnt much about the art and civilization and economy of Helladic and Mycenaean Greece. But the degree of historical accuracy in Homer's picture is calculable only in so far as archaeological discovery offers material evidence. The elements of fiction, especially where thought and manner of speech are concerned, remain an unknown quantity. Even the discovery of Mycenaean Greek as a written language has not helped us much here, since it has not yet shown us whether there was such a thing as a written literature in Greek between 1500 and 1000 B.C. Mycenae and Pylos have not yet given us anything comparable to the Hittite documents and chronicles of Boghaz Keui. One should not expect the mimetic accuracy of an epic poet to be so complete that he will not make mistakes in describing even a contemporary aristocratic society, of which after all he is a member only by courtesy.

Furthermore, most critics who have written about the vocabulary or the thought or the social conventions of the Homeric poems (even those who wrote before the great age of archaeological discovery) have been disposed to regard different parts of these poems as representing different stages in social and political development.[2] Some parts of the poems may have an earlier origin than others, some scenes and details of description may apply more properly to earlier ages. It is not important for the present argument whether this lack of homogeneity is to be explained by different dates of composition and different authors or by the persistence of conventions in language and description that a single author has inherited from a long and well-established tradition of epic narrative.[3] In the present state of our knowledge, ethical conventions and literary fashions in the second millennium B.C. cannot be dated like technique and style in armour or architecture or pottery. One can say that epic poems are always intended to present the exploits of great men in bygone days, that many details more appropriate to the poet's own day than the past will inevitably be introduced, and that the similes, in particular, are likely to be drawn from the world with which the poet is familiar. But one cannot say how far custom demanded that a poet should be consistent or accurate in the setting that formed the background, how far it permitted him to mix elements that belonged in different settings[4]—as different as the court of Phaeacia is from the palace of Odysseus in Ithaca, since (in so far as either setting is depicted with historical accuracy) the Phaeacian palace represents an earlier and wealthier period than the Ithacan.

Homer, or the two or more poets who are responsible for the *Iliad* and the *Odyssey,* may be more consistent and more accurate historically in some respects than in others. Accuracy in the description of mental processes and character cannot be checked. But it happens that a remarkable consistency will be found throughout both poems in the language used to describe mental processes.[5] It is this consistency that enables us to talk of Homeric man and the Homeric way of thinking, and that enabled the Greeks of classical times to do the same and to regard Homer as a moral teacher; the accuracy of the setting, the correspondence or lack of correspondence between the intellectual and the material background of different episodes, did not concern them. Greek readers and teachers did not apply modern standards of historical criticism to Homer; and for the present purpose we need not do so either.

It cannot be expected that a poet who is not himself an aristocrat will describe or expound the code of behaviour by which nobles are bound. Nor is it likely that his principal object will be to illustrate it by his poem; no code, moral or legal, covers all situations, and an epic poem in which the characters were confronted only by situations that were covered by a code would interest no one and have little chance of survival. On the other hand, popular morality, which is less exacting and less strictly logical than philosophy, does not reject a traditional code because it fails to cover every situation; it will still continue to describe both justice and moral excellence within the framework of a community and a code. In this respect there is no difference between Homer and the Athenians of the fifth century. But the terminology will differ, and only by a careful examination of the Homeric terminology can we discover where the differences in emphasis lie.

Popular morality rarely, if ever, defines its terms. But much can be learnt by investigating the etymology of the terms that are used and considering the imagery which they imply. In classical Athens, indeed throughout classical Greece, great emphasis was laid on moderation; μηδὲν ἄγαν, "avoid all excess," was a favourite aphorism, supposed to be hallowed by Apollo of Delphi. In Homer's language a similar idea is expressed more vividly and picturesquely by the insistence that a man act "according to his portion," "not beyond his due"—his *moira, moros,* or *aisa.* This language appears even in situations in which one might expect much stronger expressions. After the Cyclops has killed and eaten some of the comrades of Odysseus, he is charged with acting "not according to his portion" (ἐπεὶ οὐ κατὰ μοῖραν ἔρεξας, ix.352). Zeus complains that mortal men, by their criminal folly, "suffer woes beyond their portion," like Aegisthus, who went "beyond his portion" when he married Clytaemnestra, killing her husband Agamemnon when he returned from Troy, though he knew that disaster would follow:

> σφῇσιν ἀτασθαλίῃσιν ὑπὲρ μόρον ἄλγε' ἔχουσιν,
> ὡς καὶ νῦν Αἴγισθος ὑπὲρ μόρον Ἀτρεΐδαο
> γῆμ' ἄλοχον μνηστήν, τὸν δ'ἔκτανε νοστήσαντα
> εἰδὼς αἰπὺν ὄλεθρον.
>
> (i.34–37)

Nothing can be learnt by listing the various passages in which these phrases or some equivalent occurs. It is no surprise that brutal murder and adultery are considered beyond a man's due portion of behaviour. Deceit and overconfidence are censured in the same terms. Penelope tricked the suitors by asking them to wait for her decision until she had finished weaving a winding sheet for her father-in-law, Laertes, and then unwound each night what she had woven during the day. The suitors complained that her device was "undue" (οὐκ ἐναίσιμον, ii.122). The same word, "portion," is used for man's destiny or fate, or simply for death, which is indeed his due portion.

When gods or men disapprove of an act that is beyond the due portion, their indignant reaction is described by the word *nemesis.* Literally, this word also means "distribution" or "apportionment." The imagery is clear; when men blame or gods punish a man for his misdeeds, they are thought to be giving him his due portion. If men's behaviour is limited by their due portion—a limitation which they must recognize since they are mere mortals—so also their success or wealth is regarded as a portion allotted to them in due measure by the gods. Sometimes, however, it appears to men as though this allotment bears no relation to a man's deserts; the system according to which good or bad fortune is meted out to men is a mystery known only to the gods, since everyone knows that worthy men often fail and unworthy men succeed in the struggle for prosperity. It is therefore no criticism of a man that he is poor, as Nausicaa tells Odysseus when he is cast up destitute on the shore of Phaeacia: "Stranger, thou dost not seem like a worthless or a witless man; and Zeus himself allots prosperity to men, to good and bad, to each one as he wills; so it is that he has given thee these troubles to bear, which thou needs must bear" (vi.187–90). If there are times when the distribution of rewards and punishments seems understandable and just, there are other times when it looks like the arbitrary behaviour of jealous gods. Hence the notion of "apportionment" is not always vividly present in usage when the word *nemesis* is employed; the notion of anger or even of jealousy may predominate.

In Homer the word nemesis normally denotes human, rather than divine, indignation or censure, and the verbs derived from it, νεμεσάω and νεμεσίζομαι, are used for the feeling of disgust or disapproval, as when Nausicaa says she would disapprove of a girl who had intercourse with men before marriage: "For any girl who did such things I would have nemesis" (vi.286–88). It is not necessary for her to add that such a girl would be acting "beyond her due."[6] But in Aeschylus and Herodotus and in classical Greek generally, the word nemesis denotes the divine retribution that overtakes a man who has been guilty of *hybris*—the man who is arrogant or self-confident beyond his due.[7]

Faults of behaviour or character are often indicated by words denoting excess, and adjectives beginning with *hyper-* are common, such as ὑπέρβιος, ὑπερφίαλος. Generally such words imply blame, unless used with reference to an occasion when a certain excess is to be desired, as warriors cannot be too brave or servants too eager.[8] The exact due measure of a human impulse cannot be laid down for every situation. There are times when a man should be modest; there are also times when he should be bold and put shame aside—for example, Odysseus points out that for a beggar in need shame (*aidos*) is "not good" (xvii.347).[9] If taken in isolation, this remark might seem like a jest, a deliberate paradox suitable to a king disguised as a beggar but not to Odysseus in his own character, appropriate only to the most abject kind of beggar who has lost everything, even his sense of shame.

One could point to passages in which the appeal to nemesis and aidos is unanswerable, as when Telemachus appeals to the suitors, bidding them refrain from their destructive behaviour in the name of nemesis and aidos:

> Have some sense of nemesis yourselves,
> Feel shame before your neighbours who live near,
> And fear the anger of the gods.
>
> (ii.64–66)

The suitors cannot defend their lack of shame; their behaviour is sufficiently condemned by Odysseus when he says that they have "no share of aidos" (xx.171). And yet when Telemachus is asking Nestor and Menelaus to tell him the truth about Odysseus, even if they know that he is dead, he says to each of them: "Do not try to spare me, out of aidos, or out of pity for me" (iii.96; iv.326). Shame is a double-edged restraint on a man's behaviour; it can make him tell lies as well as the truth. It can even cause him to fail in his duty. Telemachus fears that shame will restrain him from questioning Nestor, though he knows that he should overcome this feeling (iii.22–24); and Peisistratus explains to Menelaus that Telemachus, who should be questioning his host about Odysseus, is stopped from doing so by his sense of nemesis (iv.158–59).

It is easy to say that one should feel shame and respect in face of an individual or institution that deserves respect; and it is right and proper that a young man should have such feelings towards his elders. But these feelings do not offer an absolute and infallible guide to conduct. There are times when the traditional code of good manners must be disregarded and the risk taken of exceeding one's "due portion."

It might be thought that *themis* and *dike* are more absolute in their demands on men. In classical Greek these are abstract ideas or ideals of justice; they seem to correspond to the *fas* and *ius* of the Romans, which no man may disregard, though there can be times when he must disregard the statute laws of his state. But in Homer these two words are not abstract but concrete; and they are often used in the plural (*themistes, dikai*). Like *nomos* in classical Greek, they denote the demands of a society, set by established custom and precedent, rather than any moral obligation. The Cyclopes are complete and utter savages. Their lack of civilization is shown not only by their violent and intolerable arrogance, but by the fact that they neither have nor recognize any themistes: "They have no gatherings where they deliberate nor any themistes, but each one sets his own themistes for his women folk and his children, and they have no regard for one another." They are also uncivilized in the sense that they plant no crops and live apart from their neighbours in caves on the mountains (ix.106–15). Polyphemus is more brute than man, knowing only lawlessness (*athemistia*), with no understanding of dikai or themistes: οὔτε δίκας εὖ εἰδότα οὔτε θέμιστας (215). He has no intelligence beyond a sort of animal cunning, and it would be absurd to expect any moral sensibility in such a monster. Even the universal custom of showing kindness to strangers means nothing to him. Since he recognizes no themis, the only thing that could restrain him would be fear, either of gods or of men stronger than himself; he has no fear of either, jeering at Odysseus when he bids him have shame before the gods and remember that Zeus defends and avenges suppliants and strangers (269–78). It means nothing to him when Odysseus tells him that he has acted "not according to his due (351–52).[10] The only kind of order or "due measure" that he recognizes is in caring for his flocks (the same phrase "according to their due," κατὰ μοῖϱαν [342] is used to describe how he milks all his sheep and goats "in order, in their turn").

Among the gods, Ares is just as much a savage as Polyphemus is among men, since he has no concern for the civilized life of peace. "A witless creature who knows no themis," Hera calls him in the *Iliad,* when she complains to Zeus of Aphrodite and Apollo, who have "let Ares loose" to fight on the Trojan side: ἄφϱονα τοῦτον ἀνέντες, ὃς οὔτινα οἶδε θέμιστα (v.761). Dike and themis are the demands of a society, which man must accept and recognize if he is to rise above the level of animals and savages; dike is something which distinguishes men from animals, who know no law except what we call the law of the jungle. Thus Hesiod bids Perses "listen to the voice of dike and forget violence entirely, because this is the law that Zeus set for men, that fishes and beasts and birds of the air should eat one another, since there is no dike among them, but to men he gave dike which is by far the best" (*Works and Days,* 275–80).

These passages do not tell us exactly what dike is or on what sanction it is founded (except that it is the gift of Zeus). Lawless people, who "fear the anger neither of gods nor of men," are foolish to think that they can outwit the gods or escape their anger; but in many instances they can escape human retribution, and no one blames them for thinking so if, for example, they are raiding an enemy's country. The gods may even permit them to disregard the dike of a hostile people. Eumaeus in the *Odyssey* says, with reference to the suitors, that "the gods love not ruthless deeds, but respect dike and the due behaviour (αἴσιμα ἔϱγα) of men," and he can add without logical contradiction that "even enemies and hostile men, who make their living on the country of others (and Zeus grants them plunder, and filling their ships they sail on the homeward voyage)—even on them a mighty fear of wrath[11] falls on their hearts" (xiv.83–88). Such men act in fear, knowing that they will receive no mercy (from god or man) if they are caught, while at the same time they thank the gods for helping them to escape. But it is unthinkable that any god should sanction the killing and robbing of one's own people. When Amphinomus warns the suitors against any plan to kill Telemachus, he says: "Let us first inquire the counsels of the gods, and if the themistes of great Zeus approve, myself I will do the killing and urge on all the others; but if the gods turn us back, I bid you to refrain" (xvi.402–5). He is speaking in perfect confidence that the gods *will* refuse consent; and nothing more is heard of any consultation of an oracle.

One need not read far in the *Iliad* or the *Odyssey* to recognize that neither dike nor themis commands absolutely "Thou shalt not kill." But dike does distinguish between one kind of killing and another, and it is the task of judges, whether divine or human, to enforce these distinctions or at least to make them plain so that human avengers may exact punishment and no one who is not directly interested will interfere. The distinction may not always be clear. In one of the scenes on the shield of Achilles, two men are arguing a case of manslaughter before a court composed of elders: "The one was offering to give full satisfaction, making clear his offer to the people, and the other was refusing to take anything, and both were anxious to have the issue tried before an arbiter; and the people were crying their support on both sides, supporting both this plea and that, and heralds were restraining the people" (*Il.* xviii.498–503). Both these men respect dike, because, however violently each may urge his own case, they are prepared to accept whatever verdict is given. They recognize the authority of a court, even though they may think its verdict wrong or "crooked," just as Socrates in the *Crito* insists that he must accept the verdict of an Athenian court or forfeit all right to call himself an Athenian. Whoever refuses to accept the judgment ceases to be *dikaios* (a respecter of dike); like the Cyclopes, he is making his own rules. A judge cannot satisfy everyone; and, as Penelope points out, it is the dike of kings (or judges) to make mistakes (*Od.* iv.691)—not their *right* exactly, but their privilege, as with the umpire in a game, whose verdict is final no matter what the players and onlookers may think.[12]

Themis etymologically means simply something that is "laid

down" or "established," from the root *the-* (as in the verb τίθημι, "to place" or "set," English "theme," "thesis"). It is an understandable term, therefore, for rulings that are laid down either by an assembly of men or by Zeus himself (cf. *Od.* xvi.403). Dike has a very similar root meaning. Though it often appears to mean "custom," it usually means a judgment "laid down" by an authority in a dispute, a judgment that members of the community must recognize. Etymologically, dike is almost certainly connected with the root *deik-, dik-* (cf. Latin *dico*), "to point out," "to mark," so that the imagery implied is just as simple as in themis. These etymologies have been disputed;[13] but the alternatives suggested still imply that dike and themis are imposed by the will of human authority or by the gods, and are recognized by civilized men, but not by savages, as obligations which control their behaviour in their particular society.

The language of the Homeric poems, though not perhaps as perfectly consistent as a student of legal theory might wish, definitely forbids the conclusion that the words mean anything like "natural law" or "self-evident justice." In due time, as later literature shows, these concrete words become abstract and acquire ethical implications; but we cannot trace the stages of this development.[14] We do not even know how early or in what historical setting Themis and Dike emerged as goddesses who personified the ideal of justice. The first literary appearance of Dike as a goddess is in Hesiod, but Themis makes a few appearances in the Homeric poems. She is not a goddess of abstract justice, but restricts her activities to assembling the councils of gods and men. Her duty on Olympus is to summon the assembly of the gods (*Il.* xx.4); she does not pass judgment herself. When Telemachus asks the suitors to withdraw from the palace and leave him alone, he appeals to Olympian Zeus and to Themis "who disperses and gathers the assemblies of men" (*Od.* ii.68–69). He is asking them only to behave in a manner that custom would approve, just as previously he asked them to feel shame before men and to fear the wrath of the gods (65–66).

To search for a sure distinction between themis and dike in Homer is not profitable.[15] Both alike appear to mean "custom" or "judgment" or "rule" or the "rule of law," which lawless men, who are not *dikaioi,* seek to drive out when they refuse to recognize the verdicts of proper authority or when they deliver "crooked themistes." Thus, for example, Zeus is said to be angry with men "who by violence in an assembly judge crooked themistes and drive out dike, caring nothing for the wrath of the gods" (*Il.* xvi.386–88). It is a mistake to conclude that dike here means "justice," though that would certainly be the meaning in classical times, when the notion of a wicked generation "expelling justice and shame" was familiar; indeed, this meaning can already be found in Hesiod.[16] What Homer seems to have in mind is a manner of behaviour which the gods respect and men generally observe, rather than a principle or an ideal. Eumaeus tells Odysseus that "the blessed gods do not love reckless deeds, but they respect dike and the due deeds of men" (xiv.83–84).

From these two passages one might think that dike meant justice; but they are without parallel in Homer, and it is much more likely that the meaning is "lawful behaviour." So also the adjective *dikaios,* very common in classical Greek in the ethical meaning of "just," appears in Homer in the sense of "law-abiding" or "recognizing the rule of custom," in contrast to the actions of savages and criminals, as when Odysseus wonders whether the Cyclopes will be "savage and not *dikaioi*" (ix.175). Both dike and themis, then, help to indicate the *moira* which defines the proper behaviour of man in a civilized society; he must fear and respect them, as he must fear the gods. Themis gives certain unmistakable commands which must be obeyed. It commands all men to show hospitality to strangers (for example, *Od.* xiv.56–57); it forbids a man to approach the sword of Poseidon (*Il.* xiv.386); and it forbids Aeolus to help a wanderer who is hated by the gods (*Od.* x.73). But a man achieves no very high worth merely by obeying the rules. In the *Odyssey* (xvii.363), when Odysseus, disguised as a beggar, makes the round of the suitors asking alms, it is said that Athena urged him on so that he might find out which of them were *enaisimoi* and which *athemistoi*—i.e., which of them recognized and which did not recognize aisa and themis. None of the suitors are men of high character; even the better among them will do no more than satisfy the demands of custom by giving him a morsel of food. There is no suggestion that any of them will be found good or worthy men; their mere presence in that company and their behaviour during Odysseus's years of absence have already condemned them.

The demands of custom and the social order, the need to act "according to one's due" and to feel shame, respect for the feelings and rights of others, beggars and wanderers included—all these demands exercise a negative restraining influence on man's behaviour. If he disregards these demands, he becomes a social outcast and deserves no mercy, like the suitors. A more positive standard is to be found in man's need for honour and good reputation, which can be won only by excelling in some way or other, by *arete* or "excellence." In the *Iliad,* which is a world of war, one kind of arete overshadows all others—prowess as a warrior and a leader of men. But arete is of various kinds, and when Penelope praises Odysseus, she says he is "distinguished by every kind of arete among the Greeks, a worthy man whose fame extends widely":

> παντοίῃς ἀρετῇσι κεκασμένον ἐν Δαναοῖσιν,
> ἐσθλόν, τοῦ κλέος εὐρὺ καθ' Ἑλλάδα καὶ μέσον Ἄργος.
> (iv.725–26)

And when Odysseus makes his final farewell to the Phaeacians, he prays that the gods may grant them every kind of arete and no evil may be among the people (xiii.45–46). His meaning is: "May everything that they do be well done, and may nothing go wrong with them; may there be no strife, no sickness, no poverty."

Usually the context makes it clear what kind of arete is in

question. When the ghost of Agamemnon, after hearing the fate of the suitors, breaks out into praise of Penelope and extols her arete, saying that its fame will never die, it is her loyalty and faithfulness as a wife that he has in mind, in contrast to the faithlessness of Clytaemnestra, who killed her husband on his return, thereby bringing ill-repute on all womankind (xxiv.191–202). The wife of a king like Odysseus or Agamemnon has greater opportunities for arete than the wife of an ordinary man. In modern language it would be usual to say that her opportunity is greater to the degree that her responsibility is greater.

The Homeric manner of expressing this notion is to insist on the link between arete and fame or reputation (*kleos*). Penelope complains that when Odysseus departed for Troy, "the gods destroyed my arete and my beauty and my form" (xviii.251–52), and she adds that if he should return to take charge of her life, "my fame would be the greater."[17] As the widow or the wife of a lesser man, she would have less arete because her fame would be the less. Eumaeus has a similar thought in mind when he says that far-seeing Zeus takes away half a man's arete when the day of slavery seizes him (xvii.322–23). Taken out of context this famous saying might be interpreted in a modern sense, as though it meant that a man's character was broken by his loss of freedom or that the humiliation of slavery impaired his powers. The context shows that the meaning is different. Odysseus's old dog Argus has just died, a poor, helpless, neglected creature who has suffered sadly as a consequence of the absence of his master. "The women in their carelessness have not looked after him; and servants, when their masters are no longer in command, are no longer willing to work in due measure; for one half of a man's arete far-seeing Zeus takes away when the day of slavery seizes him." Servants, like dogs, can have little or no arete, because they have no standing by themselves. Whatever fame they can win will be from the reflection of their master's fame; without a master they have nothing at all, and a dog has not even a name.

In Homer, arete does not denote a quality of character inherent in a man. There is never any discussion of hidden, unrealized arete, because it does not exist until it is recognized by others. The persistence of this idea in Greek thought and speech is shown by the phrase that is commonly used to describe bravery in battle: ἄνδρες ἀγαθοὶ ἐγένοντο, "they became good men." This traditional phrase implies that men are not good men until they prove it by winning a good name. And if the respect of others or the source of their respect is withdrawn, as when a woman loses her husband or a dog its master or a man his freedom, arete is likewise lost in great part. The story of Achilles and his distress in the *Iliad* is properly intelligible only on such terms; the whole meaning of his life is lost if he is no longer held in honour.

The same point is brought out in Hector's reply to Andromache, when she begs him to stay behind in the city, so that his child will not be made an orphan and his wife a widow. He grants the force of her argument: "In truth all these things are before my mind, wife; but I feel terrible shame before the Trojans and the women of Troy, at the thought that I should shrink from war like a coward; nor does my spirit so bid me, for I was taught always to be a worthy man and to fight among the foremost of the Trojans, winning great fame for my father and myself" (*Il.* vi.441–46). He has learnt well the same lesson that Glaucus learnt from his father: "Ever to excel and be preeminent before others, and not put to shame the lineage of his fathers" (vi.208–9). Brave action and the good name that it wins are linked so closely that the words of Hector, if taken at face value, might give the impression that he is fighting only to win fame, and not to postpone the inevitable fall of Troy and the captivity of his wife and child.[18]

Even a man of little real worth, if he happens to command respect, may lay claim to arete. We find that the suitors are credited with it. Antinous and Eurymachus, their leaders, are called "by far the best in arete" (*Od.* iv.629; xxi.187), not because they are the worthiest characters among them, which they are not, but because they enjoy widest fame. The suitors think it right that Penelope should choose a husband from their number in accordance with his arete: "We await all these days," they say, "striving in a contest of arete,"

ἡμεῖς δ' αὖ ποτιδέγμενοι ἤματα πάντα
εἵνεκα τῆς ἀρετῆς ἐριδαίνομεν.

(ii.205–6)

"A contest of arete" seems a curious way to describe the suitors' daily life of idleness; their unruly and unseemly behaviour is hardly consistent with any effort to display "excellence" or to impress Penelope with the fitness of any one of them to be her husband. But their use of the phrase shows very clearly what they mean by arete. They expect Penelope to make a choice on the basis of their past achievements, their wealth and lineage and social prestige and the respect which they command among their own people. This kind of arete is something that is already established; as they see it, their present behaviour can have no influence on it. In the poet's opinion, on the other hand, this kind of arete is not really pertinent and their judgment is totally wrong.[19] They are worthless men not because they lack arete (if they had had none they would have been beggars or common labourers), but because they act in outrageous fashion with no respect for other people or fear of the consequences. The verdict is given clearly in the words of Odysseus after he has killed them: "The due destiny of the gods and their own shocking deeds struck these men down, for they had no respect for any man on this earth, mean or good, who came to them; so it was that by their outrageous folly they drew on themselves a hideous fate" (xxii.413–16). This folly is something for which they can blame no one but themselves; they cannot say that "a god took away their wits," as the poet says of Glaucus when he exchanged golden armour for bronze. They have not acted from anger or in a momentary impulse, which they might regret, as Agamemnon regretted his anger with Achilles, saying that *ate* ("infatuation") had seized him.

They have acted from pure "witlessness" (*aphrosyne,* cf. xvi.278; xxiv.457); they lack real intelligence.

Throughout Greek literature a man's moral worth is estimated largely in terms of his intelligence; the virtuous man "thinks right" and has "sound intelligence"; even the famous virtue of *sophrosyne,* commonly translated as "self-restraint," really means "sound intelligence." It does not mark a revolutionary change in Greek thought when Plato insists that only the wise man can be just; his interpretation of wisdom is different from the current interpretation, but Greeks could never have any admiration or sympathy for a "virtuous simpleton." Their mythology knows no "pure fool" like Parsifal. There is no pity for the crewmen of Odysseus who bring on their death by their folly, "fools, who ate the oxen of Hyperion, the Sun-god, and he took away from them their day of return" (i.8–9). They should have known better than to disobey Odysseus.

If moral judgments are sometimes passed in Homer in terms of what other people think or the due portion that society demands, a man's more permanent worth or character is regularly described in terms of his intelligence. Modern readers might be inclined to say that Odysseus's men, though intelligent enough, were weak-willed and could not resist temptation. But the familiar modern distinction between will and intellect is alien to Homer. Why, then, do Homer's characters resist temptation? Sometimes because they feel shame or respect for others, as the suitors did not; this is the first reason that Hector gives for not playing the coward. And when the Greek leaders are urging on their men to fight bravely and not lag behind, they tell them to "feel shame before one another" (ἀλλήλους τ' αἰδεῖσθε κατὰ κρατερὰς ὑσμίνας, *Il.* v.530).

But when Anteia, the wife of Proetus, tries to seduce Bellerophon, it is his intelligence that makes him reject her: "She did not persuade him as he had good thoughts,"

ἀλλὰ τὸν οὔ τι
πεῖθ' ἀγαθὰ φρονέοντα.
(vi.161–62)

The phrase "to have good thoughts" (ἀγαθὰ φρονεῖν) sometimes means "to be well-disposed or kindly," as when Hermes "with kind intent" tries to dissuade Aegisthus from the folly of murdering Agamemnon,

ἀλλ' οὐ φρένας Αἰγίσθοιο
πεῖθ' ἀγαθὰ φρονέων.
(*Od.* i.42–43)

But where self-restraint or resistance to temptation is concerned, many passages show that "intelligence" is meant. Clytaemnestra was not easily persuaded by Aegisthus to betray Agamemnon, because "she had good intelligence," φρεσὶ γὰρ κέχρητ' ἀγαθῇσιν (iii.266).[20] The archer Pandarus, on the other hand, is easily persuaded by Athena to shoot at Menelaus and break the truce, because he is not intelligent: τῷ δὲ φρένας ἄφρονι πεῖθεν (*Il.* iv.104). And when the ghost of Agamemnon, in the last book of the *Odyssey,* praises Penelope for her constancy to Odysseus, he insists on her good intelligence (ἀγαθαὶ φρένες) as well as her arete (xxiv.194).[21]

The plural noun *phrenes,* used here in the sense of "wits" ("poor fool, Athena took away his wits"), as it is in many other Homeric passages and throughout Greek literature, is also used to refer to one or another of man's internal organs. In the classical writers it is the term for the diaphragm, and in Homer it may possibly mean the lungs.[22] The word is not used with complete consistency, and there are times, in Homer, when it is difficult to be sure whether a physical or a psychic process is being described, as in *Od.* iv.661–62: μένεος δὲ μέγα φρένες ἀμφὶ μέλαιναι / πίμπλαντο, "his phrenes, darkening, were mightily filled with anger." Or when it is said that wine affects a man's phrenes by "coming around them," as when Odysseus made the Cyclops drunk: ἐπεὶ Κύκλωπα περὶ φρένας ἤλυθεν οἶνος (ix.362).

In any case, a man's phrenes are within him and not open to public view; the working of his mind is often contrasted with his outward appearance, and qualities of intelligence and character are contrasted with strength or beauty. Thus, phrenes are often contrasted with *erga,* "works," which are observable. When Agamemnon says of Chryseis that "she is in no way inferior to Clytaemnestra, my wedded wife, neither in build nor stature, neither in her phrenes nor in her works" (οὐ δέμας οὐδὲ φυήν, οὔτ' ἄρ φρένας οὔτε τι ἔργα (*Il.* i.115), one is tempted to believe that by her phrenes Agamemnon means simply her cleverness and skill, as illustrated by her womanly works. But it is hard to believe that Agamemnon is so much attached to Chryseis simply because she is beautiful and a good housekeeper. He must be thinking of all her qualities of character that endear her to him; the mention of "works" (*erga*) is an afterthought, not intended as an illustration of her phrenes.[23]

The term phrenes, it must be admitted, is used with a certain vagueness in Homer, in much the same way as terms like "heart," "mind," and "feelings" in modern English; it is not used to denote intelligence as opposed to feelings, and the corresponding verb, *phronein,* can mean "feel" as well as "think." But some consistency in usage can be seen.[24] A man's phrenes may be lacking or "not firm" or they may be good and "even." For example, the thoughtless Elpenor, who falls asleep on the roof after drinking too heavily and is killed when he walks over the edge, is "not well-fitted in his phrenes" (οὔτε φρεσὶν ᾗσιν ἀρηρώς, *Od.* x.553). This sort of language suggests the imagery of building, as though a man's intelligence were part of his inner structure, his *demas.* The adjectives derived from phrenes show that Hephaestus, the skilful craftsman, has no lack of intelligence (πολύφρων). Penelope, like the Phaeacian queen Arete, excels others in this quality (περίφρων) and holds fast to it (ἐχέφρων), just as Odysseus is "enduring in his phrenes" (ταλασίφρων), in contrast to others who are lax or have a loose hold on them (χαλίφρων). Other characters are described with reference to their *thymos,* their "spirit" or "impulses"; thus, Aphrodite cannot control her thymos, she is οὐκ ἐχέθυμος. In brave, confident, and vigorous men, spirit is plentiful, even excessive (μεγάθυμοι, ὑπέρθυμοι); in some it is sharp (ὀξύθυμοι), in others it is lacking (ἄθυμοι).

Very often, adjectives from the root *phren-* denote not a man's permanent quality of intelligence and character, but his immediate attitude towards another person. A man who has good and kindly intentions is "well-minded" or "forward-minded" (εὔφρων, πρόφρων), or his mind may be on destruction like Aetes (ὀλοόφρων) or Circe (δολοφρονέουσα), or on gain, as Achilles in his anger complains against Agamemnon (κερδαλεόφρων). Attitudes may be permanent or temporary, the result of some quality of character or merely of the immediate circumstances. But when strangers meet, what each wants to know immediately about the other is his attitude towards him: is he friend or foe, gentle or savage, trustworthy or deceitful? To a far greater extent than the *Iliad,* the *Odyssey* is a poem about strangers meeting. Odysseus, the great traveller, "saw the cities of many men," and learnt, often by bitter experience, whether their citizens were friends or foes. His immediate concern when he approaches them, whether in Phaeacia or the land of the Cyclopes, is to learn the attitude of the people—will they help or hinder him, show him hospitality or seek his death? His question follows a standard formula: "Who are these men? Are they violent, savages who know not the rule of law, or are they kindly to strangers and have they a god-fearing *noos*?"[25]

The traditional English translation of *noos* is "mind," as in the opening lines of the *Odyssey,* where the Muse is asked to sing of the man who "wandered much, after he had sacked the holy citadel of Troy, and saw the cities of many men and learnt their mind (noos)."[26] In classical Greek the word (in its Attic form *nous*) means "intelligence," and this meaning was established at least as early as the Ionian philosophers, since Heraclitus can say: "Accumulation of learning does not teach intelligence (noos)."[27] A distinction between noos and phrenes would be difficult to draw in classical Greek usage, except that phrenes, unlike noos, can be used to denote a physical organ of the body. In classical Greek a man who is well-disposed, kindly, or loyal is said to have "good noos"; the adjective *eunous,* unknown to Homer, has displaced the Homeric *euphron,* and the opposite is *dysnous,* "unkindly," "disloyal."

These are the adjectives normally used in political language to describe men who are loyal or disloyal to their cities; they describe the attitude of a man to his city, just as the "god-fearing noos," which Odysseus hopes to find among the strangers whom he visits, is a matter of attitude rather than intelligence.[28]

It is equally clear that the suitors are complaining of Penelope's attitude towards them when they declare that they will continue to devour the property of Odysseus by eating and drinking, so long as Penelope maintains the noos which she has shown by her trick of never finishing the winding sheet for Laertes:

> τόφρα γὰρ οὖν βίοτόν τε τεὸν καὶ κτήματ' ἔδονται,
> ὄφρα γε κείνη τοῦτον ἔχῃ νόον, ὅν τινά οἱ νῦν
> ἐν στήθεσσι τιθεῖσι θεοί.
>
> (ii. 123–25)

Since she had promised to make up her mind and choose a husband among them when it was finished, but never intended to finish it, it is her deceptive intention of which they are complaining. "Intention" or "plan" is often the meaning of noos, and sometimes a better translation than "attitude." One of the suitors speaks of "accomplishing our noos" by killing Odysseus and Telemachus (xxii. 215); and Helen says that when Odysseus came into Troy disguised as a beggar and she alone recognized him, he told her "all the noos" of the Greeks (iv. 256)—evidently their plan or intention, not their attitude.[29] The noos of Zeus, which men cannot escape or thwart, is his intention or purpose, like his *boule* or "plan," which is accomplished by the events of the *Iliad* (i. 5). The two words, boule and noos, are sometimes used synonymously, as when Odysseus asks the ghost of his mother to tell him the "plan and intention" of his wife (xi. 177–79; cf. xii. 211).

When strangers meet, one may try to conceal his noos—his unfriendly attitude or intention—from the other. When Odysseus wakes up in Ithaca, Athena approaches him disguised as a young shepherd, and Odysseus at once reveals his own friendly noos by the form of his address: "Friend, since thou art the first to meet me in this place, hail to thee! Do not answer me with evil noos" (xiii.228–29). Sometimes the noos is a more permanent state of mind, an attitude towards the whole world. When Odysseus, still in his beggar's disguise, starts giving orders to his own serving women, Melantho is astonished at such apparent insolence and asks him: "Does wine hold your phrenes or is your noos always like this?" (xviii.331–32). Earlier Odysseus had told an imaginary story of his life, combined with a sermon on the weakness of man, whose outlook on life is determined by the success or misery which the gods grant him; he is confident so long as the gods grant him arete (which in this context means success), but submissive when they make him suffer: "The noos of earthly men is like to the day which the father of gods and men brings upon them. I, too, once thought to be prosperous among men, and many outrageous deeds I did, yielding to my strength and might, trusting to my father and my brothers" (xviii.136–40).[30] Thus the confident noos of a prosperous man is contrasted with the humility of a beggar. A man's noos can be changed for better or for worse by circumstances or persuasion; it can be "turned," though the noos of the gods is not so easily "turned": οὐ γάϱ τ' αἶψα θεῶν τϱέπεται νόος αἰὲν ἐόντων (iii.147).

These passages are from the *Odyssey*, but there are passages in the *Iliad* in which the word is used in exactly the same way. A man's noos is equally important in the world of the *Iliad*. Paris praises Hector for his fearless noos (iii.63), and when Eurypylus is wounded and badly hurt, his noos nevertheless remains firm (xi.813). When Zeus is favouring the Trojans in battle, he soothes or charms the noos of the Greeks (xii.255) so that they become less bold, and Zeus speaks of Poseidon "turning his noos," changing his attitude or purpose (xv.51–52).[31]

The word *ethos* in the sense of "character" does not occur in Homer, but it is clear from the passages cited that a man's noos, whether considered as a permanent attitude or a reaction to particular circumstances, is an important sign of his moral worth. Hector's fearless noos sets him apart from Paris the weak coward, and the lack of any god-fearing noos among the Cyclopes is one of their characteristics as savages. And when Odysseus is angered by the Phaeacians, who taunt him for not competing in their games, he tells Euryalus that, despite his fine appearance, his noos is worthless (*Od.* viii.177).

The original root meaning and the etymology of noos have long been matters of dispute. It cannot be derived from the root *gno-* ("to know"), although it acquires a meaning close to "knowledge" in classical Greek and the cognate verb *noein,* which is common in Homer, means "to perceive," generally by sight. Since a consonantal *u* has been lost between the vowels and the older form would therefore be *nowos* (νόϝος), the root must be *new/now,* unless (as been argued) an initial *s* has been lost and it is *snew/snow.*[32] It is possible that there is a connection with the verb *neuo,* "to nod" (cf. Latin *nuo*), and that *noos* and *neuma* ("a nod") are originally similar in meaning, just as *rhoos* and *rheuma* both mean "stream," "flow." There is no immediate connection between nodding and thinking or perceiving, but the nod of Zeus was proverbial as indicating his purpose or will, and ancient Greeks, like modern, indicated assent or dissent by "nodding down" or "nodding up." Thus a nod can indicate purpose, attitude, good will or ill will. And noos, like rhoos and other words of similar form, could denote a movement or inclination rather than a physical or psychic organ (such as phrenes), an action ("willing," "thinking," "inclining") rather than an agent ("will," "mind").[33]

Even if this etymology is correct, it is not to be expected that the imagery of movement will always be respected in Homeric usage, and it has apparently been forgotten altogether in classical Greek. But there are many instances in Homer when the imagery of movement can be seen plainly. When anyone's purpose is changed, it is said to be turned, as Poseidon turns his noos and Calypso agrees to let Odysseus go "either because of a message from Zeus or because her own noos turned" (vii.263). The poet's choice of a theme depends on the direction in which his noos moves: "Why dost thou grudge a poet to delight men in whatever direction his noos moves?" Telemachus asks Penelope (i.346–47). The imagery in Latin and English "intention" is very similar; Calypso might be said to have changed the "intention" or "direction" with which she "aimed her purpose." The range of a man's thought is also a matter of some importance if it is conceived as movement. The noos of one man is said to be "shorter" (βράσσων) than when two take thought together (*Il.* x.225–26). And the movement of thought is swift. The ships of the Phaeacians move swiftly "as a bird or a thought" (*Od.* vii.36); and when Hera hurries from Ida to Olympus, she goes "as darts the noos of a man, who fares over much country as he thinks with shrewd phrenes" (*Il.* xv. 80–81). Here we see clearly that noos is a process performed by a man's phrenes. When Hephaestus made his automata to serve him, he put noos in their phrenes (*Il.* xviii.419).[34]

If a man's reason is impaired, temporarily or permanently, it can be said of him that the gods took away his phrenes (*Il.* vii.360) or even that he has lost his noos, as Athena says of Ares: "Mad creature, with thy mind destroyed, thou art ruined; to be sure thou hast ears to hear, but thy noos is lost and thy sense of shame" (*Il.* xv.128–29). Circe protests that Odysseus's noos cannot be bewitched (*Od.* x.329), but she has no intention of destroying it, because even the men who have been turned into pigs still retain their noos "unimpaired as before" (x.240). It is the human noos in the animals on Circe's domain that makes them behave in such a strange way, instead of attacking men as real wolves and lions would. And just as these bewitched men retain their intelligence, so does Tiresias, alone of all the dead: "His phrenes are unimpaired; to him alone in death Persephone granted noos (x.493–94).

Intention, purpose, attitude, even imagination, if the noos of a poet may be so described—all these are important elements in determining the quality of a man. They are all workings of his mind, which may at times be masked by outward behaviour. A man's immediate usefulness or friendliness may be assessed by his actions at the moment; but his usefulness for the future can be judged only if one can fathom his noos, which (unless it is turned or bewitched or otherwise affected by circumstances) will determine his behaviour. Sometimes a man's noos is described by saying that he "knows deceitful things" or "knows kindness"; knowledge is a permanent possession and is not easily lost. Hesiod uses the same kind of language; when Zeus creates Pandora, he orders Hermes to put in her "a shameless noos and a deceitful character (*ethos*)" (*Works and Days,* 67–68).

Some readers may think that this discussion of Homeric language and usage, with its brief excursion into etymology, has little direct relevance to the main theme—that it makes little difference to our understanding of popular ethics whether its conclusions are correct or not—and that in any event it was more detailed than necessary. It seemed worth while, however, to enter into details in order to make it as clear as possible that Homeric characters judge one another in terms of noos, and that no treatment of Homeric ethics is complete which confines itself to an exposition of the heroic code of arete and the limitations of man's "due measure." And, in view of the disputed etymology, the actual meaning of noos seems to deserve at least as much attention as that of arete and moira, if its application is to be properly understood.

Some interpreters of Homeric society and Homeric psychology are inclined to believe that the code of observable behaviour mattered above everything else, and that greater emphasis was placed on "excellence" than on kindliness or loyalty (though perhaps to a lesser degree in the *Odyssey* than in the *Iliad*). Such a view is not easy to maintain if, without disregarding the exhortations to arete, one studies the language that Homeric men and women use in passing judgment on the character of others. Antinous, the typically undesirable character of the *Odyssey,* shows his character by his name; his noos is hostile, and Telemachus says that he "is accustomed ever to provoke men unpleasantly by harsh words and urges others to do the same" (xvii.394–95). Antinous is the chief of the suitors, and no matter how unpleasant he is to the other suitors they have no redress. Kindness and gentleness, on the other hand, are qualities that constantly receive praise, especially in the *Odyssey,* where the relentless warrior is out of place. "He who is harsh himself," says Penelope, "and knows harshness, on him all mortal men call down curses while he lives, and when he is dead all men mock him; but he who is noble and knows noble thoughts, his fame strangers carry far and wide to all men, and many call him good" (xix.329–34). Penelope constantly bears witness to the kindness of Odysseus, who never did or said anything unseemly to any man (though kings often will; cf. iv.690–91). It is a sorry world in which good deeds are not appreciated (iv.695) and there is no incentive to do them. Athena herself, whose verdict must surely be taken as final when she speaks to Zeus on Olympus, expresses this thought most vigorously: "Father Zeus, and ye other blessed gods who live eternally, now let no sceptred king gladly be kind and gentle any more, nor know due behaviour, but let him be harsh and do deeds of violence—for no one among the people over whom he ruled is mindful of god-like Odysseus, and he was kindly like a father" (v.7–12).

The importance of winning a good name is not forgotten. Just as fame and reputation are always linked with arete, and no one acquires arete without acquiring the good opinion of others, so the incentive for a king to show kindness and good will towards his subjects disappears if his kindness is not appreciated and recognized. If neither gods nor men return the good will shown to them, the ethical structure of life collapses entirely. It is one of the tragedies of war that a man's acts of kindness may be of little use to him when death threatens; his grateful friends may not be at hand to help him. Axylos, who was "dear to men, because he showed friendship to all, living as he did near the road," did not escape death at the hand of Diomede; none of those whom he had befriended "warded off grim destruction for him then" (*Il.* vi.12–16).

The tradition of hospitality and the obligation to return the favour of a kindly host are so constantly illustrated in Homer that it is not necessary to cite any particular passages. Kindness to strangers is an important part of man's due behaviour; and because Diomede kills the hospitable Axylos, it is appropriate that he should soon afterwards redeem himself by sparing Glaucus, when he discovers that they are bound by a tie of hospitality which their fathers established. The abuse of hospitality is not the least of the sins of the suitors. Apart from the fact that such abuse was a violation of the code, it tended to undermine the whole basis of good behaviour when they tempted men to withhold hospitality by their insults and their plot to murder their host. The tie of loyalty between husband and wife is no less important than the tie between host and guest. Clytaemnestra's crime caused the ghost of Agamemnon to tell Odysseus "never to be gentle with a wife" and not to trust her (xi.441–42); he advises Odysseus to arrive unnoticed in his native land, "since women can no longer be trusted" (xi.456). But he makes amends for his loss of trust in marriage as an institution by the praise he lavishes on Penelope's loyalty in the last book of the *Odyssey* (xxiv.191–202).

The *Iliad* and the *Odyssey* are not moral treatises; they do not attempt to say why a king should be kindly to his subjects or a man hospitable to strangers or a wife faithful to her husband. Just because we are told that anyone who violates these fundamental rules will earn ill fame after death, it does not follow that desire for a good name was considered the principal motivation for good behaviour. A goddess says that dire results will follow if due behaviour is not rewarded, if this incentive to royal kindliness is removed. But the poet cannot analyze or expound the aristocratic code. It would be an impertinence for him to say that this was the only incentive to due behaviour. It might not occur to him to distinguish between incentive and moral obligation, but he does not say or even imply that it is as important to be honoured by men as to be kindly and loyal.

In telling the story of Achilles, he shows how a man who recognizes the obligation to win great renown is likely to be angry or even disloyal if honour is withheld from him; and how a man like Agamemnon, who already possesses great distinction, is liable to forget how easily he can lose respect if he pays no attention to the claims of others. Honour or the desire for honour can explain why such men behave as they do; but the poet is explaining, not condoning, their behaviour towards each other. Thetis does not moralize on the subject as Athena does, but Achilles recognizes his error in the end no less than Agamemnon; his obligation to be a brave and loyal fighter does not cease because Agamemnon has insulted him. The poet does not imply that the obligation to help those who cannot help themselves ceases when the chief incentive is withdrawn—if it seems that no one will hear of it.

Hybris, the lack of respect for one's fellow men, whether they are great or small, is the one sin the gods cannot forgive; and it is a fault that is in the noos of a man, a matter of thought rather than word or deed. But a man reveals his noos to others only by his deeds and words; it is by his outward behaviour, whether actually observed or known merely by hearsay, that a man's worth is assessed. In passing judgment, it is often enough to say that a man acted according to his due portion, according to dike or themis, or that he acquired arete and won fame. Since a man's fame lives after him, the question might arise whether a good reputation is as important as a good noos, as sound a basis for judgment as knowing what he really thinks in his heart. The question is not actually raised in Homer, though Hector comes near to raising it in his farewell to Andromache in Book VI of the *Iliad.* He admits that he is leaving her and going out to meet his death because of what men will say and what the custom of war demands; he does not say that he is doing the better thing. But there are other occasions when the contrast between outward behaviour and inner intention is clear, as when the suitors gather about Telemachus, "speaking goodly words, but plotting evil in the depths of their phrenes"

(*Od.* xvii.66). The arete that the chief suitors have acquired is no indication of their real noos; and their evil noos far outweighs anything that is admirable in their arete.

The way is prepared in Homer for the questions that are agitated in Attic literature, especially for the question: How is a man to estimate the true worth of another? Homer shows the alternative methods which are available, since a man cannot actually observe the noos of another unless he reveals it. A man may be guided by another's reputation or talents, as shown by his deeds; he may judge another's conduct in relation to a norm of behaviour or custom, or an inexact prevalent notion of what is due or fitting; or he may concentrate his observation on certain kinds of behaviour, taking note whether the other is loyal or deceitful, whether he rewards the favours done to him and by persistent good faith encourages others to follow his example. There can be occasions when one of these methods will give an answer which conflicts with the answer given by another, if, for example, a man who follows the established norm of conduct is nonetheless censured by others. And once the possibility of conflict between one method and another raises serious difficulty—as it does in Attic tragedy—men must ask whether one method is in itself better and more trustworthy than another. When doubt arises in the epic, any hint of apparent hybris gives the answer; good faith and kindness and respect for one's neighbour or guest or spouse are more important than any reputation that can be gained or maintained only by hybris. It does not follow that "the men of old" always found matters so simple and straightforward, or that this was the constant decision upheld by thoughtful men. But popular morality, as subsequent chapters show, was very unwilling to abandon this simple answer.

THREE. Hesiod, Solon, and Theognis: Persistence and Development of the Old Ideas

Since every poet and indeed every educated person throughout classical antiquity was influenced in some degree by the reading of Homer, the reappearance of Homeric ideas and words and phrases in the literature of the archaic age is scarcely a matter for comment. It is difficult to imagine a Greek poet unaffected by Homer's language and style, and the persistence of Homeric ideas is the most natural thing to expect in a literature with a strong sense of tradition. But it will be a more significant matter if the poets from the seventh and sixth centuries, as well as Hesiod, use an ethical vocabulary which is almost exclusively Homeric, and if most of their ethical ideas can be traced back ultimately to a source in the *Iliad* or the *Odyssey*. This will not mean that these poets are mere imitators of Homer, or that they are devoid of any individuality or original thought of their own; though they use Homer's ethical terms, they can develop or extend the meaning of them to suit different contexts or limit it by emphasizing one aspect of a word to the exclusion of others. Thus their work will provide a bridge between Homer and the literature of the fifth century, in matters of ethics as well as in language and style.

It is the use of a common ethical vocabulary which justifies the discussion of Hesiod, Solon, and Theognis in a single chapter. They are very different poets if regarded as individuals, and the differences between them are plain to see. Theognis, though the latest in point of time, is the most aristocratic in spirit, full of complaints about the poor quality of the new ruling class and the decay of old standards. Hesiod, the earliest of the three, has the least sympathy for the nobles, whose corrupt and "crooked" judgments are depriving humbler men of their rights. One cannot assign precise dates to Hesiod and Theognis, beyond saying that Hesiod belongs to the eighth (or possibly the early seventh century) and Theognis to the sixth century. But Solon's reforms in Athens are dated definitely in the first decade of the sixth century by Athenian tradition. He holds an intermediate position between Hesiod and Theognis in time and also in spirit, advocating a spirit of compromise and balance between nobles and commoners in order to maintain existing institutions and prevent the rise of a tyrant. He emerges as a much more distinct historical personality than the other two, since some of his poems are closely connected with his public activities and are in fact quoted by Aristotle, in the *Constitution of Athens,* to illustrate and document his reform movement. Later democratic tradition contrived to surround Solon with the mists of legend; even before Aristotle's time the orators liked to present him as an idealized "father of democracy," a title to which his claim is not at all well established. The details of his career provide some puzzles for the historian; but at least there is some external evidence in Greek literature to supplement what can be gathered from his poems, whereas nothing whatever is known about Hesiod and Theognis apart from the poems attributed to them.

Solon is an Athenian, the first writer from Athens whose name and works are known to us at all. But his poems have survived only in quotations made by Aristotle and Plutarch and others; one can only guess at the total quantity of his original poetic composition, and since only extracts of his work are preserved, the form and length of individual poems are uncertain, as well as the manner in which they were made public. The poems attributed to Theognis of Megara have survived in a manuscript tradition, but most critics would agree that they cannot all be attributed to a single author, that an attempt must be made to distinguish between the genuine poems of Theognis (the original nucleus of the collection) and later additions. The collection, as it is preserved, is a jumble of short poems in completely random order, including fragments from earlier poets with or without slight modifications. Here again, therefore, the original form of individual poems, as well as the extent and purpose of the original collection, can only be conjectured. The two poems of Hesiod which concern us, the *Works and Days* and the *Theogony,* have also been preserved in manuscript tradition (in contrast with other works of Hesiod that are known only from fragments in papyrus texts). These two works are preserved as ostensibly continuous poems of substantial length, but their continuity is broken in many places, and many lines preserved in the manuscript tradition are probably not part of the original composition. A similar difficulty thus presents itself with respect to all three authors: there is almost no hope of recovering their works in the form in which they were originally composed.

These would be very serious obstacles if one were trying to pass judgment on the work of these poets as individuals; the task of reconstruction is almost as difficult and as unsatisfactory as trying to reconstruct earlier versions of the *Iliad* and the *Odyssey* or the rhapsodies that bards of the Homeric tradition may have recited in the days before poetry was normally written down. But when one is concerned with the elements these three poets had in common, rather than with their differences or with the form or artistic quality of their work as individuals, these uncertainties become less important. Just as the previous chapter was concerned with the common stock of ethical thought that runs right through the *Iliad* and the *Odyssey,* without regard to the problem of authorship or the date of composition of different books, so the purpose of this chapter is to show that surviving poetic literature from the eighth to the sixth century used a common stock of ethical ideas and a common ethical vocabulary. For this purpose it would make no difference if the poems of Hesiod, Solon, and Theognis were divided in the manuscript tradition between ten distinct authors or if they were all attributed to one single writer, real or imaginary.

Our knowledge of the literature and thought of the archaic period is not of course confined to these three authors. Other poets, notably Tyrtaeus, Mimnermus, and Xenophanes, must not be forgotten, and their work will be introduced into the discussion as the opportunity occurs; often it will be seen that they conform to the same ethical pattern. But it is from the poems attributed, rightly or wrongly, to Hesiod, Solon, and Theognis that most can be learnt about ethical ideas current in the archaic period.

For present purposes the archaic period may be considered as extending over three centuries, from 800 to 500 B.C. Within that period there were naturally great political and social differences between one area and another, as well as notable divergence and development in literary fashions and styles and taste. But our knowledge of the history of this period is so fragmentary that we cannot call the work of any one poet specially typical of the spirit of his time and place. These poets are more concerned with personal grievances and admonitions than with an attempt to describe their own age. And in any event their poetry is so heavily flavoured with Homeric idiom, of thought as well as of language, that an individual political or intellectual setting does not emerge very clearly. This vagueness of background is one reason why it is difficult to decide whether a particular extract is "genuine" Hesiod or Theognis or Tyrtaeus. In fact, consistency or accuracy of historical description is not to be expected of the gnomic poets any more than in the *Iliad* or the *Odyssey*. But a consistent loyalty to a literary tradition is very strongly in evidence.[1]

The readers of later Greek times—for example, the young Athenians of the fifth century—were not greatly concerned with the accuracy or consistency of poets like Hesiod or Tyrtaeus. Their interest in such a poet as Tyrtaeus is better explained by saying, as Werner Jaeger does,[2] that they "rediscovered their own ideals" in his poetry. When a later age rediscovers an older poet and finds his tone appropriate and timely, it does not worry whether his tone was in fact timely at the moment when he wrote. Can we determine whether it was? Was the ethical code, strongly traditional in flavour, which emerges from the writings of poets like Theognis and Tyrtaeus, really in conformity with the ethical code of their times that was instilled by word of mouth, the practical teaching that parents expected their children to absorb? There is no certain answer, no sure way of satisfying a questioner who raises the doubt. But there are some considerations worth bearing in mind.

The gnomic or semi-proverbial character of this poetry, especially that of Theognis, is some guarantee that it represents popular, though old-fashioned, thinking. It is widely believed that some of the poetry attributed to Theognis was written by different and later poets; if this belief is correct, we have a further guarantee that the collection presents a cross section of current ideas rather than the opinions of an unorthodox individualist. Moreover, when the Theognis collection is compared with other poetry more or less contemporary, a fairly consistent pattern of thought emerges, and there should no longer be any doubt about accepting such evidence as a guide to the opinions of the time. Finally, all doubt can be discarded if this pattern of thought is seen to be a logical and natural link between the Homeric pattern and the pattern of the classical world revealed by Athenian literature of the fifth century. Literary tradition may be responsible for the long life of some ideas in poetry when they have become outmoded in real life. This is the only risk that need be recognized.

In the Homeric poems one of the most important limitations on human conduct is the "due portion" that must not be exceeded, the moira beyond which a man must not go if he is to avoid disapproval or nemesis on the part of gods and men. Insistence on this due portion of conduct implies a society with a firmly established traditional code, an aristocratic or at least a stable society in which variation from the norm is automatically condemned. Since great social changes in the framework of the community took place in the course of the eighth, seventh, and sixth centuries, it is understandable that the notion of a man's due portion should become less prominent. Indeed, the word moira is used by post-Homeric poets almost exclusively to denote man's destiny, the portion of life allotted to him by the gods, which he must receive without fear or complaint:

What is our moira to suffer, Cyrnus, we cannot escape;
And what is my portion to suffer, I am not afraid to endure.
(Theognis, 817–18)

A man's portion includes death, which no one can escape, though he may wish that it will come to him at the time of his choosing, as when Solon says that a man would receive his portion of death in due season after passing his seventieth year, or when he scolds Mimnermus for his complaints and invites him to say: "May death's destiny come to me in my eightieth year" (19.17–18; 22), or when Theognis wishes for the "portion" of death when he is in the depths of misery (819–20). Some unwelcome gifts of the gods must be accepted without complaint, and a man must recognize that they are not necessarily given according to his deserts. Wealth or success, therefore, are not matters of ethical importance; and if good fortune calls for rejoicing, misfortune calls for courage.

Sentiments of this kind need no particular comment. But if moira or *moros,* as a measure of man's behaviour in general, ceases to play the prominent part it had in Homer, it is still important as a limit to man's acquisitiveness. The Greek word *koros* describes the behaviour of a man who oversteps this due measure and is guilty of sating himself, selfishly taking more than he needs, like a greedy man who stuffs himself when he is no longer hungry. The word itself and the ethical recognition of its importance can be found in Homer. In the *Iliad,* for example, Menelaus complains that the Trojans seem never to have their fill of fighting, but always to want more of it; he says that there is a *koros* (a "point of satiety") in everything—in sleep and love, in song and dance—but the Trojans are insatiable in their appetite for battle (xiii.636–39). To pass beyond this point, to "know no satiety," is dangerous, even disastrous. According to Theognis,

Many more men than hunger koros has ruined before now,
Men who were anxious to have more than their share to possess. (605–6)

And there are the famous lines of Solon, which are included also in the Theognis collection:

Koros breeds hybris, when wealth grows thick and fast,
In men whose noos is not rightly set.[3]

(τίκτει γὰρ κόρος ὕβριν, ὅταν πολὺς ὄλβος ἕπηται
ἀνθρώποισιν ὅσοις μὴ νόος ἄρτιος ᾖ).
(Solon 5.9–10; Theognis 153–54)

We can see, then, how the old idea of moira as a due portion of conduct has given way to the idea of a due portion of possessions. Solon is more particularly concerned with political power than with wealth. He has to prevent any party from holding so much power that it will breed hybris, and like Theognis he fears the lack of self-control of the common people:

If this city falls, it will not be by the destiny [aisa] of Zeus or the purpose [phrenes] of the blessed immortal gods. See who holds out her hands above us, so great-hearted a protector, Pallas Athene, child of a mighty father! No, it is the citizens themselves who would destroy this great city in their witlessness, yielding to wealth. The noos of the people's leaders is unjust; they will suffer many ills for their great hybris. They know not how to restrain their desire for more [their koros] nor how to grace the good things offered them in the peaceful banquet (3.1–10).

A translation into more idiomatic English would obscure the abundance of Homeric terms that are used. They come thick and fast, and the poet darts from one way of describing behaviour to another. First he says that Athens cannot blame destiny, aisa or moira, for its disaster. The time is not ripe; this is not some heaven-sent calamity to be accepted with resignation. Rather, it is the citizens themselves, in their witlessness, their lack of phrenes, who are to blame—in their search for gain, their wrong-headed attitude, their noos with no regard for dike, their hybris inevitably bred by koros. Because of his fear of hybris which might result from koros, Solon tried to divide power between nobles and commons, as he tells us in another poem, "throwing a stout shield about both parties and not allowing either to win in despite of justice"; he "gave the people only as much power as suffices" (5.1–6).

All the standards and restraints of conduct familiar from the *Iliad* and the *Odyssey* appear in these passages, and very similar language can be found in Theognis, as in the following lines in which he describes his fear that a tyrant will rise:

> This city is pregnant, Cyrnus; I fear it may breed a man who will put a check on our base hybris. Our citizens have sound phrenes still, but the leaders are ready to fall into the depths of baseness. There never was a city, Cyrnus, that good men destroyed; but when it pleases base men to be hybristic, and they corrupt the people and give verdicts in favour of the lawless for the sake of their own gain and power, then you may expect that city not to be at peace for long, not even if it lies in the deepest calm now (39–48).

For Hesiod, as for Solon and Theognis, the greed and corruption of the men in power is the worst evil of his time—the "gift-eating kings" of Hesiod who pass crooked judgments (*Works and Days,* 263–64) are the base men of Theognis whose noos is insatiable and the leaders who give verdicts in favour of the lawless. Wealth does not necessarily corrupt. It is the danger, rather than any actual offence, in exceeding the due portion that these writers stress. "Listen to justice, Perses," says Hesiod, "and do not practise hybris. Hybris is bad for a weak man, nor can the good man bear it easily; he sinks beneath its weight" (*Works and Days,* 213–15). There seems to be a distinction between the criminal kind of hybris, which ignores justice and the claims of one's fellow men, and the kind which results from extreme prosperity and is likely to harm no one except oneself. The story that Herodotus tells about the Egyptian king Amasis, who fears that Polycrates is doomed to disaster because of his unbroken prosperity, illustrates it exactly (iii.40).[4] Though insistence on moderation persists right through classical literature, there are times when moderation is not a positive virtue, but a cautious counsel for the inexperienced and the unstable, who cannot be trusted to deviate from the norm. No one, least of all a gnomic poet, would ever recommend or approve koros or hybris; but in special circumstances, perhaps, it may be inevitable and even pardonable, just as Odysseus reminds us that there are times when shame (*aidos*) must be discarded—"shame is not good in a beggar" (xvii.347). Tradition and traditional standards are not sacrosanct, except in a perfectly stable society. But a man will disregard them at his peril.

There is no positive merit in remaining within the limits of one's due portion; most men are never tempted to do anything else. Likewise it is not difficult for an inconspicuous man to avoid the censure of his fellow citizens. But is it always a good thing to seek and win their acclaim? Arete, not only in Homer but in these poets also for the most part, is bound up with kleos, with reputation and what people say. Most men whom Theognis knows seem to regard arete as almost equivalent to distinction or success; and distinction does not always imply justice or desirable character. It is not, therefore, something that is to be sought in all circumstances and at all costs. Theognis advises Cyrnus not to seek honours or aretai if they can only be won by base or dishonest lawless deeds (29–30, cf. 129–30).

The inadequacy of public opinion as a true test of a man's worth is much more clearly set forth by Theognis than by any earlier poet. Arete, it is clear, can be earned dishonestly, just as the arete of the suitors in the *Odyssey* was hardly worthy of respect, a mere matter of social standing that they barely deserved to enjoy.[5] So Theognis tells Cyrnus to earn arete, but not to aspire to more than he deserves:

Strive not too much; the mean in all things is best; and thus
You shall have arete, Cyrnus, which is a hard thing to win.
(335–36)

An alternative version of the poem contains the variation: "Often a man strives for arete seeking his own gain, whom a god purposely draws into great error" (401–4).[6]

The second version, whether by Theognis himself or not, modifies the first by a more definite warning that arete is not to be sought at any price. It sounds as though a disillusioned old noble is advising a young man against a life of leadership and distinction because he will meet unworthy competitors. The alternative to what the world considers arete is the middle path (and that is real arete according to Theognis); but the direct opposite of arete is abject failure, the fate Hesiod fears may befall Perses if he does not bestir himself. For Hesiod, there are only the two alternatives, arete and failure (κακότης): "The immortal gods have put sweat in front of arete. The way to it is long and steep, and rough to start with; but when you come to the top of the hill, then the road is easy, though it is a hard climb" (*Works and Days,* 289–92).

The alternative road, which leads to failure, is smooth and easy. The choice for a man is whether to achieve something or to take the road of least resistance and be content with less than his portion. Arete here is no more a matter of morals or character or inborn qualities than it is in Homer. It is a matter of making one's way in the world, of "becoming a good man" and realizing one's potentialities, whether as a farmer by the sweat of one's brow and by following a rigorous programme of work (which is what Hesiod has in mind), or as merchant, politician, or soldier.[7]

Arete, in Hesiod's sense, may be something which the ambitious peasant respects without any qualifications, just as the aristocrat with only one path of life laid down for him must respect it. For Tyrtaeus, on the other hand, there is only one kind of arete worthy of respect, which a true Spartan should seek to win, the arete of a soldier:

> I would not praise nor hold in account a man
>   For speed of foot or skill in wrestling bouts;
> Not if he be as big and strong as a Cyclops
>   Or outstrip Thracian Boreas in the race;
> Not if in beauty he surpass Tithonus
>   Or wealthier than Midas be or Cinyras;
> Not if more kingly than Pelops he be
>   Or speak with tongue far sweeter than Adrastus,
> Or every fame enjoy but that of warrior.
>   In war a man is not accounted good
> Unless he looks steadfastly at the slaughter,
>   And pushes forward towards the foeman's line.
> True arete this, the best of all man's tasks,
>   Here is the fairest fame young men can win.
> (9.1–14)

Tyrtaeus, in the martial tradition of Sparta, is insisting that other kinds of distinction are not really true arete, not at least for a man who is young enough to fight in the battle line. He may also be deliberately contradicting a different point of view (the point of view, for example, of the Lacedaemonian farmer with little appetite for war), which would maintain that other ways of achieving distinction are just as praiseworthy as the warrior's way. Hesiod would have little patience with this praise of the warrior's life; his lines on arete have nothing to say of war, and he never implies in any of his precepts that a farmer may have to play his part in defence of his country.

It is not accurate to say that Tyrtaeus is defining arete or setting up the state as the standard of arete.[8] He is merely setting the Spartiat hoplite above the other classes of the Lacedaemonian community, proclaiming that the warrior's arete more truly deserves the name than the farmer's or the merchant's or the politician's. Nor does Hesiod define arete or say that only a farmer can win it; he thinks that farming is the preferable, perhaps the only practicable, way of making a living in Boeotia.

He thinks that a farmer's arete is hard to achieve but that other ways are even harder, and it is for this reason that he does not recommend seafaring. Theognis would add that success is not really arete unless it involves some difficulty:

> What the gods grant readily is not great or good;
> A deed must be hard to win praise,
> (463–64)

or

> Wealth to a worthless man a god may give;
> The lot of arete, Cyrnus, falls to few.
> (149–50)

Theognis is well aware that "To most of men arete means simply wealth" (699–700), and Solon talks of most men taking bodily strength as a sign of arete (19.8). Theognis, therefore, makes a distinction between material success and something more praiseworthy:

> Many a man grows rich with never a wit in his head;
> Others, with poverty's burden, seek the nobler ends.
> (683–84)

The same distinction emerges from some lines of Solon, which are repeated in the Theognis collection:

> Many base men are rich, while good stay poor.
> We for our part will never exchange arete
> With them for riches—giving a lasting prize
> In exchange for wealth, that now one has, now another.
> (Solon 4.9–12; Theognis 315–18)

When Solon and Theognis talk of "good" (ἀγαθοί, ἐσθλοί) and "base" or "bad" men (κακοί, δειλοί), we may suspect that they often mean the political and social groups which they like or dislike, the *boni* and *improbi* of Cicero, the established people as opposed to the trouble-makers. But in complaining of the revolution, Theognis admits that these titles have been reversed. Men who not long ago were mere outlaws,

> Now they're the good men; they who were good before
> Are now the bad. Who could endure this sight?
> (57–58)

In a well-established society, where the lines of class distinction are thought to be fixed permanently, it is understandable that the same word should be used for "undistinguished" and "worthless." But with the breakdown of the old aristocracy things have changed. Both in Hesiod and in Theognis we find the words used sometimes in one sense, sometimes in the other. When Theognis hears the men he respects called "bad," he naturally finds an apology for them:

> No man is rich or poor or bad or good
> Without some god to make him so.
> (165–66)

Here the terms good and bad clearly mean successful and unsuccessful. Similarly,

> One man will blame the good, others will praise them,
> But never a word is said of the bad.
> (797–98)

The "bad" are not positively vicious, but they have failed to achieve arete. And when Theognis speaks of making friends with a bad man, he is not thinking of someone who will prove to be a false or treacherous friend, but of someone whose friendship will be of no value or assistance (for example, 955–56).

Gnomic poetry is a mixture of practical advice and more genuinely ethical precept. Theognis says that arete is not worth winning at the price of injustice, and that distinction and success deserve no respect if they are the result of chance. What does deserve respect then? What kind of arete does he really respect? Perhaps "justice" is the answer:

> Rather be willing to live with modest possessions in piety
> Than be rich by gains unjustly won.

All arete is included in justice, Cyrnus, I tell you;
A man is good if he is just.

(145–48)

But what is justice, and who is the just man? In Homer he is the man who has respect for dike—the law-abiding man who fears the judges, and the law-abiding judge who observes the precedents of law and gives his judgments without regard for his personal advantage. Justice, in Homeric language, is one of the marks of civilized society, and Theognis is using this language when he complains that the new citizens are "men who hitherto no dikai knew nor laws" (54). Justice in this language is not so much a positive moral quality as a mark of civilized, well-ordered society. One must stop, therefore, and consider whether this is a new ethical definition of arete—"all arete is included in justice"—or whether it is simply a preference for one kind of arete over another. Tyrtaeus, who preferred the arete of the brave soldier to other kinds, might have said "all arete is included in bravery," and he did say "all arete is lost by cowardice." It seems, then, that just as Tyrtaeus regards bravery as a prerequisite to arete, so Theognis regards justice as a prerequisite. He has no use for the man who seeks arete by unjust means; arete won by such means does not deserve the name. Justice is the key, but it is not in itself arete.

No poet of the archaic age could say that "justice is arete," unless he were prepared to alter the meaning of the word arete and remove from it the connotation of "distinction," which it had always possessed, because certainly a man can be just without achieving distinction. Arete, in the old sense of the word, is a *telos,* an end or consummation which man does not achieve unless fortune and the gods favour him. And even though the gods favour him for a time, they may withdraw their favour. Thus arete, in the old conventional sense, is not won by man's efforts alone and its permanence is not guaranteed; it can be diminished or even destroyed by time. What the gnomic poets seek is the mark of true, permanent arete, which nothing, neither time nor the gods, can destroy, something without which no arete can be permanent, though it may be too much to ask that it will guarantee fame. Inevitably they pick on an inner quality of man, disregarding the externals of wealth and power; it has to be a matter of his noos. Instead of bravery or justice, others might prefer wisdom as the key to arete. Thus Pindar, in the second Pythian ode, is anxious that the arete of Hiero shall be guaranteed for all time. He does not forget the truism that one must not strive with the gods, who give glory now to one man, now to another (88–89); but he also does not shrink from predicting "unbounded fame" for Hiero, because in addition to the might of his fighting men he has "wiser counsels which make this word of mine less dangerous." Wiser counsels should ensure arete, no matter how fortune may change. Hiero will be able to ride out any storm.[9]

But the insistence on justice or some other inner quality of man as the essential prerequisite of arete has important consequences. It will eventually destroy the old meaning of arete, which will no longer denote "success" or "distinction," but will have to be identified with "true human excellence"; and the kind of success that is measured by temporary human approval will have to be designated by other words.

The just man will of course avoid koros and hybris, which are obstacles to true arete, though not necessarily to short-lived success; and he will preserve proper aidos, due respect for men and gods. He will do so the more readily if he is a child of parents "to whom holy dike is a care" (Theognis 131–32). Such parents are just parents, though they may not achieve fame or "become good men" in the old heroic sense of the term. They will teach aidos and self-restraint or "sound-mindedness" (sophrosyne), which are akin to justice; they will inculcate qualities of mind and habits of behaviour; but they cannot teach arete in the older sense of the word, when it is a telos, an end. They can only teach the means that lead to the end. Hence a discussion of whether arete is teachable is unthinkable until the word ceases to denote an end and is identified with a means, a quality of mind and character and a mode of behaviour. In the world of Hesiod and Theognis, it is unlikely that the discussion would arise.

The meaning of a word does not change overnight. The shift in meaning is likely to be a gradual process, and while the process is going on, some ambiguity in speech is inevitable. In fact, Theognis himself can be found using the word arete in three distinct meanings, which correspond to three stages in its development: (1) distinction and acclaim; (2) true distinction, which is not adequately measured by public acclaim; (3) true worth, which is independent of public opinion. In some passages it is hard to say precisely which meaning is intended, but in others there can be no doubt at all. Thus the first meaning is clearly intended in lines 129–30: "Pray not to excel in arete or in wealth; / Good fortune is all a man needs," and equally clearly in lines 699–700: "Most men recognize only one arete, wealth." Wealth may be considered a kind of distinction and contrasted with other kinds of distinction—political, military, athletic, artistic. But there is little or no ethical element in this kind of distinction or arete; and to cynical minds it may seem to be the result of pure luck.

A shift to the second meaning may be seen in lines 149–50:

> Wealth to a worthless man a god may give;
> The lot of arete, Cyrnus, falls to few.

The element of real worth in arete is clear in these lines, as also in lines 335–36, where it is said that arete is hard to win, or in lines 971–72:

> What arete is this, to win a contest of drinking?
> Often the mean man wins here, not the good.

But when arete is coupled with justice or wisdom (as in lines 789–90: "Let arete and wisdom be my foremost care") or when the poet says (as in lines 793–96), "Be just and content in thyself," ignoring what men may say in praise or blame, he is thinking of an arete totally independent of public opinion. Arete in the first or second sense cannot be hidden; but when we read (1061–62): "Some men with wealth conceal their meanness, / Others with cursed poverty hide their arete," a quality of character is meant, something totally independent of fame or recognition.[10]

Hesiod has nothing to say about the relation between arete and justice; though he has much to say about both, he has a way of using the words in separate paragraphs, as though they were of importance in different contexts. But it is instructive to examine the story of the five ages with both arete and justice in mind. Hesiod's despair with the present age, the age of iron, is tempered with a belief that the reign of hybris will not last forever; dike will prevail over hybris in the end (*Works and Days*, 217–18). It is the hope of a just world in the future that relieves the gloom. But in the golden age the conception of justice or injustice had no meaning. There were no evils in the world, there was no scarcity of anything that man needed, "and quietly men did their work with all good things in plenty" (119). The word "quietly" is important; since there was no need of hard work, neither kind of strife played any part in the golden age—neither the bad strife of contentiousness nor the good strife of healthy rivalry. There was nothing to test the qualities of a man, so that the distinction between good and bad did not exist or at least was not recognized. There was in fact no arete in the golden age at all; there was no need for it, and no need for justice where there was no strife.[11]

There was no arete in the silver age either, but strife had come in and men had no self-control. They were not tempted to commit hybris in the golden age, and once the temptation has taken hold of them they have no defence against it. The need for justice has arisen, and the age is helpless for the lack of it. In the bronze age men develop great strength, which might be considered a primitive form of arete or at least a means of winning recognition and fame. But it is only in the fourth age, the age of heroes, which is "juster and better" (δικαιότερον καὶ ἄρειον), that the distinction between good and bad first arises; here it must be supposed that both justice and arete are present. The iron age sees all these gains lost. No respect is shown for the just or the good man or the man who keeps his word. The only kind of arete that men recognize is a perverted one: "They will honour rather the doer of evil and hybris" (191). Dike exists only after a fashion; it is a matter of taking what you can, "taking the law into your own hands" (δίκη δ' ἐν χερσίν); and aidos and nemesis, the two powerful restraints on behaviour, will soon have left the earth.

But the iron age is not like a return to the ages of silver and bronze. There is some good left in the world; the better man is still there, though he is cheated and mistreated by the worse man, unable to achieve his telos of arete so long as hybris prevails over true justice. But time will bring a change, since justice is bound to triumph in the end; dike cannot be postponed indefinitely. A city cannot prosper except under the rule of justice, and such arete as a man may think to win without justice will be of short duration. Justice, which is denied to the animals, is "by far the best," and if a man is willing to speak words of justice, knowing what they are, to him far-seeing Zeus grants prosperity (276–81). Very similar sentiments will be found in Solon:

Possessions I would have, but win them unjustly I would not;
Ever does judgment follow at last."

(1.7–8)[12]

If in Hesiod dike distinguishes man from the animals, in Homer it distinguishes civilized man from savages. Savages, possibly even animals, may win some sort of arete (it might be attributed to the horses of the great heroes of the *Iliad* or horses who win victories at the games); but once it is made dependent on justice, neither savages nor animals can win it. Hesiod's myth of the five ages represents arete (of a primitive kind) as preceding justice in the development of civilization. Once it is made dependent on justice—once the rule of justice and law is established—it lies within the power of any just man. It may not be won without sweat, but it is there for him to win. Perses may be thwarted by the unjust judgments of the nobles, for the day of justice has not yet come. But the hope for the future is there.

It is quite unnecessary to regard Hesiod as a serious and accurate historian of ethical change, or to think that Homer's characters or the actual men of the late Helladic age in Greece were primitive in their thinking, like savages respecting success without justice, and that justice was "introduced" as a new idea by Hesiod.[13] Nor need we imagine that Hesiod supposes any changes of this sort.[14] The only change that can be substantiated between Homer and Theognis is a shift in the meaning of words. Perhaps, however, this shift should be explained as the result of a social change. These centuries saw a transition from aristocracy to a less clearly defined form of oligarchy, in which the rule of a traditional code no longer sufficed as a guide to conduct. A true aristocratic society, which stresses arete, will take justice for granted, regarding it as the minimum requirement if a man is to be tolerated in the society at all. But a new ruling class, not sympathetic to the old aristocracy, may have too little respect for aristocratic public opinion to accept its praise of arete, unless it is specifically associated with justice. It may even imply that aristocratic arete was not always an admirable thing, just as Theognis, a disappointed traditionalist, may feel that the notion of arete which the upstarts hold deserves little respect. Whatever the merits of either point of view, it is absurd to imagine that either party is deliberately exalting success at the expense of justice.

One consequence of this change in ethical vocabulary is that it is now easier to define arete than to define justice. No serious attempt is made to define justice, and the actual language used in passing judgment on a man's behaviour or disposition remains much the same. Aidos and nemesis still play their part, and it is by his noos that a man is judged. The word noos, however, can now be coupled with a word that will replace it in time, *ethos*; Hesiod says that when Zeus created Pandora he ordered Hermes to put in her "a shameless noos and a deceitful ethos" (67–68).

Like Odysseus in the *Odyssey,* Theognis wants to know a man's noos, and he complains that it is often difficult to be sure about it; and if a friend's noos turns out to be false and his heart deceitful, this is a worse disappointment than any counterfeit coin and the discovery brings great pain: "You cannot know the noos of man or woman until you test it, as with a mule; nor can you make a guess and wait till tomorrow to test it. How often appearances deceive!" (125–28). Zeus, who knows the kind of noos each man has (375), would make men suffer severely if he were to take offence at every shortcoming (897–900). What a man seeks in a friend is a trusty or an even noos (πιστός, 74; ἄρτιος, 154), not one that is fickle, changeable, or light, like the noos of a bird (498, 580). Wine unsettles, lightens (498), or unsteadies a man's noos, but it also reveals it (500). So also Solon complains of the unjust noos of the people's leaders (3.7), and how the noos of the immortal gods is hidden from men (17.1); and he talks of a harsh (23.18) and even of a gaping noos (χαῦνος, 8.6), apparently in the sense of loose and unsteady. These adjectives are different from those that Homer uses; they are more appropriate to a substance than a form of movement, to an organ of thought than the process of thinking.[15]

Noos is still the real essence of a man, as it always was; it carries a man's inner thoughts in contrast to his tongue (cf. Theognis 759–60),[16] and poverty in making a man cast shame aside causes him to disgrace both his body and his noos (649–52, cf. Solon 19.13–14). But there are synonyms for it, as when Theognis says: "Praise not a man until you know clearly his temper, rhythm, and way" (ὀργή, ῥυθμός, τρόπος, 963–64). And the change to the meaning of "intelligence," "good sense," which it has in Aeschylus and Herodotus (though not always) as well as in the philosophers, may already be found in Theognis. Theognis can speak of noos as the element in a man which should control anger if it is not lost; the man "whose noos is not more powerful than his anger" (631) will be constantly in trouble.

Theognis still judges men by their noos in the Homeric

manner, but he has more specific terms for particular qualities than were available in Homeric language. It matters to him not only whether a man's noos is friendly or hostile, but whether he is a good friend or whether it might be better to think of him as an enemy. His bitterest complaint is that his friends have betrayed him (811), and he regrets the scarcity of trusty companions in the world (209, 415–18, 645–46); a trusty man, he thinks, is worth his weight in gold (77). He himself has kept faith:

> Nor have I betrayed a friend and a trusty companion,
> Nor is there a slavish taint in my soul.
>
> (529–30)

In more bitter mood he writes:

> Through faith I lost my goods, through lack of faith I saved them:
> A gloomy thought to ponder, either way.
>
> (831–32)

Darker still is his picture of the world deserted by faith:

> Hope is the only goddess left among men;
> All other gods have left, to Olympus gone.
> Faith, the great goddess, is gone, Sophrosyne, too,
> Has disappeared; the Charites left the earth.
> No more may one put faith in fair-sworn oaths,
> Nor is there anyone who fears the gods.
> The breed of pious men has perished; none
> Revere tradition or the pious rules.
> And yet, while a man still lives and sees the sun,
> Let him stay pious and stand fast by Hope,
> Pray to the gods and burn the white thigh bones,
> And first and last to Hope make offering.
>
> (1135–46)

Sophrosyne, "sound-mindedness," is a powerful restraint on a man because it makes him recognize the consequences of his actions; it is a thinking element in him that controls and conditions his behaviour; men commit hybris more readily when they do not think what may follow. But *Pistis* (Faith), *Elpis*

(Hope), and *Charis* are of a different order from Sophrosyne; they are more like virtues in the Christian sense (though it would be dangerous to equate them with the Christian faith, hope, and charity) or qualities of character or of the noos. Just as certain situations may take away a man's noos or prevent it from functioning properly, so also faith and charis may disappear from his life. Hope stays longer, because it is one-sided. A man can hope independently of what other people think and do. But faith and charis are reciprocal: a man is loyal and trustworthy, kind and grateful, in the confidence that the trust and the kindness will be returned. If they are not returned:

> A thing I have suffered not worse than ugly death,
> But the most grievous thing besides—
> My friends betrayed me!
>
> (811–13)

Pistis and *elpis* need no special explanation; but it is hard to find the right English word for *charis,* which is both the initial favour that one person does for another and the gratitude or recognition that is shown in return. It plays a very great part in popular thinking and in all discussions of friendship; it not only makes friendships but also maintains them.[17]

A man's public behaviour, his behaviour as a citizen, may be regulated by considerations of justice. He must obey the laws, respect his fellow citizens, pay his debts, and so on; and if he is to earn respect, he must show that he excels others in some way or other. But neither justice nor arete is relevant where relations to family or friends are concerned. This is the realm of charis. In the literature of the fifth century, friendship also is regulated by justice, and the disappointed friend may complain that he has been "unjustly" treated; and in turn the vocabulary and reasoning of friendship is applied to public relationships, even to relations between states. This is democratic thinking, appropriate to a society of equals and perhaps inevitable in communities in which every man is expected to play some part in public life, so that all his fellow citizens are either friends or enemies and his importance will depend on the number and the influence of his friends.[18] Thus the conceptions of justice and friendship are blended; but in Theognis, as in preclassical literature generally, the distinction between public and personal relationships is still maintained, and justice and friendship belong under separate categories.

When Socrates asked for a definition of justice, it was to be expected that he would be offered the old formula, "helping one's friends and hurting one's enemies." But in earlier literature the idea of justice plays no part in such matters; this is simply what a man expects to do:

> Fall on me, great broad heaven above,
> In brazen mass, affrighting earthly men,
> If I fail in helping those who love me
> Or fail to bring my enemies woe and pain.
> (Theognis 869–72)

A man's friends are more vulnerable than his enemies:

> Even an enemy can hardly cheat his foe,
> But, Cyrnus, a friend can easily cheat a friend.
> (1219–20)

And even sufferings are to be deplored because they bring pain to one's friends and joy to one's enemies:

> Unlucky me! a joy to my foes in truth
> And woe to my friends my sufferings are.
> (1107–8)

The sharp distinction of friend and enemy, as though the relation of enmity was natural and permanent, is a remarkable feature of Greek literature. In the *Odyssey* (vi.184–85) when Odysseus is praising the happiness of a contented married couple, he describes their happiness as "great sorrow to their enemies and joy to those who love them," and the echo of this passage is clear in the words of Theognis just quoted. The contrast of friend and enemy is constant in Theognis, most striking perhaps when he prays to Zeus to let him repay his friends for their favours and prevail in strength over his enemies:

> And thus a god among men I should seem,
> If I could repay, and then due death would come.
> (339–40)

In similar style Solon prays "to have ever good repute before all men, and so to be sweet to my friends and bitter to my foes, a sight for those to revere and these to dread" (1.3–6). Theognis has no scruple about hurting or humbling an enemy:

> When he comes into thy power,
> Punish him; thou needst no special cause.
> (363–64)

But if a friend gives offence, this is no reason to make an enemy of him: "Hurt not a friend on pretext slight" (323). Dike should have no part to play, when strife is absent, as it is presumed to be between friends. In Hesiod's golden age, when there was no strife and all were friends of everyone else, there was no place for it; as Hesiod tells the story, justice does not even exist until strife and injustice and hybris have asserted themselves.

Friendship, however, like justice, is supposed to depend on a balance, a returning of like for like; you are not making a true friend if he cannot return your favour, because if there is no interchange of favours there is no charis. Friendship is also a matter of equality. A man who is put under an obligation and cannot return a favour finds himself in an inferior position to his benefactor, and the relation of friendship is in danger of being destroyed. Aristotle laid great emphasis on the importance of equality in friendship and found some difficulty in making "friendship between unequals" seem a practical possibility.[19] We should not be surprised that Theognis insists on careful choice of friends, when he knows how difficult it is to be sure about another man's noos. There is no warrant for Jaeger's view[20] that this insistence on carefully chosen friendships is a "protective attitude" into which the social revolution had driven Theognis. In any age except a golden age men suffer if they make friends rashly and carelessly, the more so if they regard friendship as a permanent relationship and if, like the Greeks, they think the possession of loyal and grateful friends one of the most important elements in a happy life.

FOUR. Justice and Revenge: The Tragedies of Aeschylus

With this chapter the discussion has reached a new stage. It would be absurd to pretend that the ethical and religious ideas of Aeschylus are a mere reflection of popular morality, and yet it is equally wrong to look upon him as an isolated individual completely independent of his time. Some of the issues in his tragedies may have been as obscure and difficult to his audience as they are to us, but his success as a dramatist shows that he was not out of touch with his age. In addition to original contributions and strange new ideas in his dramas, we should expect to find a fair measure of familiar or even conventional ethical thought.

For one thing, the inheritance of epic thought, as well as epic language, is still plain to see in all fifth-century writers, as it is in the poets of the sixth and seventh centuries. Aeschylus is supposed to have said that his tragedies were "slices from the feast of Homer."[1] Since he did not in fact take his themes from the *Iliad* and the *Odyssey,* or even adapt episodes from these poems as scenes in his plays, he must be thinking of thought and style rather than subject matter. His debt to Homer cannot be set forth all in a moment. It is something the poet shares with his audience, a common heritage of thought and language that enables innovations to be presented and understood as deviations from or improvements on a traditional pattern. If, like the other dramatists, Aeschylus is to be considered a moral teacher, he deserves the title because he invites the Athenians to question and refine their traditional ethical ideas; he does not merely re-state these ideas or illustrate them by tragic examples.[2]

It is hard to believe that a critic has correctly explained an Attic tragedy if he finds that its main theme is the illustration of a familiar moral maxim. Certainly the *Suppliants* of Aeschylus would scarcely qualify even as a rudimentary tragedy, if it was designed simply to show the rights of suppliants to protection. Nor does classical tragedy regularly show the virtuous rewarded and the vicious punished. On the contrary, in so far as tragic heroes are worthy characters, it seems to suggest the opposite. Greek tragedy, as Aristotle recognized, is full of moral paradox. But the greatest paradox of all, perhaps, is to be seen in the *Prometheus Bound* of Aeschylus, which shows Prometheus suffering for his benefits to humanity and, stranger still, appears to present Zeus, the father of the gods, as an ungrateful tyrant. Ingratitude and treachery, in the popular ethics that has emerged from the discussion in earlier chapters, are unforgivable offences; and so the impression given in this play, taken without the sequel, is that Zeus has failed in the most elementary test of good character.

Many tragedies present situations in which a character has to choose between alternatives, both of them unpleasant but one more completely and explicitly forbidden by the ethical code than the other. If a character chooses this alternative and is nonetheless eventually justified—like Zeus in the Prometheus trilogy, who must in the end have proved to have had a large measure of right on his side despite his apparent ingratitude and cruelty to Prometheus—this does not mean that Aeschylus is criticizing popular ethics for its condemnation of ingratitude. The implication is, rather, that moral issues are not as simple as popular ethics would suppose and that the current code cannot provide adequate answers to every moral question.

The present chapter does not claim to offer a comprehensive

discussion of Aeschylean tragedy, since justice is not done to any single tragedy if it is discussed solely in terms of popular ethics. Even to the critic whose main concern is to discover the relation between the poet and the opinions prevailing among his audience, political and religious ideas are important as well as ethical thought. The political and religious issues in Aeschylus have attracted much attention (especially interesting is the political relevance of the *Oresteia*); but it is not easy to relate the earlier plays to the current political and religious ideas of the earlier fifth century, because our other evidence for political and religious thought in Athens comes from the second half of the century. It is very doubtful whether one has any right to identify traditional ideas about politics in Athens until as late as 440. The background of traditional ethics, however, can be discerned more clearly. It has not changed from the Homeric and Hesiodic patterns as fundamentally as have ideas about religion and politics; even at the end of the century Aristophanes and Thucydides can show us that much of the old pattern still remains. Friendship, gratitude, trust, respect for law and justice, the sense of moderation, self-restraint described in terms of sound-mindedness—all these elements are still there. Indeed, they will continue to appear in Aristotle's *Ethics,* because in his day they still represent a recognized starting point for more searching discussion. We can be sure that they were part of the ethical heritage which Aeschylus shared with his audience.

We certainly should not imagine that traditional ideas had always been accepted without question. On the contrary, we must be ready to admit that Aeschylus was understood when he appeared to be criticizing them. His audience must have recognized what he was doing when he presented situations in which conventional morality was found inadequate; indeed, if they had not understood what he was doing, it is hard to see how the work of his successors could have been understood, since in this respect they certainly followed his lead faithfully.

It is usual to say that Aeschylean tragedy is preoccupied

with the problem of justice. Some modern scholars have supposed that Aeschylus knew what he meant by justice—a justice immanent in the cosmos or a justice guaranteed by Zeus.[3] But it is safe to say that the tragedies of Aeschylus, like the dialogues of Plato, take for granted that people are uncertain and unsatisfied about the nature of justice. Popular ethics had certain rough and ready definitions that met many situations. One definition was that justice meant returning like for like, evil for evil and good for good. It is easy to see that the extant plays of Aeschylus are largely concerned with this definition, with problems of reward and punishment and with the illusion that justice and revenge are necessarily the same thing. The search for so-called justice—for revenge, that is—often ends in disaster, whether the seeker attains his end or not, in the *Persians* and the *Seven against Thebes* no less than in the *Oresteia*.[4] It is proper to wonder whether the themes of justice and vengeance play an equally large part in the lost plays, but in the present state of our knowledge it will be necessary to restrict the discussion to the seven extant plays.[5]

Each play of Aeschylus will be discussed separately in this chapter. The plots of these plays are well adapted to illustrate problems of reward and punishment, and it is worth while to notice what Sophocles and Euripides make out of plots which have the same elements in them. Both of these dramatists wrote an *Electra,* and it will be found that the treatment of justice in their plays is definitely not the same as in the *Choephoroe*. But the plot that would be the most obvious choice for a vigorous treatment of the theme of revenge is the plot of the *Medea*. There are other plays in which the motif of revenge plays some part, notably the *Antigone* and the *Trachiniae* of Sophocles. But a brief analysis of the two *Electras* and the *Medea* of Euripides will be enough to show how much the fashion of thought concerning revenge and justice seems to have changed in the twenty or thirty years that followed the production of the *Oresteia*.

The Suppliants

Many tragedies are concerned with a conflict of duties. In the *Antigone* of Sophocles two characters are in conflict—Antigone, who insists on her duty to her dead brother, and Creon, who insists on her duty of obedience to the laws of the city—and the clash between their wills leads to disaster. In the *Philoctetes* there is a conflict not only between Neoptolemus and Odysseus, but in the mind of Neoptolemus himself, who is torn between the obligation of obedience to Odysseus, who wants him to trick Philoctetes, and the obligation of friendship and kindness which binds him to Philoctetes. Here a god appears in the end to resolve the difficulty, just as in the *Eumenides* the clash between the Furies and Orestes is resolved by Athena. The possibility that one obligation might conflict with another can hardly have escaped the notice of all Greeks before Aeschylus; but it is noteworthy that earlier literature did not exploit the conflict of duties, or even the apparent conflict of duties, as a theme. Thus in the sixth book of the *Iliad,* Hector knows that by going out to battle he is deserting Andromache and, in a way, abandoning her to her fate; but there is never any doubt in his mind, or in Andromache's or the reader's mind, that he must go out and face death on the battlefield. Andromache does not plead with him, and Hector gives no outward sign of wavering himself. The way of duty or the path of arete which he has to follow is not smooth and easy, but there is no doubt in which direction it lies.

The obligation of a host towards suppliants and helpless strangers is almost always clear and imperative. In the *Odyssey* (x.72–75), Aeolus, the master of the winds, refuses to give Odysseus help only when he recognizes that by so doing he is acting in defiance of a god's wishes, and that Odysseus after all is not one of those suppliants who can claim the protection of Zeus Hikesios; and Odysseus, when dismissed, is in no position to complain, since he knows very well how obstinately Poseidon is obstructing his return and that Zeus will not give him much help against this opposition.

Possibly Aeolus might be considered a prototype of Pelasgus, the Argive king in the *Suppliants,* who is doubtful whether he can offer sanctuary and hospitality to Danaus and his daughters, since he fears that by receiving them he may anger the Egyptians and involve his countrymen in a war. His dilemma is the greater because he is a king; whether he acts with or without the consent of his people, he will endanger his country by receiving them, and if he rejects them, the curse of the gods will fall on his country as well as on himself. His decision is to receive them, and he easily persuades the people of Argos to agree. Indeed, he could hardly have decided otherwise, since a religious obligation normally takes precedence over a political one; a serious conflict of duties can hardly have been said to exist. Herodotus provides several examples of the short shrift shown by oracles to individuals or states who asked whether they could betray suppliant refugees when it was politically inconvenient to continue protecting them.[6] So far as the story goes in the *Suppliants* Pelasgus has no choice.

But in reality he has made the wrong choice, and his error is revealed in the subsequent plays of the trilogy, when Danaus and his daughters act with unforgivable treachery. To protect a group of so-called suppliants, who were ready to go through a form of marriage and then murder their new husbands, was an error of terrible dimensions. Such suppliants did not deserve a kind welcome. Pelasgus was wrong to have done the right thing. The later plays of the trilogy are lost, and we do not know exactly how Aeschylus handled the character of Pelasgus nor how prominently his responsibility for the disastrous sequel was emphasized. It turns out that the situation facing Pelasgus was like the one Socrates imagines in the opening discussion of the *Republic*: Current ethics says you must give back to each man what you owe. But would you give a madman back his sword? It appears that by fulfilling the duties of a host, Pelasgus has, unwittingly, given back a madman his sword.[7]

In the *Suppliants,* however, the error of Pelasgus is not revealed and neither his character nor his problem really holds the centre of the stage. The ethical interest of the play is centred on the chorus, the suppliant daughters of Danaus themselves. Together with their father they have fled from Egypt to avoid forced marriage with the sons of their uncle Aegyptus, a union they regard as impious. Danaus has chosen Argos as a place of refuge because it is the land from which they trace their origin, from which Io came to Egypt where she gave birth to Epaphus, her child by Zeus and the founder of their family. The theme of the *Suppliants* is their reception by the Argives, who protect them in the face of an attempt by the Egyptians to carry them off. The Danaids do not form a prudent, balanced chorus such as often appears in tragedies. They see only one side of the question, and are quite unmoved by the difficulties that a quarrel with Egypt may cause the Argives. They demand their rights from Pelasgus relentlessly and unscrupulously; the fierceness with which they demand his help and the help of the gods, threatening suicide if it is denied them, offers a hint of the violence that will follow in the later plays of the trilogy. They appear to have a horror of marriage, whether with the sons of Aegyptus or anyone else; their hatred for the sons of Aegyptus is extravagant, and they have a rabid faith in the righteousness of their cause.

The manner in which they present the rights of their case by appealing to popular ethical rules deserves close attention. If one turns to the opening scene of the *Suppliants* after reading Homer or Hesiod or Theognis, every term and turn of the argument is familiar. In Homer the exile from his country, like Phoenix in the *Iliad,* is often guilty of manslaughter. The Danaids are quick to anticipate any such accusation; they are "not driven out by vote of the people for any spilling of blood, but self-condemned in flight from husbands" (6–8). Their flight is from an impious marriage, which themis forbids. They have followed the advice of their father, so that no one shall think them disobedient or wilful. And Danaus has not taken the step lightly. Since the Argives are their kinsmen, the Danaids expect to be treated as children of Argos with the affection and fondness that is granted to members of the family; they tell the story of Io's wanderings and the birth of Epaphus in order to establish their kinship. So long as their plea rests on kinship and friendship, they make no mention of justice; it is only when they turn to the gods, asking them to right a wrong, that dike is invoked—when they ask the gods, "who see the just so well" (78) and who hate hybris, to uphold the traditions of marriage and punish the Egyptians. Dike has no part to play in their plea to their friends; its part is to be in countering the impiety of the sons of Aegyptus.

Zeus is invited to take note of the Egyptian hybris; if he does not, the Danaids threaten to hang themselves, thus abandoning the Olympian gods in favour of the Zeus of the underworld, "who receives many guests," and Olympian Zeus will find himself liable to the charge of injustice (68–69). Thus they are threatening to judge Zeus, an act of impiety against which Theognis gave due warning:

> Mortals with immortals may not fight;
> Nor may they judge them; no one has this right.
> (687–88)

Danaus is more cautious than his daughters. After reminding them that they must restrain their tongues and behave as helpless suppliants should, he finishes with the thought that any man who seeks a woman in marriage by force must surely meet due judgment in the world below, if not in life—"and there, so we are told, another Zeus sits judging men's misdeeds" (230–31). Justice appears in his argument only at the point when punishment of the wicked is concerned; he is not asking the Argives for justice.

The same procedure can be observed in the dialogue between the leader of the chorus and the king, who now appears.

Pelasgus is satisfied that the Danaids are of Argive descent. He asks why they have come and is told simply: "To escape enslavement by Aegyptus' sons" (334). And when he asks explicitly what piety demands of him, the reply is: "Thou shalt not give me up at their demand" (340). When he demurs, fearing war with Egypt, the leader of the chorus tries a threat: "Justice stands guard to defend allies" (342). Dike is invoked only when the king seems to refuse help, since desertion of an ally will call down the judgment of men as well as gods; but the king quickly shows that the threat has no force: "Quite right, had I been with you from the start" (343). So the leader of the chorus changes ground, returning to the safer and unanswerable plea of a suppliant, without respect to the details of the story. Pelasgus cannot deny the suppliants' plea, "I shudder seeing how the place is decked with boughs" (345), and the leader of the chorus replies: "Yes, dread is the wrath of Zeus, the suppliant's god" (346).

Pelasgus accepts without question the Danaids' religious claim as suppliants, but denies their political claim. Again in lines 395–401, when the Danaids ask him "to take justice for his ally," he refuses to give judgment in their favour:

> 'Tis not a matter for easy judging;
> Choose not me for judge.

Each time the Danaids appeal to dike or "the just" (τὸ δίκαιον), as they do once again in lines 405–6, the king disregards their appeal. Nothing really weighs seriously in their favour with him except the fact that they are suppliants. He insists on the distinction between the religious and the political issue; and since he is not a tyrant, he cannot decide the political issue without consulting his people.[8]

After the verdict is given in favour of the suppliants, they sing a hymn in praise of Argos, ending with three special prayers for the Argives:

May they ever have a stable and far-seeing government (698–700).

May they grant justice [or: judgment] without harm to foreigners before arming for battle

> (ξένοισί τ' εὐξομβόλους,
> πρὶν ἐξοπλίζειν Ἄρη,
> δίκας ἄτερ πημάτων διδοῖεν, 701–3).

May the people honour their gods and children honour their parents, for this is the third command of Dike (704–9).

The first and third prayers need no particular comment, but the second prayer is specially relevant to the occasion. It is not always possible to pass judgment, as one thinks it should be passed, without unpleasant consequences or even war. Despite its apparently archaic features, it is no longer permissible to assume that the *Suppliants* is the earliest extant play of Aeschylus;[9] but even so, this is perhaps the first hint in Greek literature that justice and political expediency (or patriotic statesmanship) may be incompatible.

The rest of the play is of little concern to the present discussion. The Egyptian herald considers that he is acting with justice in claiming the daughters of Danaus and asserting his claim by force, but he is told bluntly that he is not following the correct legal procedure; he should make a claim in proper order, using his local representative (his *proxenos*) to plead his cause. The ethical issue is set aside; the herald intends to seek Ares as judge, and his judgments are never painless.

Prometheus Bound

The *Prometheus Bound* is a play concerned with punishment, and it introduces the notion of dike in the opening lines. Kratos and Bia (Power and Force) enter with Hephaestus, bringing Prometheus to the desolate rock where he is to be fastened in adamantine chains, and Kratos at once explains to Hephaestus his opinion of the guilt of Prometheus:

> Thy flower, O god, the flashing craftsman's fire,
> He stole and gave to men; this dike, then,

He pays in turn to the gods for his misdeed,
So he may learn to recognize in Zeus
A master, and no longer favour men.

(7–11)

Hephaestus, though far from happy that he must make his fellow god suffer, makes no direct protest against the legality or justice of the proceedings. He admits that in helping men as he did Prometheus went too far, "beyond dike" (30), and he excuses the severity of Zeus by saying: "Every new ruler rules with hand severe" (35). Kratos has no patience with soft-heartedness; when Hephaestus says that blood ties and friendship have some claims, he counters with the reply that the commands of father Zeus must be obeyed, that fear of Zeus is surely a stronger deterrent than fear of hurting a kinsman. Hephaestus in this opening scene is almost a prototype of Neoptolemus in the *Philoctetes,* torn between the command of authority and the claims of friendship and kindness; but he is soon convinced by Kratos that he has no choice, that he cannot refuse when Zeus commands.

We know very few details of the later plays in the Prometheus trilogy. The story of Prometheus and his relations with Zeus presents religious difficulties and complications that cannot be discussed here. But whatever the right solutions are, it is clear enough that in the opening scene of the extant play the audience is expected to sympathize with Prometheus and to understand the distaste of Hephaestus for his cruel task. This does not look like the working of justice. Unlike Pelasgus in the *Suppliants,* who did what seemed right and brought on disaster, Zeus here seems to be doing something distasteful, if not actually wrong; but since he is Zeus, we should be ready to believe that it will turn out to be right in the end.

It is Kratos who speaks of dike; and the mere fact that the word is used by him, the personification of Power, who has Force for his associate, is enough to warn us that it is being misused, as blatantly misused as by Polyneices in the *Seven against Thebes,* whose shield bears the figure of Dike saying:

"I will bring back this man to his native land." As Hephaestus says in his opening words:

> Power and Force, for you the command of Zeus
> Is final; nothing beyond it stands in your way.
> (12–13)

For them there is no distinction between might and right, no further obligation, no standard they can recognize beyond the orders that they receive; they are totally devoid of ethical thought, untouched by the compunction that Hephaestus feels. It means nothing to them that Hephaestus addresses Prometheus as "son of straight-counselling Themis" (18); they would not understand the difference between the verdict of an upstart tyrant, whose power rests on force alone, and a respected, conscientious judge and king. Prometheus stole something; he must be taught that it is useless to resist authority; this is all they know.

The opening of the *Prometheus* is a terrifying scene. The two characters who have any sense of an obligation beyond the fear of authority are helpless. The cruelty that man can inflict on man many Greeks in the audience would know; the thought that gods were capable of equal cruelty was enough to fill them with terror. The grim mockery of Kratos as he leaves, making fun of the name of Prometheus, "the foreseeing," is a cruel parting blow. Prometheus is beyond the hearing of men, but he calls all nature to witness "how I a god am treated thus by gods" (92). He cannot deny that complaint is useless; he has no choice but to accept his portion (103–4). This is familiar conventional language. But he cannot keep silence; the so-called misdeeds for which he is being punished are benefits that he has conferred on mankind. He is being punished because he has been "too friendly with mortals" (123).

When the chorus of Oceanids enters and they agree that the ruler of heaven is acting like a tyrant, Prometheus goes further. He cannot resist the time-honoured complaint that his enemies will rejoice over his sufferings (158), and the chorus is quick to reply that no god except Zeus could be so hard-hearted as to rejoice at such suffering. Gradually Prometheus becomes more communicative. Not only is Zeus severe and arbitrary, he says, "recognizing no justice beyond himself," but he has failed to show gratitude for the help Prometheus gave him when he deserted the Titans and helped Zeus to conquer Cronos:

> Such benefits had the tyrant of the gods from me,
> And with such punishments he favours me in return;
> It seems that one sure mark of tyranny is this:
> A tyrant never trusts his friends.
>
> (221–25)

Zeus, it seems, has neither gratitude nor trust, neither charis nor pistis. Nor did he care for mortal men or trust them; he wanted to destroy them too, but Prometheus countered him by giving them hopes, "blind hopes" (250); and he gave them fire, so that they were no longer utterly dependent on Zeus.

The chorus and Prometheus both recognize that the theft of fire was a mistake, "a conscious mistake, I cannot deny it" (266), says Prometheus. He had known that punishment would follow, though not such punishment as Zeus in fact decreed. His only hope now is in the knowledge that in time Zeus will need his help again. He is beyond the reach of any help the human race might give him in gratitude for what he did for them. In due time, however, in the closing play of the trilogy, *Prometheus the Fire-bringer,* the gratitude of men will be shown when they establish a festival in his honour.

Prometheus is not the only one who has suffered from Zeus's ingratitude; he is quick to recognize Io when she appears:

> Who warmed with love the heart of Zeus,
> And now, by Hera hated, goes perforce
> On endless journeys, ever driven on.
>
> (590–92)

Io made the mistake of doing what Zeus wanted, as conveyed

to her by the oracle of Apollo. Neither she nor her father followed the advice willingly, but he thrust her out of the house as Apollo ordered, and now she is changed into a cow, driven all over the world by the gadfly. Prometheus compares her treatment with his own:

> See how
> The tyrant of the gods to all alike
> Is cruel; with this woman he, a god,
> Sought union, and these wanderings are her prize.
> (735–38)

As Prometheus tells his story, it does indeed seem as though Zeus is a cruel tyrant; but his behaviour cannot lack justification, and it is no surprise that Prometheus fails to hold our sympathy to the end of the play. He begins to shout at the father of the gods, frightening the chorus by his wild language:

> Yes, flatter him, fawn on the reigning power;
> I care for Zeus—less than nothing at all.
> (937–38)

He declares that he hates all the gods, who enjoyed his benefits and now are glad to see him suffer (975–76); such arrogance towards the gods, like the threatening attitude of the Danaids, is a fair warning to the audience. He defies Zeus to do his worst, though warned by Hermes that Zeus keeps his word. Despite the ugly behaviour of Hermes, who is almost as objectionable a satellite of the tyrant as Kratos, Prometheus's final protest, "Thou seest how unjustly I suffer" (1093), is less convincing than his complaint at the opening of the play. Before the trilogy ends the issue that seemed so simple will appear neither simple nor absolute; even ingratitude, that most unpardonable form of betrayal, will have its explanation, and Zeus's credit will be re-established, so that both he and Prometheus will command respect again and the conflict between their claims will be reconciled. Just as Pelasgus proved to be mistaken in his kindness that he showed to suppliants, so will Zeus prove to be justified in withholding gratitude from a benefactor.[10]

The Persians

In the *Persians,* unlike the *Suppliants* and the *Prometheus Bound,* the drama itself includes a final judgment, a judgment that popular Greek sentiment no doubt regarded as just, a proper penalty for the hybris of the Persians and their desecration of the holy places of Greece. Some modern readers are content to think that this judgment constitutes the main theme of the tragedy[11]—the inevitable fall of Persian might because it aimed too high, Xerxes led to his fate by his lack of sophrosyne, the jealousy of the gods for every plan or design that exceeds the due limit. But the conception of judgment reveals itself very slowly in the play. In the opening scene the motif of the chorus, both in Parodos and in Stasimon, is one of trust—which suggests another contrast to the two plays already examined, in which charis was on the whole more important than pistis. The chorus consists of the "trusted councillors of the king, guards of the treasure houses" (1–4). They in their turn put their trust in the might of the great expeditionary force and the god-like man (80) Xerxes, its commander:

> Irresistible is the Persian host,
> Its brave-hearted men.
>
> (91–92)

If Xerxes' great undertaking against the Greeks should fail, it could only be because the gods have tricked Xerxes, because the Persians' trust in the gods has been misplaced. Their own position of trust and their loyalty to the throne are re-emphasized when the queen addresses them as "trusted elders" (γηραλέα πιστώματα, 171), and above all when the ghost of Darius addresses them in similar terms: ὦ πιστὰ πιστῶν, ἥλικές θ' ἥβης ἐμῆς (681) ("Most trusted of all, companions of my youth").

The part that trust plays in the whole structure of the Persian empire is a significant element in the tragedy. The chorus does not rebuke Xerxes for his failure; and, before the news of disaster arrives, the queen is confident that even if he has failed, his life and throne will not be in danger:

> And should he fail, he is not liable to the people;
> If he save his life, he still shall rule our land.
> (213–14)

It is tempting to find criticism of tyranny at every turn in the *Persians,* as in the *Prometheus,* but nothing that the members of the chorus actually say suggests that Xerxes is a tyrant or that they are dishonest satellites or oppressed nobles. On the contrary, they are trusted and loyal councillors, whom Atossa expects to be loyal to Xerxes whatever happens. Xerxes has not disregarded all advice and forfeited the good will of his people; rather, he is the victim of deceit, tricked by Themistocles and the envy of the gods (361–62). Nor did his men fail him. His orders may have been wrong, but they were carried out in true obedience and discipline (374). In the Messenger's account of the battle of Salamis, there is no suggestion that the Persian crews were cowardly or slow, but they were helpless and never had a chance against the clever, aggressive Greeks. It was the same with the group of soldiers sent to occupy the island Psyttaleia, the bravest men, of noblest birth, whom their king trusted more than any (443). They had no chance against the Greek hoplites who surrounded the island; but it is not implied that they betrayed their trust.

Indeed, if there has been treachery, it seems that the gods are guilty of it:

> O grim cruel god, how hast thou tricked the minds
> Of Persia. Bitter vengeance has my son
> On "famous Athens." Not enough, it seems,
> Were the deaths that Marathon claimed in time gone by.
> (472–75)

This is how Atossa interprets the disaster of Salamis; and again, on the retreat, a deceitful frost tempted the Persian army to cross the frozen River Strymon, and when the sun came out the ice gave way beneath them. One might have expected Atossa to rebuke the members of the chorus for misinterpreting her dream; but while she admits that they did so (520), she does not lose her trust in them, and reminds them of the task that lies ahead: "Trusty counsel to give to them that you trust" (527–28). They must give help and encouragement to Xerxes when he arrives.

It is only when the ghost of Darius appears, in response to the prayers of the councillors as their courage begins to fail, that Xerxes is made to appear at fault.[12] Darius explains everything in the terms that Herodotus has made familiar: Xerxes was not a helpless victim of divine deceit, but challenged the wrath of the gods by such impious acts as bridging the Hellespont and sacking Greek temples; full requital for all this hybris will come with the disaster of Plataea; Zeus punishes excessive ambition, and he strikes heavily. These sentiments would no doubt be approved by an Athenian audience, but in the play they are practically ignored by Atossa and the chorus. Atossa rather weakly tries to excuse Xerxes by saying he has given in to the advice of "bad men"—not a very convincing explanation after the insistence on the trustworthy character of the councillors—and Darius pays no attention to it. He still trusts the chorus to give the advice that Xerxes needs, to help him learn the lesson "Mortal man, think not too high" (820).

In fact, however, the chorus does nothing of the kind. When Xerxes appears, full of self-pity for his misfortune, the chorus agrees with him that the disaster was "unlooked for"; in the closing scene there is no hint of the warning or the lessons on which Darius had insisted, no suggestion of new distress or further troubles to come. Though the Persians—the members of the chorus, that is—have received a direct revelation of the truth, they fail to understand why such a disaster has fallen on them. Here, it seems, lies their tragic fault, though they are certainly "good" men, as Aristotle requires a tragic hero to be. They are certainly not unjust men. Indeed, although the Persian disaster might be considered a judgment of the gods, the play itself is not concerned with judgment or justice, and the very words *dike* and *adikia* are conspicuously absent from the text. There is no attempt to contrast just Greek with unjust Persian; nor is the justice of the punishment that the Persians suffer a question at all. And so far as the actual characters of the drama are concerned, there is no occasion to speak of justice, since they are friends who have no grievances against each other.

The Persians are not unjust, any more than Pelasgus and Prometheus are unjust. But they have been led astray by a loyalty which proves to have been misguided, a loyalty to an unworthy king and an excessive loyalty to the traditions of the past, which has caused them to maintain, wrongly, as Darius tells them, the old aggressive policy against Greece. Just as in the *Suppliants* and the *Prometheus* the weakness of charis as a complete guiding principle of conduct is revealed, so pistis here has proved an untrustworthy guide.[13] If this is the correct interpretation of the play, we should regard the chorus as its central tragic character, and it is its failure or *hamartia* that is the real theme of the tragedy. In that case the title of the play, the *Persians,* refers not to the Persian nation but to the members of the chorus,[14] the Persian elders (just as the *Phoenissae* of Phrynichus, which was produced only a few years earlier, was named after the chorus of Phoenician women). And as in the *Suppliants* and the *Eumenides* (though not the *Choephoroe*), the acts and the suffering of the chorus demand as much attention as those of the individual actors. Indeed, if the *Suppliants* is now to be accepted as a later play, the chorus of Persian elders has a fair claim to be regarded as the first tragic character, in the Aristotelian sense, in extant dramatic literature, and its tragic error or fault is its failure to see when loyalty to a king should be withheld or modified.

The Seven against Thebes

The *Seven against Thebes,* like the *Persians,* opens on a note of trust and confidence, with Eteocles displaying his confidence of victory thanks to the "trusty bearers of shields" (19), the unfailing divination of the prophet, and the scouts and spies who, he is sure, will not fail in their task (37). And when the Messenger announces the advance of the seven Argive leaders against the seven gates, he finishes by saying he will keep "a trusty day-watching eye" on everything (66–67). The members of the chorus are less confident; in their appeals to the gods they show not only piety but terror, for which they are duly rebuked by Eteocles. But when they remind him that the power of gods is higher than that of men, he shows his piety too. He has no intention of neglecting the duty of sacrifice and prayer.

So far, at least, there is no sign of hybris in Eteocles; but he is doomed, as everyone in the audience knows, an inevitable victim of the curse on the house of Laius. He will have to take the fatal step, the fatal wrong step, that will bring him into direct conflict with his brother, Polyneices, at one of the seven gates where the attack on Thebes is being made; the curse will not be fulfilled until he makes that move.[15] He will, in fact, deliberately choose to fight against his own brother; and as soon as the Messenger starts his account of the seven Argive champions, it is easy to guess that Eteocles will wait until the last one, who will be Polyneices, to choose his own opponent. But why will he make this choice? What mistaken notion of patriotism or bravery will drive him to take this terrible step?

Enlightenment comes gradually as Eteocles names the Theban defenders at each gate and justifies each choice. There has been no mention of dike, either as justice or as judgment, in the opening scenes,[16] but since the defending champions are avenging a wrong to their own country, they might be considered as representing or executing justice. The first, Melanippus, who is to oppose Tydeus, is descended from the Spartoi and is almost literally a child of Theban soil rising in defence of his mother. *Dike Homaimon* ("the justice of kindred blood") is said to push him forward (415), and the chorus agrees that he "rises justly as champion of his city." Tydeus is boastful enough, but the second attacker, Capaneus, goes much further, defying the will of Zeus to stop him from burning Thebes, and it is simple for Eteocles to pray that Zeus's thunderbolt may strike him "with dike." It is the same with the third and fourth. Against Eteoclus, who boasts that "not even Ares shall throw him from the towers" (469), the chorus prays that Zeus Nemetor may direct his glance in anger, so that his arrogance shall receive its due nemesis. Hippomedon, who has the image of Typhon on his shield, is worthily matched by the defender Hyperbius, on whose shield Zeus himself sits, thunderbolt in hand. The fifth Argive champion, Parthenopaeus, also defies Zeus to stop him from sacking Thebes; and Eteocles and the chorus can pray that the gods will punish such impious boasting as it deserves. There is no tragic or ethical interest in the fate of such scarcely human savage assailants; their impiety makes them seem less formidable.

It is very different when the Messenger starts his description of Amphiaraus. No raging frenzy drives him on; he is a brave man, but sound and prudent in thought (568). He finds fault with Tydeus, "a source of evil counsel to Adrastus," for urging this attack on Thebes; he knows that a divine judgment in favour of these men is impossible, since no god would support Polyneices' attack on his own native city: "What justice ever will dry a mother's spring?" (584). The description of Amphiaraus draws immediate tribute from Eteocles, and a cry of regret for the fate that "links a just man with the impious" (597–98). Amphiaraus is a just man doomed by the company he keeps; the scourge of the gods that punishes the others will strike him too: "By Zeus's will he too shall be dragged low" (614). Within thirty lines the word dikaios is used four times, but it does not characterize Amphiaraus completely; he is σώφρων, δίκαιος, ἀγαθός, εὐσεβὴς ἀνήρ (610). He shows soundmindedness in contrast with the raging frenzy of the others; he is just and pious, where they reveal a disregard for the will and judgment of the gods; and he is a good and brave warrior, a man with arete, like the rest, except that they strive to display, even to flaunt, their valour with boastful images and mottoes on their shields, while his aim is different: "Not brave to seem, but brave to be he wills" (592).

Despite all his virtues Amphiaraus is doomed, and since

his destiny is known it is a mere matter of form to set up an opponent for him. The chorus's prayer is in more general terms than usual, as it asks the gods to hear its just plea.

Amphiaraus is silent and makes no boast of seeking justice; but Polyneices, the seventh assailant, calls on the gods of his native land to restore him to his own, and his shield carries an image of Dike, who says:

> I will bring back this man, and he shall dwell
> In his own city and his native haunts.
> (647–48)

This claim draws forth a furious outburst from Eteocles; Dike, he says, would lose all right to her name if she stood by such a man, who would dare anything (671). He offers himself as the most just opponent; that is, the opponent whom justice would most properly choose:

> King against king, brother resisting brother,
> Enemy confronting enemy I shall stand.
> (674–75)

Amphiaraus, it seems, has shown him the way. Both will have justice on their side; both will be victims of their curse. Eteocles will claim to behave justly, but incur the ghastly pollution of killing his brother all the same. The tragedies of Amphiaraus and Eteocles (of Polyneices too, if one could accept his claim) show the paradox of justice, as the story of Zeus and Prometheus shows the paradox of friendship and kindness. There are times when neither justice nor friendly behaviour can save a man, times when these obligations must be neglected. Theognis found that arete was not always a safe guide, and it is noteworthy that it plays little part in the ethical vocabulary of Aeschylus. Is justice an equally uncertain guide to conduct?

It is easy to answer the question in modern terms by pointing out the difference between the abstract ideal of justice and a particular judgment or sentence carried out after quarrels and violence, which is what dike means in Aeschylus. A sentence has to be carried out against Polyneices,[17] but because Eteocles insists on carrying it out himself, it becomes sheer impious horror, an act of impious quarrel. The chorus applies the word Polyneices ("man of strife") to both brothers, as it describes their death:

> οἳ δῆτ' ὀρθῶς κατ' ἐπωνυμίαν
> καὶ πολυνεικεῖς
> ὤλοντ' ἀσεβεῖ διανοίᾳ.
> (829–31)

The end is reached, the curse fulfilled, the quarrel ended by death; Ares and the dark Fury have had the final word.[18] There is no mention of dike now, for this disaster cannot be called a judgment, and it certainly is not justice. As becomes clearer in the *Oresteia,* the question for man is not whether he should seek dike, but how he should seek it, and what he should do when the search seems to involve a contradiction and a denial of the ethical code. To insist on personal redress for a wrong may not be true justice, for the gods cannot always return a favour, and loyalty cannot always be rewarded.

The Oresteia

The *Oresteia* is concerned in great part with actions that are wrong from one point of view and right from another; and since we have the complete trilogy we can observe how Aeschylus resolves the puzzle. Like the *Prometheus,* the *Oresteia* is concerned with dike, with questions of justice and retaliation and charis, and like the *Seven against Thebes* it shows a curse bringing a succession of calamities upon a family. The curse is to be finally resolved not with the extinction of the family, as in the Theban legend, but with a real solution; Orestes is saved from the pursuing Furies and a new, ordered system of resolving quarrels and injuries is established by the wisdom of Athena. The *Agamemnon* provides the setting and the preliminary deeds of violence; these create the dreadful task for Orestes and present the problem that is too great for mere human minds to solve.

From the very beginning the *Agamemnon* is full of contradictions, a justice that is not justice, a charis that is thankless and graceless. The Guard in the prologue wavers between despair and rejoicing; he knows that the beacon which announces the fall of Troy means release for himself from his lonely vigil, but fears that it will not be the end of tragedy for the house of Atreus. And when the chorus enters, one issue after another is raised and the threads of the argument are soon tangled, because the story cannot be set forth simply except by those who see only one side of it.[19] The notion of dike is introduced without delay. Menelaus and Agamemnon claimed dike from Priam, backing their claim with the thousand ships that sailed to Troy, confident of the support that Zeus, the god of hospitality, must give to a host so basely cheated by a guest as Menelaus was by Paris. But the long years of fighting, with many losses on both sides for which Agamemnon cannot deny responsibility, have made them less sure. The omen of the eagles and the hare, if Calchas was right, foreboded both good and evil. How should they know whether they can discard their feeling of dread? Zeus is their only refuge, who has set mortals on the road to understanding, making the rule that "by suffering you shall learn" (176–78).

Certainly, men must depend on the favour of the gods. But even the favour of the gods may be double-edged or "violent"—δαιμόνων δέ που χάρις βίαιος (182)—as indeed the sequel will show. The contrary winds at Aulis could be stilled only if the favour of Artemis was won, and it could not be won without shedding the blood of Iphigenia. Agamemnon had to make a far more terrible choice than Eteocles, but a choice similar in kind; only by betraying his child, by violently denying to his daughter what he owed as a father, could he keep faith with the others. He could not keep faith with both.

> A heavy lot if I am disobedient;
> Heavy, too, if I slay my child,

The darling of my house,
Staining a father's hands with streams of maiden blood,
By the altar standing.
Evil? What can there be here without evil?
How should I desert my ships
And fail my allies?
This sacrifice to stay the winds, this maiden's death—
With fierce desire Themis demands it.
So may all be well.

(206–17)

It is, of course, a ghastly illusion that Themis should really desire any such thing. Agamemnon should know that this is the curse of his family fulfilling itself, and that he gains little by appeasing Artemis. He will learn in good time; that is the judgment which lies in wait for him:

The scale of judgment swings; by suffering shall they learn
(δίκα δὲ τοῖς μὲν παθοῦσι μαθεῖν ἐπιρρέπει).

(249–50)

The weight of dike will indeed fall heavily on Agamemnon; it may be the judgment of Zeus, but Clytaemnestra will imagine herself as the instrument of dike. Of this the members of the chorus know nothing as yet; but in the meantime dike (in the sense of custom or legal duty) requires that they honour and respect their queen Clytaemnestra:

Dike it is that we honour the wife
Of a man who rules, when he is far away.

(259–60)

They do not know it, but they cannot honour Clytaemnestra without betraying Agamemnon. The contradictory claims of dike are multiplied. Whether a man chooses with eyes shut (like the chorus) or open (like Agamemnon), he will suffer for his choice just the same.

Perhaps it is an awareness of these contradictions in dike that prevents the chorus from hailing the fall of Troy as justice or judgment. To them it seems a charis, a return or reward for their toil and suffering, a favour of the gods which demands due thanks:

> Let me now thank the gods in prayer;
> No small reward for our labours have we won
>
> (θεοὺς προσειπεῖν εὖ παρασκευάζομαι·
> χάρις γὰρ οὐκ ἄτιμος εἴργασται πόνων).[20]
>
> (353–54)

It is the gods, not Agamemnon and the Greeks, who are credited with the victory. Zeus, the god of hospitality, has shot his bolt at Paris, and only impious men think that gods ignore transgressions. The choral ode that follows Clytaemnestra's departure (354) is punctuated with proverbial or gnomic thoughts: the middle course is best, deeds that no man should dare engender a curse. The language is partly gnomic too, borrowed from Solon and Theognis or from the common stock of gnomic poetry. Paris and Helen, misusing the power of wealth, are said to have rejected dike, to have put it out of sight, kicking aside its great altar. But Agamemnon is far from guiltless himself, and the chorus is too cautious to speak of his victory as the work of dike.

It is usual to think of Aeschylus as almost obsessed with the notion of dike in the *Agamemnon*; but, as in Theognis and the *Prometheus,* charis plays almost as large a part, especially in this choral ode. The story of Agamemnon and Iphigenia, of Paris and Helen, can be told in terms of charis as well as in terms of dike. Agamemnon denied charis to Iphigenia, just as Helen denied it to Menelaus; and Paris scorned the charis that Menelaus showed him. The Messenger, who enters next, represents the fall of Troy as a penalty that the family of Priam paid for its misdeeds (537), a judgment passed by Zeus, who lent his mattock of judgment to Agamemnon so that the buildings might be levelled to the ground (525–29). But he does not neglect the motif of charis; his second speech closes with the words:

> So praise the city and our generals,
> And honour the charis of Zeus.
> Thou hast the tale.
>
> (580–82)

In plainer language, the gods have entered their judgment against the Trojans, but to the Greeks they have shown their charis. And to anyone who looks ahead, the future can be viewed in terms of charis as well as dike; from Clytaemnestra Agamemnon looks for charis, but he will receive only what she claims to be dike.[21]

The Messenger leaves the stage; but the chorus is still thinking of those who withhold charis, like the lion cub who is ungrateful when the time comes for him to show charis to those who fed him; savagery is the return he makes to the house for the kindness that he has received there. The ode ends, however, with familiar sentiments about dike; and, as though to drive the point home, when the leader of the chorus hails Agamemnon he has both charis and dike in mind:

> How shall I hail, how show respect,
> Neither exceeding nor falling short
> Of due measure of charis?
> Many a man thinks only of seeming,
> And thus transgresses dike.
>
> (784–89)

Agamemnon seems to re-echo this greeting:

> First to hail Argos and the native gods
> Dike demands,
>
> (810–11)

and his emphasis on dike is very strong, as he speaks of the judgment that the gods executed on Troy, while not forgetting the gratitude that he owes them. The chorus had insisted in its greeting on the element of true friendship and good will, warning Agamemnon that in time he would learn the difference between his true and his false friends (805–9), and in his speech he makes some rather sententious comments on these remarks (838–40). They might have put him on his guard against any excessive display of warmth; and when Clytaemnestra, in her speech of welcome with its fulsome flattery, certainly oversteps "the due measure of charis," one might imagine the chorus pondering the warning it has just given. Not content with false charis, she ends on the note of dike, inviting Agamemnon, with grim irony, to tread the purple carpet on the path that dike leads him (910–11). Her plans to exact what she calls justice from Agamemnon are fully made; all that is needed is for Zeus to grant fulfilment in answer to her prayer (973–74).

Both Agamemnon and Clytaemnestra speak with great assurance of the justice which they claim to have executed or to be executing. Their assurance is in contrast with the bewilderment and uncertainty of the chorus and the language of Cassandra, who in all her catalogue of blood and vengeance has no thought of dike. Her terms are more savage and primitive. If Clytaemnestra kills her, it will be an act of retaliation, a price exacted from Agamemnon for bringing Cassandra home with him, an act of revenge by an injured wife and mother; and when Orestes comes in due time to kill Aegisthus and Clytaemnestra, she sees him as "punishing" or "exacting payment" and vindicating her own honour:

> οὐ μὴν ἄτιμοί γ' ἐκ θεῶν τεθνήξομεν·
> ἥξει γὰρ ἡμῶν ἄλλος αὖ τιμάορος,
> μητροκτόνον φίτυμα, ποινάτωρ πατρός.
> (1279–81)

She knows, nevertheless, that Orestes is only "putting the coping stone on evils" (1283). There is no justice in the succession of events as she sees them; they may follow one another in accordance with a decision of the gods, "a great oath sworn by the gods" (1290), but this does not mean that such events must be called "just," and she never uses the word at all. In the brief anapaestic interlude before the cry of Agamemnon is heard, the chorus re-echoes her language:

If now Agamemnon shall pay back
His blood in return for blood shed earlier,
And if by his death he shall bring other deaths
In payment to the dead—
What mortal who heard such news could claim
To be born with a blameless destiny?
(1337–42)

It is only when Clytaemnestra exults over her deed that the notion of justice is re-introduced, and to the chorus her self-righteousness seems insupportable. Aegisthus is equally conscious of exacting justice from Agamemnon. "O joyous light of judgment day" (ὦ φέγγος εὖφρον ἡμέρας δικηφόρου, 1577), he begins, before telling the tale (so familiar to the chorus) of Atreus and Thyestes. He presents himself as "the just contriver of this bloody deed" (1604), and declares that "justice from exile brought me back" (1607). And he finishes:

Happy now would I be to die,
As I see him caught in dike's net.
(1610–11)

But for Aegisthus, as for Kratos in the *Prometheus,* justice is simply a matter of power, so long as he holds the power. When the members of the chorus threaten him with judicial procedure, he laughs at them: he is stronger than they are, and they are fools to threaten him. All of a sudden we are in the world of Thrasymachus. They are helpless and can only complain that he is polluting justice (1669). Thus the *Agamemnon* ends, as the *Prometheus* begins, with the hint that the dike of which powerful men speak is often the merest mockery of justice.

In the *Agamemnon,* Clytaemnestra and Aegisthus speak as though they are confident that their acts are just, and Agamemnon is almost equally self-righteous. One might argue that the claims of the murderers are insincere, that they represent a kind of bravado which covers fear and uncertainty. But even if this is true, in the play it is the display of assurance that matters; and it is heightened by the fears and hesitation of the chorus. In the *Choephoroe* the situation is reversed. It is the members of the chorus now who are sure of what must be done, never doubting or hesitating; but instead of constantly appealing to justice, they are content, in the first half of the play, to emphasize the need of revenge and to repeat the "ancient law" that blood must have blood and that he who does the deed must suffer (δράσαντι παθεῖν). They appear to make no real distinction between dike and retribution (*poine*), claiming that the goddess Dike demands requital:

> Grant, mighty Fates, that this may end
> With Zeus's will in the path of justice.
> "For angry words let angry words be paid,"
> Thus Dike loudly cries, exacting her due,
> "For bloody blow let him pay bloody blow."
> "He who does must suffer."
> So runs the ancient saying.
>
> (306–14)

Later in the play, when Clytaemnestra is dragged away to her death, their language is still similar:

> Justice came to Priam's house,
> A heavy-judging punishment;
> And so to the house of Agamemnon it came,
> A double lion, a double blow.
>
> (935–38)

How, then, can they doubt that Orestes is right? When he first tells them, in the closing scene, of the Furies that he alone can see, they tell him quite calmly that he must not be alarmed, that his mind is upset by the fresh blood on his hands, that Apollo can purify him (1052–60). Only in the closing lines of the play do they recognize the question they must face—has Orestes saved the house of Atreus by killing Clytaemnestra or merely made matters worse, with a "third tempest" following upon the deeds of Atreus and the murder of Agamemnon?

Orestes, like the chorus, starts in full confidence, never

doubting that Apollo has directed him right. Praying to Zeus in the prologue, he asks:

> Help me to requite my father's death,
> And be my ready ally.[22]
>
> (18–19)

He has full confidence in Apollo—"No, mighty Loxias will not betray me" (269) – and remembers the terrible punishment threatened by the oracle,

> If I do not requite my father's slayers
> In the selfsame way.
>
> (273–74)

Besides the oracle, there are other compelling reasons for the deed:

> A god's bidding and my father's sufferings;
> And heavy, too, besides is poverty's weight;
> To think that glorious Argives who took Troy
> Should thus be subjects of two women.
>
> (300–304)

Up to this point Orestes has said nothing of dike except in the cryptic line which comes near to suggesting that it is not relevant: "Ares shall strive with Ares, dike with dike" (461). It is as though Clytaemnestra's rights were being weighed against those of Agamemnon. But finally he prays to Agamemnon:

> Send dike as an ally to thy friends,
> Or else give us some holds that we can use,
> Like those they used in their attack on thee.[23]
>
> (497–99)

If the text is correctly interpreted here, Orestes seems not to be asking for the assistance of the goddess Dike, but to be praying that the juridical interpretation of his act may be favourable to him, that he may appear to have at least as good a pretext and explanation for murder as Clytaemnestra had. It is a prayer for legal assistance rather than for moral support.[24] This is the last item in the series of requests that Orestes and Electra make of their dead father before her final prayer to him not to let the house of the Pelopidae die out (503). There is no sign yet of hesitation or doubt on the part of Orestes. Only when he is actually face to face with his mother does he hesitate and ask Pylades for advice; when Pylades says that he must obey the oracle, he is resolute again and rebuffs every plea of Clytaemnestra. But he never speaks in terms of dike, as Clytaemnestra and Agamemnon did; his final words, before he leads her off the stage, are:

> He died, who should not, at they hand;
> So suffer now what should not be
> (κάνες γ' ὃν οὐ χρῆν, καὶ τὸ μὴ χρεὼν πάθε).
> (930)

He is saying as clearly as he can that what he does is wrong, but inevitable.

It is not until after the murder that he claims from the Sun god the assistance for which he asked Agamemnon. He asks the sun to be "witness at law" for him that he killed his mother "with due justice," adding that he needs no such assistance to justify the death of Aegisthus, since the killing of a seducer is provided for by law (984–90). The legal tone of his argument continues until he is faced with the vision of the Furies. He shows evidence that Clytaemnestra was indeed the murderess of her husband, and, arguing that she had forfeited all right to be regarded as a mother, he declares boldly that he did the deed "not without dike" (1027), and reminds Apollo of his promise that "Doing the deed I should not suffer blame" (1030–32). Orestes is thinking how to justify the deed in the eyes of the world; when he uses the word dike he means "justification" or "just cause."[25] His mother's death was what his father's honour demanded, and the oracle insisted on it; and yet it was wrong for him to kill her—it was, as he said himself, what should not be.

This dilemma is something that the chorus is very slow to

understand. But Electra is concerned with dike from the start. Disturbed about the proper form of prayer to make when pouring the libation to Agamemnon, she asks the advice of the chorus and is told to ask "blessings for them that love him," that is, "for herself and all who hate Aegisthus" (109–11), and to pray that for the murderers someone may come "divine or human, who shall kill in return" (119–21). Her suggestion that the word "judge or just executor" be used is thrust aside; and when she asks if piety allows such a request as they suggest, the answer comes back: "Why not? Requite an enemy with evil" (123). The chorus can easily solve the difficulty by making the familiar distinction between friend and enemy, which plays so large a part in popular ethical thinking.

For the chorus enemies are always enemies. Not only can one properly feel hatred for them instead of charis, but any offer of charis from one "enemy" to another is to be rejected as fraudulent. To a modern mind the attempt of Clytaemnestra, at the beginning of the play, to appease Agamemnon's ghost by a libation seems either an empty, futile gesture or an attempt, however feeble, to make peace with the dead. Orestes, indeed, calls it a "feeble charis (δειλαία χάρις, 517). But to the chorus it seems "a charis that is no charis" (χάριν ἄχαριν, 43), because the enmity between killer and victim can never admit of reconciliation (48). By similar reasoning it rejects, as illogical, the possibility that the lock found on the tomb might have been put there by Clytaemnestra—an enemy (173).

To the chorus this distinction between friends and foes is final and satisfactory, and nothing is appropriate to a foe except enmity and requital. But Electra is not so sure that this reasoning provides a just conclusion. She wants to be "In mind more stable, in hand more pious than my mother" (140–41), and she prays that an avenger may come so that the murderers may be killed in their turn *with justice*.[26] She finishes her prayer to Agamemnon by asking him to send blessings "With the gods and Earth and victory-bringing Dike" (148).

There is no comment from the members of the chorus.

Their concern is with victory rather than justice, and for them Orestes is simply an avenger. But for Electra he means much more than this, and the splendid speech in which she hails him, once she is sure that he is Orestes, deserves careful reading. She greets him in terms of hope, charis, and trust. He is the hope of which they had almost despaired (236);[27] by his very presence he gives delight and joy (ὦ τερπνὸν ὄμμα, 238), reviving in her all the affection, for father, mother, and sister as well as for brother, that she thought she had lost when Agamemnon and Iphigenia died and love for her mother turned to hatred. And she can trust him: "Trusty brother thou wast" (243). But hope, charis, and trust are not enough to ensure success:

> Only let Power and Justice and for a third
> Almighty Zeus lend us a helping hand.[28]
> (244–45)

It is Electra who chooses Dike as a member of this trio. The chorus might have chosen Force (Bia), and thus have reproduced the three figures who dominate the opening scene of the *Prometheus*: Power, Force, and Zeus. Orestes for his part looks to Apollo as his patron; and, as has been shown, he does not appeal to justice but seeks rather to find legal support, in divine and human opinion, for a violent act of revenge. The way of vengeance is identified with the way of justice only by the chorus:

> "For angry words let angry words be paid,"
> Thus Dike loudly cries, exacting her due.
> (309–11)

Electra continues to ask the gods for "just fulfilment" (ἰὼ θεοί, κραίνετ' ἐνδίκως, 462), and she prays for "right after wrong" (398), only to be reminded by the chorus that this is an unreasonable prayer, that the injured parties themselves must strike the blow since blood demands blood by inexorable law (400–404).[29] But like Orestes, she knows the problem which they have to face, with its moral, religious, and legal implications.

She knows that their position is not unlike that of Agamemnon at Aulis, when he dared not neglect a god's demand and the demands of his people: "A heavy lot if I am disobedient" (*Ag.* 206). She knows that there is no happy solution, that they cannot indeed effect justice, since Ate, not Dike, has the final word (338–39).[30]

Electra does not speak after Orestes has explained his plan, and she enters the palace when Orestes and Pylades leave the stage (584), to prepare for their re-entry as strangers. When they are gone, the chorus in its ode recalls some of the most ghastly horrors of mythology and insists that it is right to gather all these tales (τί τῶνδ' οὐκ ἐνδίκως ἀγείρω, 638). Its lesson is that the sword of vengeance is forged by Destiny, not Justice, and that it is the Fury, the Erinys, who brings on the avenger, the instrument of Ate. He does not wield the sword of Justice. Indeed, the very foundation on which the altar of Justice stands is torn down: Δίκας δ' ἐρείδεται πυθμήν (646).

The reminiscence of passages in the *Agamemnon* seems clear, as though once again man was "kicking aside the great altar of Justice" (*Ag.* 383–84). These recollections remind the chorus that acts of violence and hate are never the work of Dike.[31] The next time that the stage is empty (after the scene between Orestes, in disguise, and Clytaemnestra[32]), there is no mention of justice when the chorus prays for success:

> Crooked Persuasion—now her time has come
> To join us; and Hermes of the underworld
> And Hermes of the night, to set us on the road
> In this affray of sword thrusts.[33]
>
> (726–29)

It is the "horrid work of Ate" that Orestes has to do (τλᾶθι περαίνων ἐπίμομφον ἄταν, 830), and when the chorus uses the word dike again, it is in the strictly concrete sense of "verdict," a mere synonym for revenge:

> τῶν πάλαι πεπραγμένων
> λύσασθ' αἷμα προσφάτοις δίκαις

(With sentences new pronounced
Wash away the bloodguilt of deeds done long ago).
(803–4)

When it is the turn of Orestes once again to explain himself, he says it is Agamemnon who is taking vengeance himself: "I say the dead are slaughtering the living" (886).

Both for Orestes and for the chorus the motive of revenge far outweighs the motive of justice. The chorus is inclined to confuse or identify the two at times, but Orestes knows what he is doing. He has some hopes of justifying his deed before the world, but he will never say that it was a deed of justice; he never even hopes or prays that it may be, as Electra does. It remains for Apollo, in the *Eumenides,* to state categorically that it *was* a just deed, "And, prophet as I am, I shall not lie" (614–15).

In the *Eumenides* we see the attempts of Orestes to justify his deed before the world. There is a tendency among modern readers to suppose that Apollo is under criticism, that he is on trial as well as Orestes. The opening scene of the *Eumenides* is of great importance, because it warns us that this would be a false interpretation. The Prophetess in the prologue does not merely explain the antiquity and sanctity of the Delphic oracle; she shows that Apollo is not at variance with the other gods. There is no suggestion that the orders of the oracle met with the disapproval of Zeus: "Spokesman of father Zeus is Loxias" (19). The gods of Olympus are apparently as solid in agreement as they were in the *Prometheus.* And Apollo accepts full responsibility. "I shall not betray thee," he tells Orestes (64), echoing the words of Orestes himself in the *Choephoroe* (269). But defence against his enemies, which he promises (66), will not be enough; no final solution or atonement can be won that way. Orestes cannot shake off the pursuing Fury; the only solution is to be found in dike. Orestes' deed will not of itself achieve justice. That is something which lies far in the future, for which they must search together before the court in Athens:

> There we shall find judges, and with soothing words
> A means we shall find to free thee once for all
> Of these thy sufferings. I was the one indeed
> Who did persuade thee thus to kill thy mother.
> (81–84)

The gods did not disapprove of what Apollo did. Clytaemnestra finds little sympathy either from the dead or from the gods (98–102), and it is she herself who has to stir the Furies out of their slumber.

The Furies are the ones to complain that justice is being neglected, when a god steals a matricide from their grasp: "Who shall say that any justice is here?" (154). They protest that the younger gods have become powerful "beyond the bounds of justice" (163) and that Apollo is showing too much respect for humanity, contrary to divine law (171–72). This complaint of the Furies recalls the complaint of Zeus against Prometheus; and Apollo treats their protests with as little respect as Prometheus showed for Zeus. "Speak not thus," says the leader of the chorus, "curtail not my honours." And Apollo replies: "I never shall consent to honour thee" (227–28). The justice of which they speak, he says, is of a different order from the dike that he respects. It may be a small matter that they are ready to disregard the bond of marriage in favour of the bond of parenthood, to let the slayer of a husband go free while they persecute the matricide (though it is a gross insult to human feelings as well as to the gods who are the patrons and protectors of marriage). What matters more is that their "justice" is a justice of retaliation and revenge, not of reconciliation. Athena, when she gives judgment, will reject their kind of dike altogether. The retributive dike of the Furies perpetuates violence, it leads to no end; true justice must have a finality and put an end to violence; and therefore in his prayer to Athena Orestes asks for "finality of justice" (ἀναμένω τέλος δίκης, 243).

Although the Furies reject the kind of justice that Orestes seeks as impossible and absurd, since in their opinion there can be no end in this world to the punishment that he deserves and Hades is the only judge whom they respect, they continue nevertheless to apply the proper terms of legal language to their kind of dike. They claim to be "straight in judgment" (312) and to spare the innocent as well as to pursue the guilty; and they claim a kind of finality in their pursuit:

> True witnesses, standing by the dead,
> We come to exact the guilty man's blood
> In finality.
>
> (318–20)

And twice again they insist on using the word "final" of themselves and their work.[34] When Athena appears, after first insisting that abusive language plays no part in the work of justice or themis (413–14), she shows, as we might have expected, that her eye is on finality; when informed that the Furies pursue killers, she asks what is the end to which they are driven (ποῦ τὸ τέρμα τῆς φυγῆς, 422). The Furies reply: "In a place where joy is never known" (423). This is the same as saying that there is no end, that their justice never brings expiation, that their punishment knows no end. Their other evasive replies lead her to conclude that they are not anxious for true justice, but want only to be thought just (430).

It is not always easy to distinguish the purely legal issues in the *Eumenides* from the ethical. The insistence on the validity of law courts and on their obligation to reach decisions, taking account of such things as motive, provocation, and force of circumstance—this is an important part of the play. But the ethical issue is bound up with the legal; it is man's ethical duty, as well as his legal duty, to distinguish and decide, to weigh one factor against another, and not be content with the outworn convention of the Furies, which decides issues by the old, rough classifications of acts of violence. The old, rough classifications made finality impossible, and the identification of justice with retaliation made strife endless. Thus one of the lessons of the *Eumenides* is that ethical decisions are not mechanical; they cannot be made by adhering to hard and fast rules, which was the way of the Furies—the way of primitive barbarism. The other lesson is that issues cannot be determined by threats and fear. The Furies complain bitterly that the house of Dike will collapse when the restraining element of fear is removed (515–20). The best answer to their complaint is given by Pericles in the Funeral Oration: that fear (fear of the laws) is not absent in Athenian society, but it is not the dominating element which controls behaviour. The Furies thought only in terms of punishment and deterrents; Apollo tries to tell them that a part of justice is the reward of men who have proper fear and respect: οὔκουν δίκαιον τὸν σέβοντ' εὐεργετεῖν; (725). Justice, then, is not to be regarded only as retaliation, as an unpleasant and often brutal decision which comes in the wake of strife. The novelty and real significance of this new approach to justice (which to conventional modern thinking may seem quite commonplace) is seen best when contrasted with the attitude that the poems of Theognis seem to reveal. Only when justice is presented in this new way can it take its place as the most important factor in popular ethical thinking. The insistence on arete was already on the wane in the society depicted by Theognis; if Pindar appears to be still insisting on the claims of arete, this is because in his triumphal odes he is concerned with victors rather than with ordinary men.

The insistence on justice, which means among other things (as it always did) respect for law, also means that men will now be judged principally as members of a community, as political animals. Politically and legally, justice can be interpreted in terms of the law, the constitution, and the machinery of government, but ethically it does not admit of easy definition. Even Athena fails to define it; she can only say that it is man's duty to determine what it is in individual instances. Fear and obedience, hatred and revenge, love and friendship and loyalty, charis and pistis—all these elements will continue to play their part in the search for it. But she cannot tell anyone how to reach a decision when these elements seem to be in conflict with one another.[35]

Despite all these uncertainties, some kind of final harmony

is achieved in the *Eumenides,* a measure of reconciliation between the conflicting claims that different parties make for justice. No such reconciliation is achieved in any of the other extant plays concerned with the house of Atreus. Both Sophocles and Euripides, in their *Electras,* leave the problem where it stands at the end of the *Choephoroe.* Sophocles actually lets it appear that neither Orestes nor Electra has further sufferings or difficulties to face (though this does not mean that he approved of the matricide), while Euripides brings in the Dioscuri to put everything right in a brief and hasty final scene. No general comparison between the plays by the three dramatists is intended here. But since, with certain differences which need not be described, all three are dealing with the same story, it is instructive to see how differently the theme of justice is handled in the later plays and how the interest of the story itself appears to have suffered some change. For the sake of the present argument it is of no importance whether the *Electra* of Sophocles or of Euripides was produced first; it is enough to say that neither of them produced his *Electra* until forty years after the *Oresteia* was first performed.

In the *Electra* of Sophocles, the themes of vengeance and justice appear side by side from the very beginning; there is no hint that vengeance may be unjust. The Paedagogus lets us know that he has looked upon Orestes as a potential avenger of his father's death ever since he received him from Electra's hands and took him away to a safe place; his task is almost completed now, since Orestes has reached manhood and is old enough to exact this vengeance. "This is Mycenae," he tells Orestes, "from which I took you away and brought you safely to man's estate, so that you could avenge your father's murder" (11–14). Orestes is quite delighted with his practical point of view and his wish for speedy action. He, too, has no doubt of his mission; when he went to Delphi it was not to ask whether he should seek vengeance, but how he should "get justice." He did not ask the god whether vengeance *was* justice (33–34). And it is the same with Electra; her opening lament finishes with a prayer to the gods to avenge her father's murder and to send her brother to her (115–17).

But since Electra has little hope that Orestes will come, she has another problem to solve. How should she behave if Aegisthus and Clytaemnestra continue to reign and never meet with their just punishment? Here again she has no doubt; she must persevere in her truculent, rebellious attitude. The decent, modest behaviour, the "sensible restraint and piety to her parent" (307–8), which Clytaemnestra expects and the chorus and Chrysothemis recommend, is out of the question. Chrysothemis, indeed, knows that Electra's rebellion is "just"; she advises obedience only out of expediency. She thinks Electra is foolish to continue in her angry spirit, but not morally culpable:

> The just way lies not as I am bidding you,
> But your way, as you judge it; still
> I have to live and keep my freedom—
> What can I do but what my masters say?
> (338–40)

This is a different kind of language from anything we find in Aeschylus. Even in the *Prometheus,* when Prometheus was advised to give in to Zeus, no one said that such a submission would be less *just* than obstinacy. But in the last quarter of the fifth century, Athenians were prepared to admit that at certain times justice was too great a luxury; wise counsel (euboulia), which Chrysothemis urges Electra to follow (429), must often take its place. Without power (kratos) rebellion is useless, and Electra might as well do "the will of the stronger," which many people think is the same as justice anyhow. Justice cannot prevail without kratos; Sophocles' characters know this just as well as Prometheus and the Electra and Orestes of the *Choephoroe*; the Paedagogus prays for kratos as well as victory, and the chorus predicts that justice will come "bearing just power in its hands" (477). Electra, like Prometheus, resists the authority in power, and claims that she must do so: "I am compelled by force to do these things" (256).

To most people the compulsion that drives Electra seems

nothing but folly or even madness. Chrysothemis may grant that such behaviour is just, but Clytaemnestra will not; on the contrary, she claims that justice took a hand in slaying Agamemnon and that it is Electra's duty to support this justice:

> Not I alone, but Justice struck the blow;
> Thou shouldst give aid to justice—wert thou sane.
> (528–29)

Clytaemnestra claims that intelligence or "sound-mindedness" will be on the side of justice, but what she really means is that common sense submits before power. At least, that is how Chrysothemis expresses it in speaking to Electra: "Be sensible at last; it is high time" (1013), and "A time can be when even dike brings trouble" (1042). Electra does not forget her advice. In fact it supplies her with the vocabulary that Aegisthus can understand, when she wants to win his confidence by pretending to have learnt her lesson, on hearing the news that Orestes is dead:

> In time I have learnt wisdom—
> To do what my masters wish.
> (1464–65)

It looks as though the old problem of conflict between justice and revenge has been forgotten or is no longer of sufficient interest to form the central issue of a tragedy, and a new problem—the conflict between justice and convenience—has taken its place. There is no discussion in the *Electra* about what justice actually is; the traditional definition—helping one's friends and harming one's enemies—fits well enough, and Electra is certainly as anxious to harm her enemies as to help her friends.

Euripides, in contrast to Sophocles, uses the terminology of justice in a way that would be intelligible in the time of Aeschylus; and he pays more attention to the doubts and scruples of his characters. The members of his chorus, though not greatly concerned with moral issues, are prepared to welcome Clytaemnestra's death as dike (1155, 1169), and when Orestes cries out in horror at what he has done, they try to reassure him: "Justly hast thou avenged thy father's death" (1189). Their confident certainty wavers before long; they are slow to understand, but they do think over the issue. They are, however, more bloodthirsty than either of the protagonists, until shocked out of their certainty by the actual deed of matricide. It is impossible to be sure whether Electra is actually more lacking in scruple than Orestes, since the distribution of individual lines among the speakers is doubtful in more than one critical passage. But perhaps it is not a matter of great importance. Euripides is not trying to show how persons might face and resolve their scruples, but what kind of person Electra must have been to do what she did—what character and what set of circumstances would explain her story. He begins, therefore, by showing us the kind of person who would not seek revenge and might not be unduly concerned over "justice"—a quiet, good-tempered, unambitious man, the rustic husband of Electra. The savagery and resentment of Electra are gradually revealed as permanent characteristics; in pushing Orestes on she is acting in accordance with her character. But of the actual problem which runs through the *Eumenides* Euripides takes little account; in the closing scene the Dioscuri, in simple, nontechnical language, are content to sum up the argument in a single verse: "She suffered what was just; thy deed was not just" (1244).[36]

In the *Medea* we are warned in the prologue that Medea is seeking redress for the wrongs that she has suffered at Jason's hands; and the wrongs are undisputed—he has betrayed her and made a sorry return for the help that she once gave him (17–23). But we are also warned of her character:

> Her *phren* is heavy, nor will she submit
> To unjust treatment; I know her, I am afraid,
> (38–39)

says the Nurse, and she warns the women of the chorus that it will be dangerous for them to approach her closely (102–4). Soon afterwards we understand this warning, when we hear

Medea's terrible language as she curses her own children (112–14). She is determined to obtain vengeance from Jason, determined that he shall suffer due dike for the harm he has done her, if some way can be found (261). The chorus agrees that her attitude is justified: "Yes, justly wilt thou make him pay" (267).

So far, then, there is no question raised: vengeance will be justice. But what is the alternative? And what is Jason's case and his recommendation to his wife? Medea sums up what he has to say: "What thou hast done, no doubt was done in prudent wisdom" (311). Jason, it seems, thinks in terms of euboulia and sophrosyne, like Clytaemnestra and Chrysothemis in Sophocles' *Electra*. And so Medea offers to take his advice, to "yield to the stronger" as common sense would demand; but she cannot agree that such a course is "just":

> Let me live quietly here;
> I have been wronged, but I will take no steps;
> I yield before the stronger.
>
> (313–15)

Jason knows, as well as the audience, that she is not likely to do any such thing; he does not believe she is capable of euboulia (316–17). And when Jason has left the stage, she reveals her plan of murder—a plan that may bring her what she calls justice, but will not be accepted as such by the world: "Suppose they are dead: What city will receive me?" (386).

Medea looks ahead, just as Orestes did in the *Eumenides*. And, in the famous choral ode,

> Back to their springs the sacred rivers flow;
> Justice and all else is overthrown,
>
> (410–11)

the issue is made very clear. There can be no justice in a world where pistis, charis, and aidos are thrust aside. Poets may recognize the honour due to women who retain their integrity when men have lost it; but they cannot obtain justice when kratos prevents it. The ode begins with the overthrow of dike; it ends by reminding us that superior force has made the search for justice impossible; Jason's new queen will have authority and power on her side:

> A queen more powerful than thou
> Sits now in control of the house.
> (444–45)

The situation, therefore, stands just exactly where it did at the opening of the *Prometheus Bound.*

In spite of everything and even though the chorus does its best to dissuade her, Medea persists in her determination, and prepares to make definite plans when Aegeus has offered her shelter in Athens:

> Now there is hope my enemies
> Will pay the dike they owe.
> (767)

Exultantly she calls upon the "dike of Zeus" to witness her delight, as though Zeus will really be on her side if she murders Jason and his bride; and she convinces herself that she will win the respect of the world:

> Let no one think that I am weak or feeble
> Or easy-going—no, the other way,
> Terrible to foes and kindly to my friends;
> Such are the ones whose life is crowned with praise.
> (807–10)

In attempting to dissuade her from killing her own children, the chorus claims to be helping her and "joining forces with the laws of men" (812–13). But Medea by this time is beyond the reach of reasonable argument. To kill the children is the way to hurt Jason most: "All argument to stop me is in vain" (819).

Since Medea loses the sympathy of the audience by the time the play is half finished, and since Jason never had it to begin with, the *Medea* can hardly be described as a play of serious ethical issues or problems. Justice, as the audience would understand it, is as absent on Jason's side as Medea's. The women of the chorus cannot deny that Jason has deserved punishment:

> Suffering in plenty the god has contrived today
> Justly, it seems, for Jason.
>
> (1231–32)

But they might have added the comment that the Dioscuri had to make on Orestes' murder of Clytaemnestra: "She suffered what was just; thy deed was not just."

In fact, they refrain from criticizing Medea, and it is Jason who cries out for the avenging Fury and bloody Justice to avenge Medea's crime (1389–90). And, as the audience and Euripides alike have long since learnt, fulfilment of his prayer will not improve matters, but only prolong the tale of horror. This might appear, at first glance, to be identical with the conclusion suggested by the *Oresteia,* suggested indeed in the *Agamemnon* as well as in the *Eumenides.* But there is a notable difference. In the *Eumenides* it is insisted that revenge and justice are not the same, that there is another justice by the rule of which men must learn to live, a justice that men must seek with their powers of reason, bearing in mind all the traditional claims of pistis and charis; there is no hint that justice, if rightly understood, must ever be disregarded or rejected as a guide to behaviour. This is the attitude that Glaucon and Adeimantus still cherish in the *Republic.* But in the *Medea* and the *Electra* of Euripides the matter is expressed differently. Here there is no contrast between justice and revenge, but a contrast between situations where justice can and should be sought and times when the search for it will be disastrous.

The plays of Aeschylus seem to belong to an age in which the search for arete has given way before the search for justice; in the age of Euripides, even as early as 431 B.C. when the *Medea* was produced, the faith in justice seems to have weakened. It is not yet the world of the Melian Dialogue in which justice is entirely cast aside in favour of expediency, but more like the world of Cleon and Diodotus in which the claims of "good counsel" must prevail in deciding when justice should give way to expediency. Like the change in the meaning of arete and the rise of justice as the dominant factor in ethical thought between the world of Homer and the world of Aeschylus, this change in attitude must not be thought to have taken place in a moment or to be an absolute change that every Athenian would recognize as valid and real. But one stage in this shift in popular ethics should be an attempt to define justice in the traditional terms of pistis and charis, and perhaps we should add kratos, the authority that can stifle justice or enable it to prevail. Even without the explicit testimony of Plato and Aristotle, we can see from the literature of the fifth century that ethics and politics were never entirely separated, that man's relation to his fellow man is never kept separate from his relation to the state, that the laws and customs of the state are expected to control to a considerable degree his private as well as his public behaviour, and that the laws of any city-state are thought to reflect its ethics as well as its politics.

The claims of friendship and loyalty are not forgotten or abandoned in the plays of Euripides; indeed, there are some plays, like the *Alcestis* and the *Iphigenia in Tauris,* in which they play a large part. But conflicts, real or apparent, between the claims of personal obligations and the claims of the laws play a much larger part in Sophocles and Herodotus than in Euripides and Thucydides. If we are to understand the attempt of popular ethics to comprehend and define justice in terms of friendship and the laws, and the frustration of the general public when faced by apparent conflicts between such claims, it is in Sophocles and Herodotus that we must seek enlightenment and illustration. The plays of Sophocles certainly suggest that the playwright and the public for whom he thought he was writing still retained a vivid interest and faith in these older traditional terms of ethical thought; the difficulties and shortcomings of the older tradition are not disguised, but they have not led to the disillusionment which is so patent in the Melian Dialogue and the later plays of Euripides.

FIVE. Justice, Friendship, and Loyalty

Classical Greek literature seems to lay far greater stress on the obligations of friendship and the duty of returning a favour than on the virtue of conferring one. It is one's "friend" whom one is expected to love rather than one's "neighbour." And because literature appears not to offer such explicit maxims as "Thou shalt love thy neighbour as thyself" and "The greatest of these is charity," modern interpreters are often disposed to believe that the Greeks, as a rule, had less regard for the virtue and duty of charity than is normally expected in the Christian tradition. It is certainly true that the Greeks were not commanded to love their enemies. And although Seneca in the *De Beneficiis* insists that favours, if they are to have any merit and to deserve the name of *beneficia,* must be granted without thought of return, the whole ancient theory of friendship is based on the assumption that favours will be returned:[1] a man who helps his friend usually does so with the expectation that some return for his favour will be made.

One must not, however, press the evidence too far and accuse the Greeks, without qualification, of a selfish and calculating attitude. One need not search far in Greek literature to discover that they thought it their duty to show favour and compassion towards the helpless. Suppliants, above all, were under the special protection of the gods; a beggar might even be a god or goddess in disguise, like Demeter, who wandered from city to city in search of Persephone, or carry a special blessing with him, as when the blind outcast Oedipus came to Colonus. A god disguised as a beggar would, of course, repay the man who showed kindness to him.[2] Because the regard for suppliants was so great, it was a particularly grave offence to abuse the privileges of a suppliant–to ask help, knowing that the helper would suffer for his kindness, as when Pactyas sought refuge at Cyme, knowing that if he were accepted as a refugee the Persians would attack the city (Hdt. i.157–60), or when Aristagoras at Sparta, after his regular request for military aid to the Ionians was refused and he had been dismissed, made his way back into the king's presence by putting on the garb of a suppliant (v.49–51). But despite possible dangers of this kind, the obligation to help and protect the helpless stranger still remained. If one wants a classical equivalent to the story of the Good Samaritan, perhaps the tale of Croesus and Adrastus, as told by Herodotus, will serve:

When Croesus was preparing for his son's wedding, there came to Sardis a man who had suffered misfortune and whose hands were not clean, a Phrygian by race, of the king's family. Coming to the house of Croesus, he asked to be given purification according to the laws of the country (the Lydians have the same mode of granting purification as the Greeks); and when Croesus had duly done what was needed, he asked him whence he came and who he was, saying to him: "Who art thou, man, and from where in Phrygia didst thou come to sit at my hearth? and what man or woman hast thou killed?" "O king," he replied, "I am the son of Gordias, Midas's son, and my name is Adrastus. And I am here, driven from home by my father and deprived of everything, because I killed my brother unintentionally." And Croesus answered him: "Thy parents are our friends and thou hast come to friends; here thou shalt stay in our house and lack nothing" (i.35).

Croesus grants Adrastus his request before asking who he is or what he has done. He does not know that his hospitality will have disastrous consequences for himself as well as for his guest. Croesus is a man doomed to eventual disaster, and his downfall, according to most interpreters of Herodotus, is supposed to be the result of his hybris. Like Xerxes and Polycrates, he attempts too much in his pride and excessive confidence, and the jealousy of the gods strikes him down. Though he is not a cruel tyrant, like Cambyses or Periander, he falls because pride must inevitably fall; he strives for too much and does not know himself or his own limitations. Such is the usual interpretation of the Herodotean story; this is supposed to be the moral that we are expected to draw from it, as from the other stories of powerful rulers who meet disaster in the end. Croesus does not heed Solon's warnings and is puzzled rather than enlightened by his refusal to recognize him as the most fortunate man in the world. And his success blinds him, so that he misunderstands the oracle which tells him that if he crosses the River Halys he will destroy a great empire; it never occurs to him that the "great empire" will be his own. The orthodox interpretation is right, up to a point. Herodotus does draw our attention to the hybris of Croesus, just as Aeschylus expects us to recognize the hybris of Xerxes. But, as in the *Persians,* the hybris of the king is not the whole story. Croesus is a much more admirable man than Cambyses or Xerxes; his imperialistic ambition is offset by great benefactions or attempts at benefactions, but not one of them is rewarded.

The refugee Adrastus, whom Croesus receives with kindness, does his best to show gratitude; but he is a man with a curse upon him, and he accidentally kills Croesus's son. The Spartans, whose friendship Croesus had won by presenting them with gold for a statue of Apollo and with whom he had made a treaty, were unable to help him when he needed them. And even the Delphic oracle, to whom he made so many lavish gifts, had to explain that he was beyond any help that Delphi could give; the god had done his best, but could not change the decision of fate; he had postponed the evil day, and tried to warn Croesus, but his warning had not been understood. If it were not for the motif of hybris in the story, it might be possible to regard the disaster of Croesus in an entirely different light: as an example of the generous man who is not rewarded, whose favours are given in the wrong quarter, who is betrayed, however unwillingly, by those whom he thought to be his friends.

Polycrates of Samos, one of the least admirable of Greek tyrants, deserves his eventual fate far more clearly than Croesus. He is represented by Herodotus as defending his unprovoked attacks on other cities by the argument that "he conferred a greater favour on a friend by returning what he had taken from him, than if he had not taken it in the first place" (iii.39). The remark might be dismissed as an idle jest, if it were not for the rest of the story about Polycrates. He attempts to throw away his ring into the sea as a propitiatory sacrifice; the attempt fails, because a fisherman presents the tyrant with a splendid fish which he has caught and the ring is found in its belly. It is easy to be content with explaining the story in terms of familiar superstition: the man who cannot propitiate fortune by suffering loss, like Midas who cannot help growing richer no matter what he does, is expected to pay a terrible price in the end for his unbroken success. But most stories in Greek history and legend are susceptible of more than one interpretation. Polycrates had boasted that he could be a robber and a pirate and nevertheless confer favours which would compensate for his acts of aggression. Now Poseidon reveals to him his impending doom by showing that he has forfeited the privilege of conferring a favour. The man who cannot do or return a favour can neither make nor keep friends; it is one of the worst fates that can befall anyone.[3] Accordingly the Egyptian king, Amasis, recognizing the sign, breaks off friendship with him, as a man whom the gods have cast off.

Herodotus has great respect for the character of the Egyptians, and Cambyses, the Persian conqueror of Egypt, compares very unfavourably with them in the story that he tells. Some of the overtures of friendship that he makes may not really be intended as friendly gestures; thus the Egyptians refuse his request for the daughter of Amasis as a wife, taking it to be an insult, as it is if the girl is merely to be one of his harem (iii.1). He tries to show favour to Amasis' son, Psammenitus (after dishonouring his daughter and killing his son), but Psammenitus stirs up revolt against him (iii.14–15); and the Ethiopian king regards the messengers who bring him gifts as spies rather than bearers of friendly offerings (iii.20–21). It is only after these questionable efforts to gain friendship have failed that Cambyses starts openly attacking his existing friends and his family. His mind, according to Herodotus, is now quite seriously unhinged. He becomes a person whom it is impossible to please; he gives his servants orders to kill Croesus, and when they think to please him by disobeying, knowing he will repent of the order, though he is glad that they save Croesus, he puts them to death for disobedience just the same (iii.36).

It is not suggested that the failure of Croesus, Polycrates, and Cambyses to maintain a friendly relation is intended by Herodotus to be their chief or essential fault, which stamps them as "unjust" men. But readers accustomed to measure conduct by the standard of charis could not overlook these incidents, and would inevitably regard them as part of the ethical failure of these men, just as it was part of the ethical failure of Prometheus that he could not retain the favour and friendship of Zeus. It makes very little difference whether we say that this failure is considered as part of their hybris or as a symptom of it.

The Cyrus of Xenophon, in the *Cyropaedia,* offers by contrast a perfect example of the ruler who succeeds by granting favours. While he is the paragon of all the virtues, as well as being a great lover of honour, "ready to endure any danger for the sake of praise" (i.2.1), he also has great *philanthropia*; he showed great talent for making friends at an early age, when all his companions at the court of Astyages wept to see him leave (i.4.25). His ability as a ruler is made to consist mainly in his ability to win the friendship of the right people at the right time, by gifts, praise, and encouragement. He explains his policy in a speech to Cyaxares (ii.4.9–12): kind words and kind deeds are the means by which he seeks out allies and assistants. When faced with the task of recovering the loyalty of the Armenian king, who has refused to pay tribute or send his army when it is needed, he promises not only to make him fulfil his obligations but "to make him a better friend than he is at present" (ii.4.14). He takes him prisoner together with members of his family, and so is in a position to do him a great favour by showing him mercy (as the king's son Tigranes carefully points out to him, Cyrus is now in the perfect position to win a firm friend–and Cyrus follows his advice). The policy is, perhaps, not so very different from that which Polycrates claimed to follow; but Cyrus preaches the straightforward practice of charis all the way through the *Cyropaedia*; his final advice on his deathbed is: "Do good to your friends and you will be able to punish your enemies" (viii.7.28).[4]

Socrates has little difficulty, in the *Republic,* in showing that justice is not adequately defined as "helping one's friends and harming one's enemies." As we have seen, Greek literature is full of stories that accept or stress this old-fashioned code; but it also constantly illustrates the code's weakness and inadequacy. Instances are not lacking in Herodotus. The magus who rules temporarily in Persia is not a good or just ruler simply because he confers many benefits (iii.67). Again, when the Median king, Astyages, alarmed by a dream, decides that his daughter's child must die and orders Harpagus to kill the boy, the first anxiety of Harpagus when faced with this disagreeable task is not to fail in charis towards the king–such is the excuse that he makes for undertaking to carry out the order, though he knows in his own mind that this is an instance in which charis conflicts with justice (i.108). Another equally good, but more complicated, example comes in the story of the expulsion of the tyrants from Athens by the Spartans. As Herodotus tells the story, it was largely because the Delphic oracle constantly told them to "set Athens free" that the Spartans agreed to help in driving out the Peisistratids. Then they are supposed to regret what they have done, because the new popular government is "ungrateful" (ἀχάριστος), and they are disposed to restore the old tyrannical government, until the Corinthians persuade them that to do so would be "contrary to justice" (v.92), that the welfare of the Athenians is more important than their own injured feelings, and that their attack on the Peisistratids, though formally an act of ingratitude towards friends, was justified by circumstances.

Unprovoked attack, according to the conventional view, is the clearest type of injustice. Usually when one city attacks another, Herodotus explains its action as taken in return for an injury or in gratitude for some favour from another source. If no such explanation can be given, the aggressor is guilty of a blatant act of hybris. When Oroetes, the Persian satrap in Sardis, decides to attack Polycrates of Samos, Herodotus calls it an unholy plan (πρῆγμα οὐχ ὅσιον, iii.120); the same language is used, by an Egyptian, to describe both the ingratitude of Paris towards his host, Menelaus (ii.114), and the behaviour of Menelaus himself in Egypt (ii.119), when, despite his hospitable treatment, he seized and sacrificed two children in the hope of obtaining a favourable wind for his voyage. Above all, Cambyses is denounced as "unjust" by the Ethiopian king, because "if he were just, he would not have coveted land not belonging to him nor would he be enslaving men from whom he has suffered no harm" (iii.21). Darius, by contrast, is never guilty of unprovoked aggression. The expedition against Samos, led by Otanes, is undertaken in order to show gratitude to Syloson (iii.139–41); the Scythian expedition is designed to punish the Scythians for their aggression in invading Media (iv.1); and Darius's expedition against Greece is justified by the part that Athens and Eretria took in supporting the Ionian revolt, although Atossa urges it on him earlier as a means of acquiring greater glory and respect among the Persians (iii.134).

But the moral excellence of Darius, apart from his skill and intelligence as a ruler, is not confined to avoiding aggression and returning gratitude where it is due. He is a severe and upright judge, who punishes Oroetes for his misdeeds (iii.127). While he avoids "unholy" acts of aggression, he seeks distinction for his country and arete for himself. And he confers favours with proper discrimination, not hesitating to withdraw from Histiaeus the gift he has given him—the privilege of settling at Myrcinus—when he finds that Histiaeus is misusing the privilege (but he retains Histiaeus as a friend all the same, v.23–24). It would be wrong to claim that Herodotus has given a complete and consistent character sketch of Darius, because consistent and careful characterization is not the strong point of Herodotus; that would be too much to expect from a writer who has so little discrimination about accepting evidence and generally prefers to let his readers decide when an account should be denied belief.[5] But it is certainly his intention to present Darius as a worthy character, in contrast with Cambyses and with arbitrary Greek tyrants, who share some of the worse features of oriental autocrats.

There is one particular speech by Darius to which it is especially worth while to pay attention. In iii.80–82, Herodotus describes a debate on different forms of government, which is supposed to have been held by the seven Persian conspirators against the usurper pseudo-Smerdis; and he insists this time that his source of information is trustworthy, though he knows many will doubt it. It is a way of warning us that he wants us to take notice of what these men say. He gives the text of three short speeches (all of which, he says, were excellent), in which Otanes favours democracy, Megabyzus oligarchy, and Darius, naturally enough, monarchy. The speech of Darius, which comes last, is extremely interesting and contains some unusual criticisms of oligarchy and democracy. He is not content with the conventional criticisms, which are set forth in the other speeches—the dangers of an arbitrary autocrat or an ill-disciplined, hybristic popular government. He argues that in an oligarchy quarrels and conflicts result between the numerous men who are cultivating arete and striving to win distinction for themselves, but in a democracy it is the friendships that are dangerous, not the enmities. Men of the worst type make friends with one another, and their harmful influence is broken only when a strong individual rises as a true champion of the people and establishes a monarchy. He adds as an afterthought that an additional reason for preferring monarchy is that it is traditional in Persia, but this is only a subsidiary argument; his main point is that in oligarchies harm results from men following one ethical precept—"pursue arete"—and in democracies from following another—"help your friends."[6]

The arguments are, of course, purely Greek and, despite the insistence of Herodotus, no one would believe that this is a faithful account of an actual debate. But the remarks are put in the mouth of a Persian for a reason; Greek popular morality is more effectively criticized by a foreigner.[7]

Darius's point is the danger that results when the wrong people ("bad men") make friends with one another and seek to do one another favours; and this is exactly what we see happening in the *Hecuba* of Euripides. Most modern critics have found this an unsatisfactory play and have had difficulty in discovering any dramatic or ethical theme that holds the two parts of the drama together.[8] Some are content to accept it as pure melodrama, or else as a protest against the savagery of war, which would be appropriate enough historically since it was probably produced in 425 or 424 B.C., when memories of the slaughter of the Plataeans and the narrow escape from slaughter of the people of Mytilene were still fresh in the minds of the Athenians. But this interpretation has the same weakness as the explanation of Aeschylus' *Persians* as a denunciation of hybris. It was suggested in the previous chapter that the theme of the *Persians* was the loyalty of the Persian elders towards an unworthy king—a case of misapplied pistis. It is even more likely that the *Hecuba* is concerned with misapplied charis, with the disaster that ensues when favours are wrongly asked and given and returned—something which, according to Darius, is particularly common in democracies.

Certainly the *Hecuba* is a play of many killings. But what are the motivations for these killings? There seems to be no doubt about the first one. The ghost of Polydorus in the prologue tells us that he, the youngest son of Priam, too young to bear arms, was sent away to a safe place with a large stock of gold, to make sure that it would not fall into the hands of the Greeks if Troy fell. But his host, the Thracian king Polymestor, a well-established ruler of a prosperous kingdom and a friend in whom the house of Priam had full confidence, betrayed his trust and murdered the boy for the sake of the gold. Ghosts do not lie, and we accept this story of a treacherous murder for the sake of profit.

Hecuba does not know Polydorus is dead when the play opens and she is faced with the demand for the life of her daughter Polyxena. Polyxena is not to be killed for gain. The ghost of Achilles, so we learn, has appeared to the Greeks and demanded that Polyxena be sacrificed at his tomb as a favour to him; and the Greek leaders, after some uncertainty, have been persuaded by Odysseus to grant this favour. They have been convinced that it is a manner of keeping faith with the Greeks who died before Troy:

> One of the dead, it may be,
> Will stand before Persephone and say
> That Greeks to Greeks were ungrateful and left
> the plains of Troy
> With no charis for them who died in their cause.
> (136–40)

It falls to Odysseus—a typical politician, as he often is in tragedy—to explain this to Hecuba. He begins by simply demanding that the girl be given up to him, and advises Hecuba to recognize that resistance is useless. But before he raises the issue of charis, Hecuba reminds him that he owes her a charis. When Odysseus entered Troy as a spy in disguise, Helen had recognized him and told Hecuba; he entreated her not to reveal him, and she agreed. He admits that this is true, and so she taunts him with the basest ingratitude—just what one might expect from a politician:

> Ungrateful breed of men,
> All you who seek a politician's honours!
> I would have none of you—

Who care not how you hurt your friends,
If you can win the charis of the many.[9]
(254–57)

Odysseus explains that he would like to return her favour, but she must recognize how important it is to reward and honour worthy public servants like Achilles, in death as in life; the immortal fame of the heroic dead must be fostered, "so that Greece may prosper" (330). Though theoretically a good argument, like that of Creon in the *Antigone,* it is patently false under the circumstances; it may appear to be balancing one charis against another, but in fact it is defending human sacrifice, which is no different from murder, by offering charis as an excuse for it.[10]

Polyxena is sacrificed and Talthybius describes how she died; then the corpse of Polydorus is found by the shore; and when Agamemnon enters, wanting to know why Hecuba has not yet picked up her daughter's body for burial, it is going to be very difficult for him to refuse any request she makes of him, since he is himself taking another of her children from her—Cassandra. He tries to anticipate her plea by offering her her freedom, but this is not what she wants. She wants revenge, the punishment of her son's murderer. She makes this request in the name of justice and as a charis that is due to her. Perhaps, she says, Cassandra will reward him for it by love and affection. Agamemnon tries to refuse, protesting that it will offend public opinion if he kills Polymestor; the Greeks will think he is letting a charis for Cassandra outweigh the obligation that the army owes to a king of Thrace who is supposed to be an ally:

The army looks on this man as its friend,
On your son, now dead, as its enemy.[11]
(858–59)

But Hecuba gets over this difficulty by promising that his part in bringing about Polymestor's punishment will not be revealed; and he agrees to send the Thracian a message that Hecuba wants to see him.

The tally of favours asked and granted is still not complete. Hecuba tricks Polymestor into the tent, where the women are waiting for him, by asking him to do a favour, to take charge of a secret treasure that she has hidden there, so that it will not fall into the hands of the Greeks. He agrees, of course, and we need not be told why. Just as greed led him to commit murder, so it leads him to his own destruction. A simple death is too slight a punishment for him; his sons are killed and he is blinded. But instead of recognizing that he deserves to be punished for his crime, he complains to Agamemnon that his murder of Polydorus was a charis, a favour done for the Greeks for which they have rewarded him by betraying him to Hecuba:

> See what I suffer, who strove to favour thee,
> When I did kill thy enemy.
>
> (1175–77)

Hecuba tears his defence to shreds in her final tirade; but without this last plea, patently false, of charis as an excuse for murder, the play would not be complete.

As a refutation of the popular notion that virtue or justice consists simply in returning favours, the *Hecuba* is more complete and far more brutal than any of the arguments of Socrates. It is a terrifying exposition of the crimes that can be committed if the principle of charis is exploited by men for their own purposes; it shows the damage that can be done by the "friendships of evil men" which, according to Darius, are the curse of democracy. At the end of the play the women of the chorus remind us that they are departing for a life of slavery; their slavery is the justice of revenge, inflicted without pretence or hypocrisy, a cruel and terrible punishment, but less horrible than the guilty triumph of the others who were prepared to commit murder in the name of charis.[12]

In Antiphon's speech "On the Murder of Herodes," the speaker has to defend himself against the charge of murder mainly by appeal to probabilities. He explains (57–58) that he had no quarrel with Herodes and had nothing to gain by his death, since the man had no money. What motive, then, does the prosecution suggest? "They have the effrontery to say that I killed the man out of charis (λέγειν δὲ τολμῶσι ὡς ἐγὼ χάριτι τὸν ἄνδρ' ἀπέκτεινα). Now who ever did a deed like this as a favour to anyone? I do not believe anyone ever did." The parallel with the *Hecuba* is striking, because the speech must be dated between 421 and 416[13]—later than the production of the *Hecuba,* but not by many years.

An earlier play of Euripides, the *Alcestis,* is also concerned with self-sacrifice and with mistaken or undue acts of charis. But the mistakes this time are not of criminal proportions, and the charis is given in all good will and sincerity. Unworthy character though Admetus is, the loyalty of his wife Alcestis is so great that she is willing to die in order that he may live (since Death demands either his life or that of another in his place). Many times the chorus insists on her great merit; she is the best (ἀρίστη) of women, and she has said herself that she is dying because she cannot bring herself to betray her husband (180–81). Admetus recognizes her great loyalty (368, 880), but he loses any sympathy we might have for him when he berates his parents for their refusal to die in his place. This abusive interchange, however, is not designed simply to show his selfishness or their cowardice; it shows us that like the ghost of Achilles in the *Hecuba,* Admetus may not demand someone else's life as a charis for himself. With a perversity that seems contemptible at the time, Admetus actually accuses Alcestis of betraying him by dying (202, 250, 275); but the charge is in fact a true one, as he finally recognizes. Her death, instead of saving him, has wrecked his life and made it not worth living; he cannot face either the memory of the past or the contempt in which the world henceforth will hold him (935–61). The favour that he has asked and received from her is not only excessive but impossible. Her arete in sacrificing herself may be great, her loyalty admirable, but it does not really help him, and cannot therefore be called true charis.

Admetus of course cannot make Alcestis any adequate return for what she has done; it must have been a commonplace criticism of the maxim "Return like for like" that no man can adequately repay anyone who saves his life. But by an excessive or undue exercise of his own special arete—the virtue of hospitality—he can, after a fashion, match or duplicate her action. And this is what he does. When Heracles arrives, he insists that Heracles must be his guest, pretending that it is only some stranger, not connected with the family, who has died. Heracles proceeds to get drunk and to complain loudly about the lack of attention on the part of the servants. This seems like gratuitous boorishness on his part but (as in the scene between Admetus and his parents) that is not the point; the drunken behaviour and ill manners of the guest only emphasize the extreme impropriety of the favour of Admetus in offering hospitality at such a time, after Heracles had given him plenty of opportunity to let him go elsewhere. When Heracles learns the truth—how Admetus has concealed from him the fact that his wife has just died—he is shocked and horrified. Such undue hospitality is no real favour at all.

Unlike Admetus, however, Heracles is a god and has the power to make adequate return for any favour that a mortal man tries to confer on him. His decision is quickly taken:

> I must save this woman who has lately died,
> Restore Alcestis to her home again;
> I must pay back Admetus for his favour.
> (840–42)

Heracles is not content, however, to restore Alcestis directly; Admetus must be paid out for his deceitfulness and embarrassed in his turn. When Heracles brings back Alcestis, after his struggle with Death at the tomb, she is veiled, and he pretends that she is a slave woman whom he has won in an athletic contest. He tells Admetus that he wants to leave her in his care while he goes off to Thrace on his appointed task. Unwilling though Admetus is to accept a strange woman in his house (and Heracles admires his loyalty to his dead wife), he has to agree to accept what Heracles offers; he must suffer some humiliation before he can know that Alcestis is saved from death. And he also learns—as does Alcestis while she stands a silent witness to everything—that often one cannot do a favour without hurting someone at the same time, sometimes the very person to whom one is granting the favour.

This may seem an inadequate description and interpretation of the play, whose whole meaning has never been clear to modern readers and may not have been altogether intelligible even to the Athenian audience. But anyone who thought in terms of charis would be bound to notice these excesses of charis and would conclude as Heracles and Admetus do:

HERACLES: Thou wilt be in error if thou dost not do it.
ADMETUS: But if I do it, it will tear my heart.
(1099–1100)

The dialogues between gods in Euripides' plays are always of great interest. Death, as Aeschylus pointed out in a famous line, is unlike other gods in that there is no way of putting him under an obligation: "Alone of all the gods Death has no love of gifts."[14] Euripides makes the same point in the prologue here; it is useless for Apollo to ask for the life of Alcestis, because there is nothing that he can offer in return:

APOLLO: Thou art determined, then? Thou wilt not grant this favour?
DEATH: I will not, and thou knowest well my character.
APOLLO: Indeed I do; both gods and mortal men detest it.
(60–62)

Since Death can have no friends, he has no regard for gifts or charis, and there is no way of bargaining with him. It is waste of time to warn Death that he will lose Apollo's gratitude, and Death tells him so plainly: "Talk as thou wilt; thou wilt not gain by it at all" (72).

Words will not help Apollo; but unlike men he can use force against Death, and is prepared to do so in the cause of friendship, which, unlike Death, he understands and values highly. When Death, who is incapable of friendship, charges him with injustice, the charge has no validity. And when Apollo, in his opening speech, tells Death that he comes with "justice and honest arguments," he knows it will be useless to press the claim:

DEATH: What need of weapons, then, if thou hast justice with thee?
APOLLO: To carry bow and arrows is my custom always.
DEATH: Yes, and to help this house beyond the line of justice.
APOLLO: The suffering of a friend is a heavy burden on me.
(39–42)

Thus Apollo states that when it is a choice between the way of friendship and the way of Death, which some mistake for the way of justice, man should choose the way of friendship; it is a repetition of Antigone's statement of her case: "To share in friendship is my nature, not in hate" (Soph. *Antigone* 523). Alcestis, by her self-sacrifice, and Admetus, by his undue hospitality, failed to achieve the purpose of helping a friend. But their motives were worthy and admirable, not to be confused with the motivations of Odysseus and Agamemnon in the *Hecuba.*

Friendship demands loyalty and an understanding of what will really benefit one's friend, not simply give him pleasure for the moment. The distinction between the true friend and the false friend or flatterer is a commonplace in later Greek writing.[15] In Plato's *Gorgias* Socrates finds fault with the art of rhetoric, because its purpose is to give immediate pleasure, to confer charis (χαρίζεσθαι), and he calls it therefore a kind of flattery (462c–463a). So also Demosthenes, like Hecuba in the *Hecuba,* complains that some politicians seek popularity by trying to gratify the immediate wishes of the multitude and shrink from recommending a course that involves any hardship or sacrifice; the just statesman, as Demosthenes calls him, rises above such temptations.[16] The argument, of course, was in constant use by politicians, as it has been throughout the centuries; it is as commonplace as the argument that parents cannot always please their children. But it must be pointed out that the argument is unnecessary for a politician, unless his influence is largely dependent on popular favour; historically it originates with the rise of democratic government. A citizen's loyalty towards his country, as will be shown in the following chapter, is widely considered as a way of showing gratitude for favours received; a politician's integrity, therefore, may be explained in terms of gratitude, of good will (*eunoia*) and charis. In most personal relationships it is not difficult to see where one's loyalty lies and how one should bestow charis. But when the issue was not so clear, the tendency was to interpret a man's choice (if one may use an Aristotelian term, his *proairesis*) as determined by his ability to recognize where his loyalty lay and what gratitude demanded from him.

War often tempts people to be disloyal to their old friends. Thucydides tells us that in the brutal and cynical setting of a revolution, old-fashioned honesty and simplicity were laughed out of existence (iii.83.1). The dominant motivation that took the place of charis and philanthropia was of course self-interest, the search for immediate personal advantage. But, if we can trust Thucydides, another approach was often more effective in urging or defending disloyal behaviour; it was less openly immoralist and much more insidious. It consisted in asking, "Who is my true friend of the two that claim my allegiance?" Thus a man who might be called a traitor by his enemies would save face by saying that he had really shown true loyalty to his friends.

If examples of this kind of pleading in Thucydidean speeches, however numerous, are not considered trustworthy historical evidence, an example from Xenophon's *Anabasis* may be thought more convincing. The speaker is Clearchus, an old-fashioned Spartan officer, dedicated to the military virtues. When faced with a mutiny of his men, who have discovered that Cyrus means to take them much further from home than they had expected, he represents himself as torn between two loyalties: how is he to choose between the friendship of his troops and the friendship of Cyrus? He does not know how to make his choice; and when he decides to stand by his soldiers, he says he does not know whether he is doing the right thing (i.3.3–6). Xenophon admires Clearchus and certainly expects us to believe that he means what he says; his emotional outburst in front of his troops is genuine. This must mean, then, that Clearchus recognizes no obligations except those of friendship, that he decides issues by weighing obligations to different friends, rather than by examining the obligations of a contract. A man whose decision is determined by his regard for a contract would not have found it difficult to argue that Cyrus forfeited all claim to his services when he misrepresented the purpose of the expedition.

We are hardly justified in jumping to conclusions about peculiarities of the Spartan ethical tradition with only a few instances from Athenian historians to guide us. But there is no harm in pointing out that in the narrative of Thucydides, the Spartan Brasidas is singularly successful in persuading people that Sparta is their true friend rather than Athens. Thucydides makes it quite clear that the personal influence of Brasidas played a tremendous part in undermining the loyalty of the Thracian cities to Athens; the Spartans sent him to Thrace at his own request (backed by the suggestions of some cities in Thrace), and he showed himself "just and reasonable," "a good man in every way," whose arete and intelligence won him great respect (iv.81). For a man to retain a high moral reputation when he is in fact urging cities to break a solemn contract is something of a *tour de force*. The members of the Athenian confederacy were bound by an oath that left no opportunity for escape, but it was arguable that the Athenians themselves had seriously violated the spirit of the alliance by "enslaving" cities which tried to withdraw, beginning with Naxos in 470, over forty-five years before Brasidas came to

Thrace (i.98). It is curious that Brasidas, according to Thucydides, says nothing about the oaths by which the allies of Athens were bound or about any breaches of contract on the Athenian side that might be considered to nullify the oaths sworn by her allies. Instead of this he offers freedom (the cause for which Sparta was supposed to be fighting) and Spartan friendship. In his speech at Acanthus, he insists that the Spartans have proved their friendship by the risks they have taken in sending an army to Thrace; and he expects the Acanthians to show some charis in return for the Spartan efforts on their behalf (iv.86.5).

Naturally Brasidas offers arguments from self-interest as well as these ethical considerations, and according to Thucydides considerations of justice really played a small part in influencing the decision of the Acanthians to accept his offer; it was fear and the hope of immediate advantage that counted (88). Thucydides himself has scant respect for the character or intelligence of the people who were so easily convinced by Brasidas,[17] and he is particularly bitter about the citizens of Amphipolis, since his own failure to save the city led to his exile. There is a distinct note of irony in his remark that the Amphipolitans, in their fear and alarm, thought that the offer made by Brasidas was "just" (106.1).

Whatever the true explanation of his initial successes at Acanthus and Amphipolis, Brasidas apparently did not abandon the use of ethical arguments. At Torone, so Thucydides says, he made the same sort of speech as at Acanthus, but also took pains to assure everyone that those who had "betrayed" the city were not really "traitors"—they had not been influenced by money bribes and their aim was a worthy one, to benefit the city by securing its freedom (114.3). At the same time he insisted that he did not think the worse of the loyalist party because of its "friendship with the Athenians" (114.4); he thought that they preferred the friendship of Athens to that of Sparta because fear had prevented them from realizing that Sparta had more to offer and was a truer friend than Athens. If Brasidas is taken to be a "just" man, it must be because he is able to represent the Spartans as benefactors of these cities, by bringing them liberty, and to regard the cities as justly grateful to Sparta when they go over to her side. It is quite a triumph of sophistry to represent an act of betrayal as positively "just," not merely as excusable and expedient. Perhaps Euripides was protesting against this kind of argument when he wrote the *Hecuba,* because Brasidas was not the first to use it.

The Plataeans had no grievance against Athens, and they could not and did not deny the debt of gratitude that they owed the Athenians for preserving them from Theban domination; any claim that the Spartans were coming to liberate them would have been greeted with derision. They had to admit nonetheless that the Spartans had contributed to winning their freedom at the time of the Persian invasion (ii.71); and so the Spartans have some justification in their request for a return of gratitude in the year 429. The Plataeans remain loyal to Athens, however, and resist the Spartan demands. When the city finally submits in the following year after a long siege, the Spartans kill all the surviving Plataean men when not one of them can say that he gave any help to the Spartans or their allies in the Peloponnesian War (iii.52.4, 68.1). They could not of course help the Spartans without betraying the Athenians, and they easily refute the Spartan claim that this kind of gratitude is due to them (54.2). They also insist, however, that they are not at heart "enemies" of the Spartans; they are still "well-disposed" (*eunoi*) towards them, and at war with them only by a sort of accident, under compulsion of circumstance (κατ' ἀνάγκην), so that to slaughter them after surrender will be an unholy act. If the Spartans do it, it will be in order to win the charis of the Thebans, a "shameful charis" (58.1–2) that will bring them lasting disgrace (just as, in the *Hecuba,* Polyxena is killed in order to win a "shameful charis" from the ghost of Achilles). Not only are the Spartans asking too much in expecting to be valued above the Athenians as friends, but they are themselves in the wrong for valuing Theban friendship above friendship with the Plataeans. The Thebans cannot remain silent when this charge is made, and they make the new charge against the Plataeans that they are betraying the common cause of Greek freedom when they support Athens, and that this is, indeed, a shameful charis to the Athenians, different in kind from that which they received from them. The Athenians gave them freedom, and now they are supporting the Athenians against the cause of freedom (63.4).

The debate at Plataea shows the Spartans making a vigorous effort to represent any defection from Athens as a morally worthy act; they expect responsible people to recognize that the Spartans and other liberty-loving peoples are more truly their friends than the Athenians. The Mytilenians, however, in their speech at Olympia in 428 (iii.9–14), think it necessary to convince the Spartans that their act of revolt is not a betrayal of friends. "We are aware," they say, "of the established custom among Greeks. When people change sides in time of war and abandon their previous alliance, the men on the other side who accept their help are pleased enough, in so far as they are actually helped by them, but think the less of them, regarding them as traitors to their former friends." In most circumstances, they agree, such an attitude is justified—that is, so long as the former allies are bound by common interests and are equally matched in power. But since their relationship with the Athenians cannot be so described, they hope that people will not think the worse of them if, though honoured by the Athenians in peace, they withdraw from them when the shooting starts (ἐν τοῖς δεινοῖς, 9.1–3). The sensitivity of the speakers is understandable. They run the risk of being thought cowards as well as traitors; hence they find it necessary to discuss the issues "of justice and of arete" in order to show that their behaviour is reasonable, and they claim to provide both *aitiai* and *prophaseis* (13.1), adequate complaints against the Athenians and satisfactory explanations in justification of their own conduct.

Their argument consists in showing that the elements needed for true friendship were lacking in their relationship with the Athenians. Two parties cannot be expected to act in common unless they share the same character and similar intentions. "Our intention," they say, "in entering the Athenian alliance was to free Greek cities from Persian rule; the Athenian intention was to make Greek cities subject to Athens." The machinery of the Athenian confederacy (the system whereby every city, no matter how large or small, had one vote in the federal assembly) made it impossible for them to change Athenian policy. But once they realized what the Athenians were doing, they no longer regarded them as trustworthy leaders; and as other cities, one by one, lost their freedom, their own fear of Athenian imperialism increased. On the other hand, once war broke out, the Athenians became frightened of what would happen if the Mytilenian navy decided to turn against them, and consequently treated them with more respect and attention. Their relationship, therefore, has been based on mutual fear, not mutual good will; such a relationship does not deserve to be called friendship, and they are under no obligation to respect it.

Such are the ethical arguments, which take up more than two-thirds of the speech; but the closing portion, though mainly concerned with practical matters, also has an ethical implication. The Athenians, so the speakers claim, have proved themselves unsatisfactory friends; the Spartans are therefore invited to show that they are truer friends, if they will give the assistance that is needed and clear themselves of the charge that they fail to support rebels against Athens (13.7). In point of fact the Spartans, though sympathetic and apparently willing, do not succeed in giving any material help, and the rebellion fails. The Spartans show themselves to be untrustworthy friends after all, and do not return the service that is done to them.

The type of argument that the Mytilenians offer is very similar to the arguments that the Spartans put before the Plataeans, and that Brasidas puts before the cities in Thrace. Possibly it is not accidental that Thucydides shows the Spartans using or being assailed with this kind of argument,[18] whereas

Athenian taste appears to favour more practical considerations. Certainly the Athenians are not impressed by the arguments that the Spartans use when they ask for the release of the men blockaded on Sphacteria, suggesting that a display of generosity by the party that holds the upper hand is the best way of putting an end to a quarrel (iv. 19. 2). It is the suggestion that Tigranes, in the *Cyropaedia,* put before Cyrus, and which Cyrus adopted with such conspicuous success; but the Athenians, under Cleon's influence, are more interested in exploiting their advantages than in putting the Spartans under an obligation (21. 2).

The object of the Mytilenians in their speech is not simply to persuade the Spartans to support their rebellion against Athens, but also to win a good opinion for themselves, without which they cannot expect to receive the fullest cooperation; they want no one "to think the worse of them," so that the Spartans in their turn will respect and honour them as worthy friends. The Corcyraeans make a similar effort in their first speech at Athens (i. 32–36), when they seek Athenian support for their resistance to Corinth, which might be construed as disloyalty. But of all the defences of disloyalty, real or apparent, in Thucydides, none can compare with the speech of Alcibiades at Sparta (vi. 89–92). He has not simply deserted an alliance, on the ground that it rested on a false basis without good will or community of purposes. He has abandoned his allegiance to his native city and is offering his services to its enemy, the Spartans, in order to help them in breaking its power. There is hardly any doubt that his offer will be accepted, since he has much to give them in the way of information and advice; but he also wants to win their good opinion, and like the Mytilenians begins by asking his listeners "not to think the worse of me."

It is hard for a modern reader to believe that Alcibiades could have had the effrontery to deliver such a speech as Thucydides attributes to him. Of all the speeches in Thucydides, this is the one we are most likely to dismiss as purely fictional, made up of those arguments which, in the opinion of the historian, the speaker was likely to use or would have been obliged to use, rather than with any scrupulous regard for the general theme of an actual speech. It is, however, intelligible and acceptable, both as a work of art and as historical reconstruction, when its line of argument is compared with the speeches previously considered in this chapter. Alcibiades maintains that he has not deserted his country, but that his country has deserted him and his task, therefore, is to win it back. His speech is brief and highly compressed, in keeping, presumably, with the "laconic" tastes of his Spartan audience; and some of his conclusions and hypotheses are implied rather than actually stated. Accordingly, it is easier to show what he means by a paraphrase than by an attempt at close translation.

He asks the Spartans not to think the worse of him if he, who was thought a sincere lover of his country, now joins his country's enemies in attacking it; and not to suspect his motives as induced by the resentment of exile. He expects to be judged by the services he can perform, and he claims that by helping Sparta to win the war he will be re-establishing his own country and re-creating the rule of good will in place of the rule of force. The men in power in Athens, who exiled him, are in his opinion worse enemies of their country than the Spartans: whereas the Spartans have sought to damage an enemy, the Athenian politicians have made an enemy of a friend; hence an attack on Athens is really not an attack on his own city, but an attempt to recover it from them. The conclusions, which he does not put into actual words, are: (1) The present rulers are no true friends of Athens, since they deprived the city of my valuable services. (2) The Spartans will be friends, not enemies, of Athens if they remove these men from power and set up a new form of government, based on good will, with me at its head. (3) I am therefore proving my true love of Athens in joining the Spartan side. The hybristic arrogance of this argument is breathtaking; but it is not based on considerations of expediency, as one might expect from a pupil of the sophists. It is rather a perversion of the theory of justice based on friendship, which assumes (as Socrates might have taught Alcibiades to believe) that most politicians are not true friends of their country and that therefore any attempt to dislodge them is a patriotic act (though Socrates, as the *Crito* shows, would not have agreed with him there).

When old-fashioned ethical theories can be used in defence of treachery and can be so distorted as to become politically dangerous, it is no surprise that they cease to be popular in political oratory. They will not be found in any of the speeches in the seventh book of Thucydides; and in the eighth book (which in its present state contains no speeches) there is only one significant allusion to the belief that relations between states are guided by the wish to repay benefits. The Athenian Phrynichus says he thinks the Persians will prefer to support Sparta rather than the new pro-Athenian scheme of Alcibiades, when they remember that in the past Sparta did Persia far less damage than democratic Athens (viii.48.4). Characters in the later books of Thucydides seem to be guided by considerations of expediency rather than by the obligations of friendship or loyalty; or else, like Nicias, when they speak of arete, they are thinking of honours and rewards, which a man may win by serving his country without any more specific ethical code. In the years of the plague Thucydides mentions how some people, "especially those with any claim to arete" (ii.51.5), risked infection by visiting their friends who were sick, but he also notes that less conscientious persons, who tried to avoid contact with others, were just as likely to die from the disease when no one looked after them. A lack of loyalty or charis towards friends is by no means the only symptom of moral decay that appears in the year of the plague; equally serious is the tendency to seek immediate advantages and pleasures rather than persevere in the hope of achieving "what is considered worthy" (53.2–3). The emphasis in the earlier books on arguments from friendship and loyalty is much more frequent in the speeches than in the narrative.

SIX. Justice, Expediency, and Self-Interest

Whatever Alcibiades or the Mytilenians may have said in their own defence, their enemies certainly accused them of acting solely with their own advantage in view. When a man fails in his obligations, it is usually because he finds it more profitable than meeting them. Hence in ordinary Greek idiom, the unjust man is regularly pictured as the slave of his passions, more anxious to serve his own appetites or enrich himself or avoid pain than to help his friends. The bad soldier would rather save his own skin than save his fellow soldiers and serve his country in its need; the dishonest politician can be persuaded by a bribe to disregard what would benefit his country. When a Greek politician is called just, it nearly always means that he is incorruptible. Aristides, in the final stage of his career, established the sums to be paid by members of the Delian Confederacy, and there was never a hint that he accepted any inducements from cities hoping for a low assessment; his complete integrity in carrying out his task assured his lasting reputation as "Aristides the Just." The honesty of Themistocles, despite his shrewdness and political foresight, for which Thucydides gives him full credit, was not so certain. In his praise of Pericles, Thucydides thought it necessary to remark that he was beyond question incorruptible (ii.65.8); and Creon, in the *Antigone,* when he finds his orders disobeyed, is sure that the offenders were bribed to do what they did, and denounces money as the source of all evil in public life (293–301).

References to political bribery abound in the Athenian

literature of the fifth and fourth centuries, and the political historian may be content to take this as an indication that the standard of integrity in public life was not very high. But the student of popular ethics may draw the further conclusion that one man commonly judged another according to his ability to resist temptation and control his selfish desires, whether for pleasure or wealth or fame. The familiar emphasis on sophrosyne, which means sound-mindedness but always implies self-control, points in the same direction. Ordinary men and women are not disposed to think in terms of ideals, and the notion that Greeks of the classical age worshipped an ideal of moderation (as the conventional textbooks tell us) conveys a somewhat unreal impression of popular morality. Greeks were certainly not so foolish as to think that men should simply follow their desires and impulses, or that they should or could suppress them altogether. If a man's excellence or justice was determined by his willingness or ability to help his friends, it was also recognized that he must, within limits, help himself.[1] Unselfishness, if carried beyond a certain point, makes it impossible for a man to hold body and soul together. Hence, though justice is often opposed to expediency, unless it sometimes corresponds with it there is very little hope that a man will acquire the reputation of being just.

The ordinary man sees no constant relationship between justice and expediency, though Socrates in the *Republic* hopes to prove that they are, in the long run, the same thing. He maintains that whoever commits injustice harms himself more than his victim; that it is better to be wronged than to wrong someone; that the guilty man who is punished is better off than the man who escapes punishment. One could hardly expect such views to be echoed very strongly in popular thinking, least of all in the law courts when the victim of robbery or violence or fraud is seeking restitution. They are found, however, in more idealistic contexts, as for example in the Funeral Oration of Pericles. Those who died are represented there as having made a deliberate choice, not weakening in their resolve or influenced at all by the thought that, if they survived, they would be able to enjoy riches or (if they were poor) might accumulate them. They are supposed to recognize that true salvation or self-preservation lies not in saving their lives, but in saving their honour,[2] so that they face the danger to their bodies and avoid the disgrace to their memory; the spears of the enemy are visible and tangible, immediate and concrete, whereas the disgrace exists only in their minds and in the future and the threat of it comes from what men will say, not from what they will do. The correctness of their decision is a recognition that *logoi*—words, ideals, principles, lasting reputation—are more important than *erga*—immediate, temporary physical pain and pleasure. Their death, therefore, and their patriotic devotion should not be described as self-sacrifice, but as the act of intelligent men who knew where their true interest and advantage lay.[3]

The Funeral Oration is perhaps the most extreme example, before Plato, of the so-called intellectualist approach to ethics, which refuses to recognize any clear distinction between intellect and will. But this attitude, as we have seen, is rooted in early Greek thought; in Homer, as well as in the language of Pericles, the man whose desire for some immediate pleasure or advantage causes him to disregard the unpleasant consequences is not weak-willed, but simply foolish or immature, "witless," not sound-minded. In most instances perhaps, when a man helps his friend or returns a favour, no particular intellectual effort is required; superior intelligence is shown only when a choice has to be made, when he has to decide which of his friends should claim his allegiance or where his true interest lies. The need for intelligence is equally great no matter whether justice is thought to consist in charis and loyalty or in seeking one's own advantage.[4]

Although the climax of the Funeral Oration praises the dead for recognizing where their real advantage lies, the speech as a whole sets forth the various traditions of Athens which these men are supposed to have realized and illustrated. It is supposed to be characteristic of Athenians that they give help spontaneously, recognize the authority of the laws, and are not misled by the immediate attractions of wealth or outward show; in modern terminology, they recognize their obligations, both social and political, and they have a true sense of values. Any hedonistic or utilitarian system of ethics has to weigh one pleasure or advantage against another and to consider the ultimate result, which may in fact be the very opposite of the immediate consequence of an action. Croesus, in the story told by Herodotus (i.32–33), was warned by Solon to look beyond the present to the end, but unfortunately he was not prepared to take this advice and thought Solon a fool to give it. Solon's advice to Croesus is no different from the warning that Demosthenes, in the speech "On the Crown," gives to Aeschines, when he tells him that traitors who sell their services to the enemy are not really seeking their true advantage; they will lose more than they will gain, if they look to the final result.

It is nearly always possible to argue that a just action is expedient, if one looks far enough into the future; and it is also easy to condemn people for furthering their own interests when they neglect their obligations to others. Inevitably, therefore, popular ethics is inconsistent on the issue of justice and expediency, so long as the standard of friendship and its obligations is recognized. Thucydides seems to show, however, that as the Peloponnesian War progressed, appeals to friendship and charis and the obligations of a contract became less frequent, presumably because they were found less effective than appeals to expediency.

As was pointed out in Chapter One, both the Corcyraean speaker at Athens, who made a plea for an alliance, and the Corinthian speaker, who asked the Athenians to reject this plea, tried to show that what they asked was just and in the interest of Athens; and, as Thucydides describes it, the Athenians decided the question purely on the score of expediency. On the other hand, at the Congress of Sparta there is a distinct contrast between the modes of argument used by the Corinthian and

Athenian speakers. The Corinthians, in their attempt to make Sparta support them in a war against Athens, claim that the states directly threatened by Athens will have justice on their side in taking the initiative, and that Sparta, if she fails to support her allies, will be guilty of injustice. Instead of emphasizing what the Spartans will gain by war, they insist on her obligation: "Help the rest of us and the Potidaeans, as you promised, by invading Attica without delay; thus you will not betray your friends and kinsmen to their bitterest enemies and not cause the rest of us, in despair, to look for support in another alliance. If we did such a thing, we swear, in the name of the gods who sanction oaths and the men who are our witnesses, that it would not be an unjust act, because it is just as clear a breach of a peace treaty when men fail to help their sworn allies as when they make an independent attack on others. But so long as you are ready to help us, we will stay with you; it would be an unholy act to change our allegiance, and we would not find such congenial allies elsewhere" (i.71.4–7).

The Athenians, when their turn comes to speak, refuse to argue directly with the Corinthians, saying that they do not consider themselves to be on trial nor do they recognize the Spartan Congress as a court competent to try them. But they are prepared to maintain that their behaviour in building up the empire was reasonable and normal, motivated as it was by fear, love of honour, and self-interest; and "no one grudges it to anyone if, in the face of great dangers, he arranges matters best to his own advantage" (75.5). They say the Spartans would have done the same thing in their position: "What we have done is neither surprising nor contrary to normal human behaviour, if we accepted an empire when it was offered to us and refused to relinquish it, driven on as we were by three powerful incentives, love of honour, fear, and self-interest. Nor were we the first to initiate such a procedure; it has always been established that the less powerful shall be restrained by the more powerful. We also claim to be worthy of our position, and have been thought so by you until now, when, though you are thinking of your own advantage, you use the 'just argument' and appeal to 'justice'; no one, when he had the opportunity to win a point by using force, ever offered this argument or was deterred by it from gaining some advantage" (76.2).

The Just Argument and the Unjust Argument are familiar from their appearance in the *Clouds* of Aristophanes. The Unjust Argument, which is one way of "making the worse case appear the better," simply denies that justice exists (902), and maintains that the appeal to it is old-fashioned and ridiculous. The scene in the comedy, in which the Just Argument is refuted by the Unjust, is of course not intended as an exact exposition of the technique of oratory; but there are more ways than one of defending oneself against an accusation, in the law courts or elsewhere. A man may simply say that his accuser is lying and present his alternative account of the facts; in many of the forensic speeches that have been preserved, the lucid narrative that we read may tell quite a different story from the account presented by the other side. Or else a man may argue that the facts have been misrepresented rather than actually falsified, and that his action, represented as an act of violence or rapacity or cowardice, is in fact nothing of the kind, but that it sprang from the worthiest motives; that he himself, rather than his adversary, deserves to be commended and called a just man. This is the Just Argument, deadly in its effect if it can be maintained, but not always advisable or applicable.

Strepsiades, in the *Clouds,* decides that if his son cannot learn both arguments, at least he should learn the Unjust Argument, "which pleads no justice but defeats the better case" (884). It is sometimes better policy to admit that one's behaviour may have been less than perfect, but under the circumstances was pardonable and acceptable, to maintain that anyone faced with equal provocation would have done the same, and that to call such behaviour criminal or even blameworthy at all is unrealistic and unreasonable. This is the Unjust Argument, which the Athenians use here. If they had wanted to use the Just Argument, they would have had to show that their imperialistic policy benefitted their allies no less than themselves, and that it was motivated by the purely patriotic desire to strengthen Greek defence against possible Persian attack. Pericles is supposed to have argued publicly that the Athenians were fully entitled to use the tribute paid by the allies for their expensive and magnificent new buildings on the Acropolis (Plutarch, *Pericles* 12); but the circumstances at the congress in Sparta were hardly favourable for that kind of speech.

The implication of the Athenian speech is that justice is too narrow a term to be the sole standard in political deliberations on such important matters as peace and war; and that the Corinthians are hypocritical in asking the Spartans to be guided by considerations of justice alone. It may be doubted whether Thucydides is historically accurate in making an Athenian speaker put the case quite so bluntly; such a speech might have been considered a major error in diplomacy, and one might think it would have aroused so much comment that the name of the speaker would be known.

The *Clouds* was produced in 423, eight years after the outbreak of the war. It is not so easy to establish with any certainty in what year the *Oedipus Tyrannus* of Sophocles was produced, but it was some time between 431 and 423. It is particularly interesting, therefore, to notice the language of Oedipus when he gives his reasons for supporting Creon in the search for the murderer of Laius:

> In justice you will find me your ally,
> Helping this land and giving the god support.
> It is not for the sake of distant friends,
> But for myself that I must clear this stain;
> Whoever it was killed Laius might kill me,
> That murderous hand might want to strike me too;
> And so, in fighting him, I serve myself.
>
> (135–41)

The irony is that he is himself the criminal whose guilt he is trying to uncover, but so long as he is unaware of this, his position is unshakable. On any theory of conduct he must do his utmost to discover the truth; he will be serving justice and avenging the dead man, furthering the interest of his country, and protecting himself. There appears to be no conflict between justice and expediency; the Just and the Unjust Arguments would be in agreement in recommending the same course of action. Thus when he makes his proclamation calling for anyone who has information to reveal it (225–32), he insists once again that he is acting on behalf of himself, the country, and the god (252–54). But he is shaken from his complacency when Tiresias refuses to speak, saying: "I do not want to hurt you or myself" (332). For Tiresias, it seems, self-interest and the wish to help a friend demand that he keep silent; and he would have kept silent, if Oedipus had not goaded him into speech by his threats and accusations.

The issue of justice and expediency does not play a large part in the *Oedipus Tyrannus*. In fact, Oedipus refuses to recognize that he has ever been faced with a conflict between the demands of justice and his own interest. When Tiresias tells him he does not know where his interest lies, he thinks the old man is taking part in a plot against him; if he had been in Antigone's position (in the *Antigone*), he would have been driven into a rage by Ismene, instead of treating her gently, and in Electra's position (in the *Electra*) he would have feared Chrysothemis instead of merely despising her. His failure to see how his own interest may conflict with other obligations is a kind of moral blindness, a special form of hybris to which successful politicians are particularly liable. The Athenian speaker at Sparta could not be accused of this shortcoming; but it is hard to imagine Pericles using the arguments which Thucydides puts in the mouth of this anonymous Athenian.

The general feeling of the Peloponnesians at the Congress, so Thucydides tells us, was soon evident; people considered that the Athenians were in the wrong and that war should be declared immediately (i.79). The obligation to declare war was apparently regarded as the natural consequence of the decision that the Athenians were "wronging" various Greek cities. The Peloponnesians considered themselves bound to help their allies against Athenian aggression; the ethical code demanded immediate war. Practical politicians, however, cannot afford the luxury of thinking solely in such simple ethical terms, and the Spartan king Archidamus offered good practical reasons for not behaving impulsively; he advised continuing diplomatic negotiations, while preparing for war vigorously at the same time. He claimed to be recommending a policy of sophrosyne: his hearers should not be carried away by their feelings; they should remember that to go to war before they were properly prepared would bring them no less disgrace than cowardly inaction, and that they could not justify attacking a city that was still ready to submit to arbitration (80–85). But the ephor Sthenelaidas could not see beyond the simple ethical issue. Sophrosyne, in his opinion, meant supporting an ally in its need, and since the Athenians were in the wrong there was nothing more to be said: "If we are to practise sophrosyne, we will not look on while our allies suffer injustice nor will we delay coming to their aid."[5] There is not a single reference in his brief speech (86) to the chances of success or failure or to the wisdom and expediency of going to war: "Do not let anyone tell you that it is proper for us to take counsel when we are suffering injustice; rather it is those who contemplate committing injustice who ought to take long and careful counsel. Vote for the war, therefore, in a manner worthy of Sparta; do not let the Athenians become more powerful; let us not betray our allies, but with the help of the gods let us advance against the aggressors."

The *Medea* of Euripides was produced in 431 B.C., the very year in which war was declared; and the speech of Jason, in which he attempts to defend his desertion of Medea and his marriage to the Corinthian princess, not only offers a good example of exactly contrary reasoning to that which Sthenelaidas followed, but is particularly striking in view of the date of the play.[6] Jason, as Euripides presents him, is not an admirable or sympathetic character, and his speech was not expected to find favour with the audience; his case was a weak one, and his abandonment of Medea quite indefensible by normal ethical standards. Medea had accused him of the grossest ingratitude, since among other things she had saved his life and borne him children, and of impiety, since he had no regard for the oaths he had sworn. He could not, she said, claim to be a man of good faith unless he re-wrote the entire ethical code:

> All trust in oaths is gone—I cannot tell
> If thou dost think the old gods are dethroned,
> Or else dost think the laws are all re-cast.
> (492–94)

Jason finds a way of answering the charge of ingratitude. It is not true, he says, that he has left her charis unrequited; on the contrary, he argues, since he brought her to Greece and enabled her to live like a Greek woman, in a civilized city under the rule of Greek law and justice, he has done more for her than she for him. But he has no such ready answer to the charge of broken pistis; he can hardly deny that he is abandoning her as a wife and planning to marry the king's daughter instead. He does, however, try to show that his behaviour is "reasonable," and he even maintains that, if she will think about it, she should have no cause to complain of it:

> In this regard I'll show first that I'm wise,
> Then that I'm sophron, then, too, that I am
> A powerful friend to thee and to thy children.
> (548–50)

He is wise, or intelligent, because, coming to Corinth under a cloud as he has (after the unfortunate events that took place in Iolchis), the sensible thing for him to do is to establish himself by making a good marriage with a wealthy princess. He is doing this, so he says, not to satisfy his sexual appetite, as Medea imagines, but so that he (and Medea as well, for that matter) can have a good home and social position; Medea and her children will be well provided for. His choice, moreover, is dictated not only by wisdom but by sophrosyne; he is sophron, temperate and self-restrained, because he is not allowing his life to be dominated by sex; it is Medea, on the contrary, who is at fault in this respect. In fact, he is actually doing her a favour by renouncing his marriage with her; he does not, of course, use the ugly word "betrayal" at all.

The sheer impertinence of his argument is breathtaking, and the leader of the chorus wastes no time in attempting to refute it; he is content to say that, ingenious though the speech is,

> It seems to me thou hast betrayed thy wife,
> And this is plain injustice.
>
> (576–78)

Jason never argues that his behaviour is "just," only that it is intelligent and serves his own interests best, and that Medea would recognize that it served her interests too, if she were not a silly woman. His reasoning may be quite offensive to good taste, and it is acceptable only if old-fashioned ideas like loyalty and respect for the obligations of a contract are set aside. The Nurse in the *Hippolytus* is equally devoid of any moral scruple. She never argues that her plan is admirable, but that Phaedra's scruples and her sense of honour will kill her if she persists in them. When Phaedra tells her to say no more, she defends her plans with perfect frankness:

> Dishonourable—yes; but better for you than honour.
> Better a *deed,* if it will save your life,
> Than this good name on which you pride yourself,
> And which you'll die in keeping.
>
> (500–502)

The drama of an earlier day had not cared to put such characters on the stage; the Clytaemnestra of Aeschylus had tried to justify her deeds, and was not content to fall back on such cynical reasoning. But it cannot be said that Euripides makes

Jason or the Nurse attractive; his presentation of them is not calculated to corrupt morality, nor is it necessary to say of these two plays, which are both early (the *Hippolytus* only a few years later than the *Medea*), that he is popularizing sophistical argument. On the contrary, the utter selfishness of Jason and the Nurse is quite without sophistication. Euripides was not revealing any secret in letting it be known that such persons existed, and the challenge to make them believable must have been very attractive to the actors. Critics might object that such characters were unworthy, aesthetically, of the tragic stage; but their appearance on the stage does not point to any decline in popular morality. The *Frogs* of Aristophanes, in which Euripides is presented by Aeschylus as a corrupter of morals, was not written until many years later. If the *Medea* and the *Hippolytus* had been produced in 411 and 408, instead of 431 and 428, they might have had a different effect on the audiences. To understand why this should be so, we must go back again to Thucydides.

But before returning to Thucydides, to watch his account of the change of moral attitudes during the Peloponnesian War, it is instructive to look ahead into the next century and to notice how Demosthenes, in one of his early speeches before the assembly, ventures to make use of the Unjust Argument. Demosthenes had been acquiring experience in the law courts for perhaps as long as ten years when he made his speech "On the Freedom of the Rhodians," but he was still a beginner in politics, and his reputation as a speaker in the assembly was by no means secure. He urged the Athenians to be firm in resisting the interference by foreign powers in the internal affairs of Rhodes, to defend its democracy against oligarchic revolutionaries, who were agents of the Persian king. This is one of his concluding arguments:

I think indeed that it is just for you to restore the Rhodian democracy; but even if it were not, when I look at what these people are doing, I still think I should urge you to do so. Why?

Because, men of Athens, when everyone is anxious to do the "just" thing, it would be shameful that you alone should refrain; but when all are in fact making such preparations that they will be able to act in defiance of justice, for you to hold back, taking shelter under the skirts of "justice," I consider not a "just" act but an act of cowardice. The fact is that every man measures "justice" with an eye on the actual powers that he possesses (28).

This last sentence is not greatly different from what the Athenians, according to Thucydides, say in the Melian Dialogue: "If we are to talk as practical people, *just* is a word to use in evaluating the actions of men when limitations, from outside, operate equally strongly on both parties, but *possible* is the word for the actions of the stronger, when they demand, and the weaker, when they submit" (v.89).[7] But the argument of Demosthenes does not strike the modern reader as unduly cynical, certainly not if applied to emergencies of international politics in which an atmosphere of distrust prevails. It is, however, in very sharp contrast with the blunt attitude of the ephor Sthenelaidas, who cannot see that any other factor is relevant except the obligation of Sparta not to betray her allies; and it is also markedly different from the arguments used by Brasidas in Thrace, when he is at pains to convince the hesitant cities that desertion of Athens is "just" because it is not really a breach of obligation.

It is easy to sit in judgment on the Athenians and condemn their attitude towards the Melians as brutal or morally obtuse. But the manner in which the Melians state their case should not be allowed to pass unexamined. The Melians, like the Spartans after the fall of Plataea, insist on regarding the discussion as a kind of trial in which the Athenians have constituted themselves as judges; and the trial, as they present it, is peculiarly unreasonable because "if we win, by proving the justice of our case, the outcome for us is war, and if we give in to your arguments the result is slavery" (v.86). It is the kind of complaint that Electra might have used to Clytaemnestra, if she had lost all hope of Orestes returning. The Athenians do not accept this juridical interpretation of the conference; they consider that they are inviting the Melians to accept the only possible means of saving their lives, as Creon might have argued to Antigone, if he had been an ordinary tyrant. They do not behave like the Spartans at Plataea, who claimed to be juridically in the right when they put every Plataean to death; they are quite prepared to admit that they are guided by nothing except considerations of expediency; if the Melians persist in using the Just Argument, it will serve no purpose except to irritate them.[8]

The Melians are represented as persisting in the moral attitude that characterized the diplomatic arguments of Sparta from the very beginning of the war: the conviction that the obligation which bound Sparta and her allies took precedence over everything else. Unluckily for them the Spartans made no serious attempt to help them; the fine words of Sthenelaidas, it seemed, no longer represented Spartan policy, as, indeed, the Athenians tried to point out (only the Melians would not believe it). Guilty though the Athenians may be of callous brutality and cynical in their refusal to recognize any appeal to justice, the Spartans are guilty of a crime which, according to the traditional code, is just as bad—they betrayed their friends. Perhaps their betrayal is not so surprising when we remember how skilfully Brasidas had justified betrayal in his speeches to the Athenian allies in Thrace. The Spartans might logically have urged the Melians to abandon their alliance with Sparta and recognize the Athenians as their true friends; but Thucydides never tells us that they did so.

When the Athenians decide to send an expedition to Sicily, they are, as Nicias warns them (Thuc. vi.10.1), taking the risk that their old enemies will regard this as a valid reason and a good opportunity for renewing the war. The Greek states, allies and enemies alike, so one would suppose, must have regarded the Athenian move as a distinct, even wanton, act of aggressiveness. But there was a "just argument" ready to hand which could be used to defend their action. The Athenians had allies in Sicily who had asked them for assistance, and if they refused, they could be considered guilty of bad faith. As Thucydides says (6.1), the true explanation of the expedition was that the Athenians wanted to dominate the whole island, but they could represent their act as respectable, even laudable, by saying that they wanted to help their kinsmen (the Ionian cities) and their allies. The envoys from Segesta, in their plea for Athenian help, were not content to remind the Athenians of their obligations under the treaty. They pointed out that their local enemy, Selinus, had secured the help of a powerful ally, Syracuse, whose imperialistic ambitions were well known, and there was a danger that the friends of Syracuse in Greece, like Corinth and Sparta, might choose to lend a hand as well. It was therefore prudent and intelligent (sophron) to stop Syracuse now rather than wait until Athens had no allies left in Sicily. These envoys must have felt that their case was unanswerable; here was an instance when the demands of justice and prudence were identical.

The situation in Athens, therefore, is a repetition of the situation in the Congress of Sparta, when Archidamus tried to explain that the more intelligent course was to refuse immediate assistance to the allies of Sparta who feared Athenian imperialism, only to be sharply contradicted by Sthenelaidas, who championed the "just" course of "not betraying our allies." An Athenian delegation was sent to Sicily to examine the situation, and was tricked into believing that the financial resources of Segesta were much greater than they really were. Later on, when the Athenians discovered this trick, they had a legitimate reason for withdrawing their offer of assistance; but for the present, they decided to send the expedition, and Nicias found himself actually appointed as one of its three commanders before he decided to come forward in the assembly and argue that it should be abandoned (7–8).

Nicias, therefore, had a more difficult case to plead than Archidamus. The only point in his favour was that no one would dare to charge him with cowardice, since his reputation for bravery in action was unassailable, as he pointed out in his opening sentences (9.2). He could not appeal to Athenian tradition, since aggressiveness was part of that tradition—as he quite readily admitted. Like the Athenians at Melos, he had to confine himself strictly to the matter in hand; and he undertook to show that the scheme was ill-timed and unlikely to succeed (9.3).

He is no more successful in pleading his case than are the Athenians at Melos. But his practical arguments, which are simple and cogent, need not concern us here. Far more important is his insistence that the Athenians must not be naïvely confident that Sparta will consider herself absolutely bound by the terms of the peace treaty (which he had negotiated himself); if the Athenians meet with any considerable setback, their enemies will not hesitate to take the opportunity of attacking them. He points out that their enemies accepted the terms of the treaty mainly because it was forced upon them by their military failures; it was dictated to them by external necessity (κατ' ἀνάγκην, 10.2). He does not take the next step and say explicitly, like the Athenians at Melos, that consideration of "justice" is appropriate only when external necessity or pressure is equally strong on both parties; he leaves his audience to draw this conclusion for themselves. He cannot go on to say that to take credit to themselves for meeting their obligations (when it suits them) and to expect others to observe all their obligations (whether it suits them or not) is as foolish as it is dishonest. Thucydides shows him carrying his argument only halfway to its logical conclusion—as far, perhaps, as a speaker in the assembly would dare to go.

The suggestion of a similarity between Nicias's speech and the Athenian argument at Melos must not be pushed too far, because Nicias does not ask the Athenians to abandon considerations of justice. On the contrary, he invites them to remember that justice makes other demands on them in addition to those that are claimed by these distant "barbarian" allies (as he calls them in 11.7). It may be just to avenge the wrongs Segesta has suffered at the hands of her enemies, but it is equally just for Athens to take vengeance on her unfaithful allies whose defection has never been punished (10.5). Athens has only recently recovered her military and economic strength; there is no injustice in using these resources for her own benefit closer to home (12.1), and there is certainly no obligation to use them to further the selfish ambitions of men like Alcibiades. Nicias finishes by answering the objections of the strict legalists, who, like Cleon in the Mytilene debate, insisted that the laws did not allow the assembly to reverse a decision they had already taken (14.1).

Nicias did not succeed in persuading the assembly to change its mind. But Thucydides makes it plain enough that ethical considerations played very little part in the Athenian decision; the expedition was motivated by hopes of increased power for Athens and personal advantage for individual participants in it. This is the last time that the issue of justice and expediency is seriously raised in the history of Thucydides. It is not perhaps an occasion when "returning what one owes" was equivalent to "giving back a madman his sword." But the historian leaves us in no doubt that it was a dishonest explanation of the expedition to say that it was undertaken because the request of Segesta could not have been refused without breaking faith. Nicias evidently had little respect for such misuse of the Just Argument; and Thucydides does not conceal his high regard for the moral character of Nicias.

Nicias does not suggest to the Athenians that they should, in their own interest, disregard the demands of justice. On the contrary, he seems to be combating a tendency in ethical argument to narrow the scope of ethical obligation, to regard each action as though it were complete in itself and each separate obligation as independent of other larger obligations that more far-sighted men take into account. "Nothing matters except the question we are asking" is the burden of the Athenian argument at Melos and also of the Spartan argument at Plataea.

Such single-mindedness, or over-simplification of the issue, may be useful as a way of evading responsibility, but it often looks like deliberate moral obtuseness or short-sightedness; and it is not always easy to be sure whether a man who presents his case in terms of the immediately apparent obligation, without regard for the larger issue, is small-minded (as the Spartans may have been) or hypocritical (as the Athenians certainly were).

There is, however, another form of single-mindedness, which consists in seeing nothing but the ultimate purpose to be achieved and refuses to recognize any scruples about the means by which the purpose is achieved. Odysseus, in the *Philoctetes* of Sophocles, finds it difficult to understand why Neoptolemus should feel any scruples about a single act of meanness or treachery, when it will contribute to a desirable end. The history of the last decade of the fifth century suggests that there were many such persons, Athenian and anti-Athenian, living at the time when the play was produced—men who were prepared to incur new obligations (whether to Sparta or Persia), which they had no intention of fulfilling, if making a promise could help to win the war for their side or faction; men who were ready to commit murder or to endorse the judicial murder of their fellow citizens in order to gain their objective. The *Philoctetes,* therefore, is a genuinely topical play, as well as the last of the great tragedies to present a man wrestling with a moral problem.

Neoptolemus is a scrupulous young man, but he is unaccustomed to facing ethical questions and expects to be presented with a quick and simple answer. The play, however, differs from the other great ethical tragedies in that the unsympathetic characters make no attempt to argue the *justice* of their cause. We may not be impressed by the ethical arguments of Clytaemnestra or Creon, we may think Clytaemnestra hypocritical and Creon small-minded, but at least they argue in ethical terms, whereas Odysseus does not. Odysseus does not attempt to deny that the plan to disarm Philoctetes involves deceit and meanness, nor does he take refuge in the kind of sophism that popular criticism associated with Euripidean characters. He does not say "Deceit is no deceit, if noble is the end" or "It was my tongue that swore, but not my mind" (a line on which Aristophanes could always count to raise a laugh). On the contrary, when Neoptolemus objects: "Dost thou not count it shame to tell a lie?" Odysseus replies simply: "No, not if telling lies can save my life" (108–9).

Neoptolemus at first is horrified, but it does not take Odysseus long to convince him; and he does so by showing that though it may be mean and ignoble to deceive Philoctetes, it will nevertheless win Neoptolemus honour and a good name.[9] The dialogue will be examined in greater detail in the next chapter, when the part played by public opinion in determining men's actions is discussed. For the present, however, it may be considered that Odysseus is offering a bribe to Neoptolemus, and a shrewdly chosen bribe; fair fame means more than riches to the son of Achilles. The obvious retort that one might have expected is not given; the young man does not scorn a good name won by deceit and treachery.

In the earlier argument, when Odysseus tried to explain the needs of the Greeks without offering this bribe, he met with no success at all. Neoptolemus made all the proper replies: he would stand by the warrior's code and uphold his father's good name by meeting Philoctetes in fair fight, but he would not stoop to trickery; better to fight fair and lose than win by fighting foul. It is only when Odysseus offers the bribe that the young man consents. One can imagine the cynical old politicians in the audience nodding their heads and smiling: even the noblest and most honourable of heroes has his price, if one only knows how to offer it. There will be some surprises for these old cynics before the play is over; but one may wonder whether Sophocles would have written this opening scene the same way twenty-five years earlier.

SEVEN. Justice and the State

Greek political theorists never found it necessary to spend much time on the problem that seemed fundamental to philosophers of the seventeenth century—the so-called Theory of Sovereignty. Aristotle is prepared to say, without fear of contradiction, that men congregated in cities because only by political association could they achieve their natural end of a "good life," but he never suggests that there was any form of contract, explicit or implied, by which the citizens surrendered a portion of their individual independence to an agency of government; he does not think it necessary to justify by argument the right of a government to rule. Homer's kings, certainly, claim to rule by a sort of divine right; their power is "from Zeus" and their sceptres symbolize this god-granted power. But in the democratic world of the fifth century we find no corresponding explanation of the power of the people over the individual, of the many over the few; nor does it appear that oligarchic theory could explain why the few should have power over the many, except by appealing to the interest of the state as a whole. The usefulness of a government seemed to be a sufficient justification of its existence.[1]

Nor was there much doubt, it seems, about the practical necessity for recognizing and obeying judges and generals and other public officials. Revolution and rebellion against established governments are frequent enough in Greek history, but anarchists, who rebel against the principle of authority and claim to be defenders of the rights of the individual, are practically unknown. The only familiar example is the Cynic Diogenes, who has neither predecessors nor successors; the later

Cynics, who look back to him as the founder of their philosophic sect, are not prepared to go as far as he does in claiming absolute and complete freedom for the individual.

Moreover, when Diogenes made his famous declaration that he was a "citizen of the world," he was not stating his belief in any ideal world-state or advocating revolution against local governments, but merely asserting the actual independence which he already enjoyed; he considered himself in fact free from the shackles and obligations of a narrower citizenship. Unlike modern revolutionaries and anarchists, he did not think any drastic act of defiance was necessary to secure his independence. He did not refuse to obey laws; he merely meant that he had no need of them, that he was self-sufficient in himself. The Stoics, who preserved a great admiration for Diogenes, were not opposed in principle to taking an active part in public life, but expected the true sage to make himself independent of the state.

The ordinary man, however, could not be expected to reach such heights; and indeed, in Greek and Roman times alike, the ordinary citizen readily recognized his obligation not only to obey the laws of his state, but to be a "good man," so far as lay in his power, by serving his country in a military or civil capacity or by putting his wealth at the disposal of the state when it was needed. The language in which public-spirited men are officially praised shows little variation; resolutions passed in their honour declare them "good men," whose model is worthy of imitation.[2]

A good citizen, therefore, was willing and anxious to serve the state because he knew how much he owed to it—his security, his enjoyment of its public buildings and festivals and other facilities, his pride of citizenship, which he could pass on to his legitimate children. Just as a good son would feel responsibility towards good parents, he felt himself bound to make some return for what he had received; the very least he could do was to obey the laws that were designed to serve the state's interests. Thus we see that at the political level, as at the personal level, justice is linked with the necessity of returning a favour or showing gratitude. A citizen's obligation to serve his state will be the greater if the state has served him particularly well. So Pericles, in the Funeral Oration, urges the Athenians to "become lovers" of Athens (Thuc. ii.43.1), as they recognize her greatness; his praise of Athens is designed to show how right and logical was the courage of the men who were ready to give up their lives in her service. Moreover, the man who refuses to serve his state is acting against his own interest. He may appear to win some temporary advantage, but in the end by damaging his country he damages himself; there can be no conflict here between the demands of gratitude and self-interest.[3]

The state in return rewards its dutiful citizens. Even if they are killed in war, the state will help to support their young children and will honour their memory; it may even try to show, as Pericles does, that they have served themselves better by dying honourably than by surviving without honour.

The high idealism of the Funeral Oration can appeal only to men who are contented with their country's tradition and proud of their citizenship; and it can be presented only by statesmen who are proud of their own achievements. The just man has no problem in obeying the just laws of a worthy city; he will never be faced by a conflict of obligations but, like Lysias in the speech "Against Eratosthenes," will live in such a way under democratic government as neither to do wrong nor to suffer wrong. But he does not take his morals from the state. Pericles never claims that the laws of Athens have made her citizens just or even made her soldiers brave, as Sparta may have claimed (ii.39.1).[4] He does not even assert that the state has made all its own customs; it certainly has not made the unwritten laws which bring shame, as all admit, on those who disregard them (ii.37.3). There is no suggestion that the laws of the state offer a substitute for morals or absolve the citizen from thinking for himself. Pericles even admits to some reluctance in conforming to one of Athens' laws—the custom of the annual funeral panegyric, which had been incorporated in the law of the land (ii.35).

Even in good states, whose laws are admirable, there are unjust men, and just men sometimes find themselves under the rule of imperfect laws. The unjust man can be punished when he disobeys just laws; but is the just man to suffer for refusing to obey laws which are, by some standards, unjust? Even in Athens it is evident that some people thought he should be punished for daring even to question the law; neither Creon in the *Antigone* nor Cleon, as presented by Thucydides, has any doubt about it. Creon says (666–67):

> You must obey the ruler whom the city sets
> Above you, even in little things, just and unjust.

And Cleon insists that a state with inferior laws which are firmly enforced is a better city than one with good laws which are not observed, that dull-witted men in authority serve their city better than clever men who will not accept the laws without question (iii.37.3). Neither would admit that a man could have a valid excuse for refusing obedience to any law.[5]

They are an ill-assorted pair, the noble Creon, whose right to rule in Thebes rests on his royal blood, and Cleon the demagogue, the champion of the common people and the enemy of aristocratic privilege. But the occasions that prompt their remarks are similar; each is trying to show that the laws against traitors must be enforced in full rigour, even though the people may find the punishment distasteful, excessive, or unduly cruel. Creon has decreed that the body of the traitor Polyneices shall remain unburied, and threatens death to anyone who defies his edict; his rule is absolute, and the chorus recognizes this: "Thou hast the power to enforce any law" (213). Cleon argues that the population of Mytilene should be annihilated, the able-bodied men slain and the women and children enslaved, as punishment for their city's attempt to break away from the Athenian alliance; he opposes as strongly as he can the proposal to alter this savage sentence.

But neither Antigone's defiance of Creon's edict nor the revolt of Mytilene is presented as an act of ingratitude. Creon has only just succeeded to power in Thebes; he has not yet had time to confer any benefits on the population; he is not even given credit for the defeat of the Argive army.[6] Nor does Cleon claim that Athens had conferred any benefits on Mytilene. On the contrary, he admits that Athenian control over her allies or subjects has been exercised by superior force, not by good will. Athenian imperial power is like a tyranny; the subjects are unwilling and untrustworthy. The question of return of benefits or betrayal of trust does not arise; their crime is presented, like Antigone's, as simple but unpardonable disobedience. It was, in fact, this very lack of Athenian good will that gave the Mytilenians courage to defend their act of rebellion before the Spartans in a speech at Olympia (iii.9–14); they argued that they were not really traitors, because the Athenians had not really been their friends. The treachery of Polyneices, of course, who fought against his own city and his own brother as well, is another matter altogether; even Antigone does not try to defend it.

There is very little ethical language in Cleon's argument. When he speaks of wronging (ἀδικεῖν), he means "damaging"; somewhat dishonestly, he represents his opponents as claiming that "the wrongdoing of the Mytilenians is advantageous to us and our losses are damaging to our allies" (38.1). He judges Mytilenian behaviour simply by the harm and help that it is to Athens, which is natural enough if his sole concern is with "the advantage of the stronger," as it seems to be; this makes it unnecessary for him to prove that Mytilene has broken faith or failed to keep a contract. Nevertheless, although it may be questioned whether Antigone was bound by any contract to help Creon, Mytilene certainly was bound by the contract of the Athenian league to support Athens in war. The precise form of oath in the original charter of the league has not been preserved; but the text of oaths sworn by other cities, who were obliged to renew their allegiance after attempts to revolt, is known from inscriptions and it leaves no room for doubt. Hence the Mytilenians, who did not want the Spartans to regard them merely as "useful traitors," tried hard in their speech at Olympia to prove that the contract did not bind them, that Athenian lack of good will had invalidated the treaty and annulled their obligation to remain loyal. Unlike Cleon, they use the familiar language of popular ethics; they recognize the necessity to speak of "justice and arete," and the old familiar terms pistis and elpis are prominent in their plea.[7]

Thucydides tells us that traditional ethical terms were ridiculed or perverted in the arguments of revolutionary times. But "the interest of the stronger," though a convenient motto for a government in power, would hardly commend itself to a revolutionary opposition. It is not until the Melian Dialogue that Thucydides shows us the Athenians pleading the interest of the stronger in an argument that refuses to recognize any alternative for the weaker party if it wishes to survive. They do not take the trouble to offer any ethical argument or to alter terms; they simply say that ethics is irrelevant in their particular situation. They will not spend time proving that they have any right to their empire or that their attack on Melos was justified by any wrong that they suffered. They advise the Melians not to try to justify their refusal to support Athens; they say that ethical arguments are applicable only when the parties concerned are subject to similar limitations of power; if the stronger party is strong enough, there is no limit to what it can do, and the weaker party has no choice but to do what it asks. Since justice has no place in the discussion, the question is not what *should* the Melians do, but what *can* they do? They can yield and live, or resist and die.[8] This is exactly what Creon said to the Thebans, except that he offered a preamble, explaining the necessity for rulers to be obeyed if the state was to survive—obeyed in every detail, without regard for what was just and unjust: καὶ σμικρὰ καὶ δίκαια καὶ τἀνάντια (671).[9]

The Melians have only one reply left to them—a reply which Antigone was too proud to give to Creon—that a too rigorous exercise of authority endangers the ruler in the long run. This was also the main burden of the reply of Diodotus to Cleon.

The Melians warn that no ruling power can dispense with good will entirely (just as the Mytilenians had reminded the Spartans); and the Athenians take the hint by declaring magnanimously that they want the Melians to do what is best for both Athens and Melos! They should "not resist persons much more powerful than themselves" (v.101).

Appeals to pistis or charis would hardly be useful in these circumstances, since there is no bond of friendship or trust between Athens and Melos; neither has ever helped or trusted the other. It only remains to try hope (elpis), which merely annoys the Athenians (103), because they are so sure that the Melian condition admits of no hope; they say (and as it happens they are right) that the Spartans will abandon them, even if it means losing the trust and good will of their allies; to hope for Spartan help is as vain as to hope for help from the gods.

The Melians never quite succeed in arguing with total disregard of ethical considerations. Yet at least they avoid telling the Athenians that even conquerors are limited by moral laws; in the atmosphere of the Melian Dialogue a protest of this sort would be almost ridiculous. Such protests, however, undoubtedly were made by many people. There is no need to suppose that the audience at the first production of the *Hecuba* (probably 425 or 424) laughed when Hecuba thus protested to Odysseus: οὐ τοὺς κρατοῦντας χρὴ κρατεῖν ἃ μὴ χρέων (282). Nor does Polyxena, though she urges her mother not to resist (τοῖς κρατοῦσι μὴ μάχου, 404), mean that she is wrong to protest. Polyxena is willing to be sacrificed only because (unlike her mother) she sees no hope of success in resistance or pleading or protesting. Haemon, in the *Antigone,* protested strongly that authority itself could not make its demands right:

HAEMON: I see thee in error; thy action is not just.
CREON: In error—when I respect my own authority?
HAEMON: Thou hast no respect for it, if thou dost spurn the gods.

(743–45)

But in the *Troades,* produced in the summer following the Melian massacre, Hecuba is resolved on submission from the start. She has abandoned hope, as well as any serious protest; she knows it is useless to do anything except let the conquerors have their way. She must consider what is possible, not what is just.

It is a misrepresentation of Greek thinking to speak of the "right" of the conqueror. Neither the Greeks at Troy nor the Athenians at Melos are represented as having any "right" to kill or enslave the defeated population; Odysseus, in the *Hecuba,* does not demand the sacrifice of Polyxena as a "right" (though he thinks it is just to grant Achilles the favour that he asks); he demands it because it is "possible," and any protests can be disregarded. It does not matter what the Trojans think; even the warning that the Melians gave to the Athenians would have no validity here. Nor does the support of the Greeks give any ethical justification for Agamemnon's consent to allow human sacrifice, whether of Polyxena or of Iphigenia; it merely made it "possible."

Agamemnon sacrificed Iphigenia in order that the Greek fleet might set sail for Troy. Demophon was told that he could not save the suppliants Iolaus and his children (in Euripides' *Heraclidae*) unless a well-born maiden was sacrificed to Demeter. In his case, moreover, the end that human sacrifice would serve was a just end, the protection of helpless suppliants; "just aid" to refugees was an Athenian tradition, as the chorus pointed out:

> Just aid to the helpless
> Our land ever wishes to give.
> (329–30)

But in his case, unlike Agamemnon's, it was not "possible" for him to make such a demand of his people; or rather, he *could* have taken this drastic step, he was in possession of power and had obedient underlings who would carry out his order, but it would probably have led to civil war and internal disaster.

Demophon does not specifically say that it will be "unjust" to demand a human sacrifice from his people; but Iolaus himself admits that he cannot do it, and bears him no ill will for refusing. Thus Demophon's refusal to help the suppliants has some ethical justification, whereas if the Argive king (in the *Suppliants* of Aeschylus) had refused because he or his people feared war, his betrayal would be harder to excuse. But in principle, betrayal of suppliants is always wrong; normally no political reason can justify surrendering a suppliant. The oracle, in Herodotus i.159, finally made this clear to the people of Cyme, when they tried to obtain divine consent for handing over Pactyas. Their political reason was overwhelming and had to be obeyed, but their action was still culpable and condemned them in the god's eyes. Only one thing could have saved the Cymaeans from their dilemma: namely, if Pactyas had surrendered of his own free will. And he ought to have done so, since he was asking too great a favour of his protectors. Fortunately for Demophon, Macaria solved his problem by offering herself as a sacrificial victim.

Agamemnon sealed his doom, and continued the curse on his family, by the sacrifice of Iphigenia. The Greeks had no legend equivalent to the Roman story of Brutus, who himself passed sentence of death on his sons for their treachery; but if they had known of such a story, they would have approved of Vergil's verdict on Brutus:

> Infelix—utcunque ferent ea facta minores;
> Vincet amor patriae laudumque immensa cupido.
> (*Aen.* vi.822–23)

Whenever, in Greek legend or history, someone obeys his country's laws or serves its interest at great cost to himself, his action is not presented as in obedience to a higher law or need, but as prompted by a greater or truer or juster love. Romans might conceivably have made Creon into another Brutus and made him the central figure of the *Antigone, infelix* perhaps, but worthy of some admiration all the same. Sophocles barely succeeded in making him a plausible human being. Antigone's great love for her brother makes the tragic theme of the play; the patriotic efforts of Creon are not even presented as made in a spirit of self-sacrifice.

When Macaria, in the *Heraclidae,* offers her life, she insists that her action is a charis, and the charis will be spoiled if she cannot give it gladly and of her own free will; she refuses the offer of Iolaus to let the lot decide between herself and others. There are many echoes of Pericles' Funeral Oration in the *Heraclidae,* and lack of any insistence on obedience to a law or demand is notable in both places. It is tempting to ask if there is a deliberate effort to differentiate the Athenian ideal of patriotic self-sacrifice from the Spartan, which was immortalized in the famous epitaph on those who fell at Thermopylae:

> O stranger, bear this message to the Spartans:
> We lie here in obedience to their laws.

Emotional statements about patriotic ideals are not perhaps the most reliable evidence for an actually current way of thinking. But one can turn to Alcibiades' speech at Sparta (in Thucydides), in which he attempts to justify his desertion of Athens and ventures to define "love of country" (τὸ φιλόπολι). Like the Mytilenians, he has to justify his desertion for fear that the Spartans will be suspicious of him and not give him a fair hearing (vi.89.1). He argues that he owes no allegiance whatever to the democratic government of Athens, which made him an exile, but he is not merely asking the Spartans to help him in a revolution, as the Alcmaeonids had done, in the days when a tyrant ruled in Athens. In some people's eyes any request for foreign intervention was an act of treachery, and the reputation of the Alcmaeonids suffered under the charge. But Alcibiades has a more difficult case to plead. His country, he says, has wronged him, and therefore he no longer owes it his love; the true lover of his country is not the man who serves it without regard for reward—in his own words, "not the man who, having lost it, refrains from attacking it, but he who, because of his desire for it, strives in every way to recover it" (92.4).

We are under no obligation to believe that Alcibiades said anything of the kind, and we may think that Thucydides is pointing the contrast between the behaviour of Alcibiades and his own behaviour, when his country "wronged" him by exiling him, and he showed his patriotism, as he thought, by accepting the sentence and refraining from intrigue during his absence. If Thucydides had finished his eighth book and completed his characterization of Alcibiades, we might be better able to understand why he put these words in his mouth. But the behaviour of Alcibiades is itself an indication that the Athenian theory of patriotism was inadequate, if it did not insist on the obligation of service without reward. Alcibiades might have appealed to Achilles as a model, since Achilles had withheld his services when he thought they were not adequately rewarded. Even in the Funeral Oration the emphasis is on the reward—the undying fame—rather than the duty of self-sacrifice. In ordinary speech, the public-spirited citizen is said to be motivated by "love of honour" (*philotimia*), and Greek cities did in fact try to honour their benefactors by voting them golden crowns, immunity from taxes, seats of honour in the theatre, and the privilege of free meals in the *prytaneum*. It would be foolish to imagine that these rewards were not highly prized; but for the humbler citizen the possibility of winning them was very remote. The ordinary hoplite or sailor was not so easily convinced that he would be rewarded for risking his life. When Demosthenes, in the *Philippics* and *Olynthiacs,* is insisting that citizens must serve and that Athens cannot rely on mercenary soldiers, he dares not say anything about the rewards of service.

If the tangible reward was usually slight, are we to suppose that the fear of ill repute and disgrace and the respect for the opinion of others were the strongest motives for public service? In the *Iliad,* Hector tried to tell Andromache that they were—that fear of disgrace and the need to uphold the good name that his father left him forced him to leave her and face almost certain death. And it is remarkable that Greek literature, before Plato certainly, offers few real protests about the emptiness of fame and honour.

Nicias is certainly a very different character from Alcibiades. He accepts the post of general on the Sicilian expedition, though he does not believe that the expedition is a wise undertaking at all. Thucydides in fact never makes it clear what his motive is in accepting responsibility. Is it the wish to preserve his military reputation and not miss the opportunity of winning new distinction, in case his initial judgment was wrong? Or is it the wish to serve his country in all things and not deny it the competent leadership and counsel that he thinks he can give? Is he in fact a cowardly time-server or a very brave man? His competence in the field does not concern us here, though Thucydides gives us reason to think that he made many mistakes, and that it would have been better if he had resigned at an early stage. He makes it clear, however, that Nicias was greatly respected, and insists that we admire his moral character and lament his unhappy fate as ill-deserved: "Of all Greeks in my time he least deserved such ill fortune because of his constant attention to what is generally considered arete" (vii.86.5). Thucydides does not define arete, and leaves it to us to decide whether Nicias was right in following the accepted norm of a "good man." Though he tried and worked hard to be a "good man," to serve his country and win distinction, would it have been better for himself and his country if he had abandoned the attempt? Unfortunately, as Thucydides knew very well, if he had resigned, his life would have been ruined; the Athenians did not condone failure in a military command. Nicias seems to be an unusually unfortunate example of a man who prefers death to failure and disgrace; he might have served his country better if his *philotimia* had been less keen and his pursuit of arete less determined.[10]

Theognis had warned Cyrnus against too great an attachment to arete; and Sophocles shows us, in the *Ajax,* the tragedy of a man whose whole life depended on honour and distinction and the respect of his fellow men. Ajax is so sensitive to the opinion of others that he cannot endure being slighted; when Achilles thought himself insulted and undervalued, he sulked in his tent; but Ajax lost his sanity. Infuriated at the decision of the Greeks to give the armour of Achilles to Odysseus rather than to himself, he started out with the intention of killing the judges, only to be thwarted by Athena, who diverted his fury against the captured flocks and herds, making him think that he was killing the men whom he hated. The intervention of the goddess makes no difference; his attempt at wholesale murder was not the act of a sane man.

The men of the chorus at their first appearance describe Ajax's character; whenever he suffers from "the stroke of Zeus or the ill-speaking tongues of the Greeks," they are terrified at what he may do (137–40); they have heard the tale of his slaughter of the herds during the night, but think it is a malicious rumour spread by Odysseus. They shudder at the effect it may have upon Ajax; great men, unlike the humble sailors that they are, are so vulnerable to insult. When Ajax, with his senses restored, sees what he has done and that his enemies are still living, his first thought is that he has been insulted again—the great warrior has been made to look ridiculous. He does not regret his attempt to murder Odysseus and the sons of Atreus. Nor is it any comfort to him that a goddess was responsible for stopping him; he resents divine intervention on principle, since it helps "the lesser man to escape the better" (456). He cannot face the prospect of returning home with no prize to compare with what his father had won. Life is insupportable if all that is left for him is to live on empty hope:

> The man of noble birth
> Must live with honour or have honour in his death.
> There is no more to say.[11]
>
> (479–80)

Tecmessa pleads with him. She, the daughter of a wealthy Phrygian, has learnt to accept the humiliation of slavery; if he kills himself, her lot, as his abandoned concubine, will be bitter indeed, and the insults she will have to bear will reflect on him and his family (505). She has learnt to love him; and while she begs him to have some respect (aidos) for his parents and pity for his infant son, the final strength of her appeal rests on charis:

> Take thought for me as well; a man
> Should not forget the joys that he has known.
> Charis begets charis, each time in its turn;
> But if a man lets slip the memory
> Of kindness he has had bestowed upon him,
> He cannot then be called a noble man.
> (520–24)

It is only the thought of his little son that strikes Ajax, since only his son can redeem his good name;

> Have better fortune than thy father, boy,
> But otherwise resemble me.
> (550–51)

But in his later speech he rejects her remarks about charis; they cannot supply for him the rule of life that she finds in them. He says that he has learnt a lesson in sophrosyne:

> I learnt one need not hate a foe forever;
> He may become a friend. And as for a friend—
> Only so far will I agree to help him;
> He will not always be my friend. Most men
> Find friendship's harbour treacherous in the end.
> (678–83)

He is not converted, therefore; he still stands by his old heroic ideal of arete.[12] Soon we learn from the Messenger that even as a boy his craving for honour went beyond reason. He believed that he could win it even without the favour of the gods; and if he cannot win the highest honour, he has nothing to live for.

The *Ajax* is the only play that presents such a character and shows his inevitable tragedy.[13] It is not simply a tragedy of hybris, but the tale of a man who attempted to live by an impossible and completely selfish ideal. His single-mindedness gives him a real heroic quality that is lacking in the other characters.[14] The chorus, after his death, describes him as "solid-minded" (*stereophron*); and Tecmessa consoles herself with the thought that his death was consistent with his ideals: "He found for himself what he craved: the death he wanted" (967–68).

The other characters—Teucer, Menelaus, Agamemnon, and Odysseus—are revealed, each in his turn, in the closing portion of the play. Unlike Tecmessa, who understands that death was the only solution for Ajax, Teucer is concerned with its effect on himself; he is crushed by the thought that he will be blamed for the death of Ajax and appalled by the strength of public opinion: "Words have changed me from a free man to a slave" (1020). But he quickly recovers his freedom under the shock of Menelaus's behaviour; though he cannot defy public opinion, he defies the authority that Menelaus claims. Menelaus, a sort of Creon in miniature, can see nothing in the tragedy of Ajax except an act of disobedience to himself; and like Creon, he demands that the traitor's corpse be left unburied. Like Creon, he is absolutely in the right up to a point, and he gives an orthodox exposition of the civic virtues, condemning hybris, only to be rebuked in turn, by the chorus, for being hybristic himself because he cannot see the limits to his power. When Teucer speaks out in the name of justice, he replies: "Is it just that the man should prosper who kills me?" (1126). Justice, for him, begins and ends with obedience to his authority.

Agamemnon is a more constitutional version of Menelaus; he appeals to the judgment of the majority rather than to his personal authority, and to the need for "sensible people" (οἱ φρονοῦντες εὖ) to prevail if the rule of law is to be maintained. Teucer counters him by charging him with ingratitude to Ajax, with forgetting how Ajax saved his life: "How quickly does a dead man's charis slip away!" (1266–67).

It remains for Odysseus to make peace, dismissing abruptly Menelaus's order to leave Ajax unburied; he must not trample on justice or ignore the gods' laws (we recognize the language of Haemon and Antigone). Despite Odysseus's personal quarrel with Ajax, he recognizes him as a good man, whose arete outweighs his own feelings. He has an answer for every objection that Agamemnon raises. His argument is lucid and simple, and he gives three reasons why Ajax must be given proper burial: (1) *charis*—respect for the advice of a friend (Odysseus) and gratitude towards a good man (Ajax); (2) *respect for public opinion*—Agamemnon is wrong in thinking public opinion will support him if he insults a dead man; (3) *justice*—which he does not define. He only knows, like Antigone and Haemon, that to refuse a dead man burial is unjust and impious by any standard. When Agamemnon grumbles (as Cleon might have done): "Piety is not so easy for a tyrant" (1350), he can only reply: "But they say well who bid you respect your friends." And this is the argument that sways Agamemnon: "To *thee* an even greater favour I would grant" (1371). It is the friendship of Odysseus, not the dead man's arete, that he agrees to respect; this is his way of saving face.

It is unusual to find Odysseus presented as an admirable character in tragedy. In Sophocles' *Philoctetes,* a play produced over thirty years later than the *Antigone* and seven years after the *Troades,* he is a less sympathetic character, but has the same part to play as in the *Ajax*: he has to convince two people to do what he wants, or rather what the state wants. The Greeks cannot take Troy except by the bow and arrows of Philoctetes in the hands of Achilles' son Neoptolemus. Philoctetes, therefore, must be persuaded to give them up (the oracle has specified that he must do this willingly, so force or trickery alone will not suffice), and Neoptolemus must agree to cooperate. For Odysseus alone the task of persuading Philoctetes is quite hopeless. Charis will not help, since Philoctetes owes no gratitude to the Greeks who abandoned him, crippled with a hideously infected foot, an embittered old man, on the deserted island of Lemnos; least of anyone can Odysseus plead the privilege of friendship, since it was he who actually deposited him there, "at the order of my commanders" (as he is careful to tell Neoptolemus in the opening lines of the play). Nor is Philoctetes likely to have much regard for public opinion, and no argument from justice seems to have much force, even if Philoctetes could be expected to listen to it. Neoptolemus, therefore, will have to do the persuading; but he is a sensitive and scrupulous young man, whose mind recoils from deceit and who cannot bear the thought of staining his reputation or that of his father. How can Odysseus persuade him that it is "just" to do what the state requires, even though it involves deceit and cruelty to an old man and behaviour that will make him appear like an unworthy son of his father?

Odysseus begins by stressing the need for obedience; it is for Odysseus to command and the young man to obey (24–25). A story has been prepared which he is to tell Philoctetes, so as to win his sympathy (Odysseus carefully points out the one detail in the story which is not a lie):

> If this thou wilt not do,
> Thou wilt bring misery on all the Greeks.
> (66–67)

The task may seem unpalatable, but

> Take heart; the time will come again when men
> Will call us just; now lend thyself to me
> For one small shameless portion of a day,
> And earn a name for piety thereafter.
> (82–85)

Neoptolemus, of course, demurs; like Ajax, he would rather fail honourably than win dishonourably. So Odysseus explains to him what is "possible"; since force is out of the question (there is no defence against the arrows), the use of deceit is inevitable. Gradually he breaks down the resistance of Neoptolemus:

NEOPTOLEMUS: Dost thou not think it shame to tell a lie?
ODYSSEUS: No, not if telling lies brings victory.
NEOPTOLEMUS: But how can one look up and say such things?
ODYSSEUS: When thou dost work for gain, thou must not flinch.

NEOPTOLEMUS: What gain for me that he should go to Troy?
ODYSSEUS: These weapons, and no others, can take Troy.
NEOPTOLEMUS: But it was said that *I* shall capture Troy.
ODYSSEUS: Not thou without them, nor without thee they.
NEOPTOLEMUS: If that be so, then I must track them down.
ODYSSEUS: Do this, and two rewards thou shalt receive.
NEOPTOLEMUS: Say what they are—and then perhaps I'll do it.
ODYSSEUS: Thou shalt be called a wise man and good.
NEOPTOLEMUS: Yes, I will do it; I'll cast shame aside.
(108–20)

So the appeal to fame and glory proves more effective than the appeal to obedience; Neoptolemus, it seems, is a true son of his father. Justice for the moment is forgotten; but the issue of charis has not yet been raised. So also when Philoctetes first begs Neoptolemus to take him away in his ship, he urges the good repute (*eukleia*) that such an act will bring to the rescuer; and he uses a form of words very similar to that which Odysseus had employed:

> The labour will mean scarcely one whole day;
> Take courage to do it; stow me where thou wilt.
> (480–81)

Accordingly, when Neoptolemus has to admit that he has no real intention of rescuing him (though he is already beginning to waver), he cannot use the arguments with which Odysseus persuaded him; he has to fall back on the need to obey authority:

> Justice and expediency
> Both bid me hearken unto those in power.
> (925–26)

It is this excuse of Neoptolemus which gives Philoctetes his last chance to make the young man change his mind (after his angry outburst has had no effect):

> Thou art not base thyself; but from base men
> It seems that thou hast learnt these evil lessons.
> (971–72)

And later he reproaches Odysseus for using as his instrument an immature young man,

> Who nothing understood except to do
> What he was told.
>
> (1010)

He can forgive Neoptolemus; but, naturally enough, he is enraged when Odysseus piously tries to excuse his own behaviour by saying:

> 'Tis Zeus, if thou must know, who ordered this;
> Zeus rules this land, and I must do his bidding.
>
> (989–90)

The story might have ended there, with Neoptolemus wanting to do the right thing, but finding it no longer possible. Indeed, Odysseus does say, when Neoptolemus wants to relent: "Though he may want it, he shall never do it" (981–82). But since Neoptolemus keeps the bow, he does not lose the "possibility"; he has the power to defy the authority of Odysseus and the good will of the Greeks; he says, when he returns in the final scene, that it was shameful and unjust to rob Philoctetes of his bow, and he intends to return it. When Odysseus protests that what he is doing is "unwise," he says that just acts are better than wise acts. Even so, his change of heart does not solve the problem. He cannot persuade Philoctetes to come to Troy with them; his last appeal fails:

> How shall I escape the blame of the Achaeans?
> What if they ravage my land?
>
> (1404–5)

It looks, therefore, as though his "just" behaviour has been to little purpose, and it takes the intervention of Heracles as *deus ex machina* to put things right.

Thus even in the end Neoptolemus never discovers what he ought to have done; the need for a *deus ex machina* shows that there is no real answer. If obedience to authority and the search for good repute both led him astray, so also did charis. Philoctetes was too deeply embittered even to be moved by kindness; no mortal plea could persuade him to abandon his quarrel with the Greek leaders, to whom he owed no debt of gratitude. It is true that Heracles, in the speech of reconciliation, has much to say about the fair fame that Philoctetes will win. But the audience would not conclude on that account that he was more readily moved by thoughts of fame than by the memory of his quarrel. The play, moreover, ends as it does not because justice demands that Philoctetes should go to Troy, but because history and the gods will have it so; it is an end for a tragedy, not an ethical solution of a problem of conduct.

Sophocles is concerned with the behaviour of his characters rather than with the justice of an actual result. The distinction is a simple one. Equally simple, one would think, is the distinction between the ethical validity of a law and a particular application or interpretation of it, between a constitutional principle and the order of a superior officer or the verdict of a court. Athenian political practice recognized the distinction by giving a different kind of validity to laws (*nomoi*) and executive resolutions (*psephismata*), both of which were voted by the popular assembly. *Psephismata* had only immediate application to a particular purpose, but *nomoi* had permanent validity and to invalidate or repeal them was a dangerous process; anyone who attempted it was liable to prosecution for making an illegal proposal (*graphe paranomon*). It is perhaps surprising that popular ethics was apparently incapable of recognizing a distinction, which was well established and understood in political practice; it is also curious that the distinction is not more sharply emphasized in Plato's *Crito*.[15]

The *Crito* is unique in Greek literature. A man who, in his own opinion and the opinion of his friends, has been unjustly condemned to death has the opportunity of escaping execution and refuses. The fact that he does not fear death and thinks it a lesser penalty than exile may influence his personal choice, but it does not affect his ethical argument. Crito wants

Socrates to escape from prison, saying that if he refuses, his friends will be blamed for not helping him, for being too cowardly or too mean to put up the money needed. When Socrates is surprised that they should care for what the ignorant general public might think, Crito says that their disapproval can be dangerous and damaging; and when Socrates denies this, Crito changes his ground and says that he and his friends are under an obligation to run the risk of saving him. He must not try to do them a favour by protecting them from this risk.

It is by careful design that Plato makes Crito use more than one argument. He appeals first to public opinion and then to justice, but justice here is really only charis in disguise; the obligation to rescue Socrates is perhaps really the obligation of gratitude and affection which they owe him. Crito is sure of what he should do, but, like Neoptolemus, he has to convince the older man that it is right for him to leave his prison: "It is not a just thing that you are trying to do, to destroy yourself" (45c). It is not right for him to abandon his sons and expose his friends to accusations of cowardice; if Socrates really cares for arete, as he says, he must act like a "brave and good man." Crito uses the conventional vocabulary of popular ethics; he expects Socrates, like himself, to recognize the obligation of charis and to respect public opinion.

Socrates, of course, reminds him that this is not the proper philosophical approach; that if they are to respect other people's opinions, they should respect the opinion of informed persons rather than those of ignorant men, no matter how numerous or powerful they may be; and that, if the obligation to return favours is real, the supposed obligation to return evil for evil is totally unacceptable. Then he tries to show what the relationship is between the laws and himself. According to the law of Athens, decisions of the courts must be accepted as binding; if he escapes their sentence, he is trying to circumvent the laws ("destroy" is the word he uses), and he represents the laws, personified, as asking him what harm they have done him that he should treat them so shabbily; what fault has he to find with them? The laws remind him of the benefits he owes them, his birth as a legitimate Athenian, his upbringing and education in the Athenian tradition. They also remind him that his relation to them is not that of one equal to another, but like that of a child to its parents; he owes them obedience, should not contradict them, should not complain if they punish him; and furthermore a man's native country is something more precious, more worthy of respect, and more sacred than a parent, so that his debt of obedience is the greater and the more solemn. Socrates uses the same word for respect (σέβεσθαι) as Creon in his dialogue with Haemon; he is still using the terms of popular ethics, and insisting that obedience to the law is a form of gratitude. He also introduces the notion of a contract which a citizen is said to make by staying on in a city, and not departing and abandoning his citizenship when he is free to do so.

Crito does not question the accuracy of this description of the relationship between a citizen and his city and the obligations by which he is bound. Finally, of course, as he must, Socrates makes the point that any wrong he has suffered has not been at the hands of the laws but at the hands of men, individuals who have been trying to apply the laws. If, because of this injustice (he does not deny that it is an injustice), he tries to revenge himself on the laws, he will belie all his own ideals, do himself harm, make himself look ridiculous, and put his friends in danger. So he says he must do as the laws bid him "because this is the way the god leads us."

Plato may have written the *Crito* with the object of showing that Socrates had no intention of undermining the laws of Athens and did not incite young men to disregard them. Its particular interest for our present purpose is that Socrates here describes, in terms that every orthodox Athenian would accept and understand, the obligation of a citizen to serve his city and obey its laws. But its importance should not be exaggerated, and if Socrates, for once, speaks the language of popular ethics, there is no need to imagine he means more than he says.

He neither says nor implies that justice *consists* in obeying the law, and he does not vindicate the judgment of the court that condemned him. There is no justification for the view, which Jaeger expresses,[16] that "Socrates recognizes in the law of the state the highest norm of man." The highest norm that Socrates recognizes is the norm of justice, the essence of which he tries to explain in other dialogues; and Crito is expected to remember something of what had been said on other occasions. It is justice that bids him obey the laws, not the laws that create justice; obeying the laws is an example of just behaviour, like returning favours or keeping contracts. Obedience to the law is nearly always, but not necessarily, right; if he could have said to the laws that they *had* wronged him, his obligation of obedience would no longer hold. There is, therefore, no conflict between the *Crito* and the arguments in the first two books of the *Republic,* where Socrates shows the weakness of the maxims of popular ethics because they cannot be applied as universal rules. In the *Crito,* he takes the opportunity of showing that he is in a situation in which popular ethics gives him the right answer.

In the *Crito,* Socrates is content to show the good side of the conventional view of the state and the citizen's obligations. Crito does not ask the questions that would reveal its weakness—for example, whether laws were still worthy of respect if they gave power to ignorant juries to do "what seemed good to them, to banish and kill good citizens," a procedure which did not really achieve the object that they sought, the political health of the city. If Crito had argued with Socrates in the manner in which (in the *Gorgias*) Socrates argues with Polus, he might have forced him into all kinds of contradictions.

Polus and Callicles, in the *Gorgias,* are not average conventional citizens but sophists. But Plato often represents sophists as holding popular views in exaggerated or extreme form. Thus Polus recognizes rhetoric as the art which makes politicians powerful and respected; but not content with the orthodox view that respects and admires fame and public service, he exalts the mere possession of political power—the ability to do what one wants. The arguments that Socrates brings to bear against him need not concern us here, except for his insistence on the distinction between "what seems good" to the politician (his immediate object) and "what he really wants" (which may be to serve the state well); this is a distinction, as we have seen, that plays only a small part in the *Crito*. It is certain that Polus's views, which are almost as immoralist as those of Thrasymachus in the *Republic*, would not have met with general approval among ordinary citizens. One might even argue that the new outbreak of tyranny, as a threat to constitutional government, in the early fourth century, tended to discredit the respect for political ambition which prevailed, if it was not actually inculcated, in the middle of the fifth century in Athens.

Arete can be identified with political ambition and political eminence only so long as the citizens are proud of their laws and their constitutional tradition. Once the Periclean era was past, Thucydides could no longer admire this kind of arete, just as Theognis, in another unhappy age, could not urge it upon Cyrnus. The disillusionment of the Peloponnesian War forced a sharp distinction between eminence and actual public service; it could no longer be assumed that the successful politician actually benefitted his city; the generation which admired Themistocles was succeeded by a generation which could still admire Nicias, but learnt to distrust Alcibiades. Polus agrees with Socrates that most men who try to achieve an end by force are not happy men. But his reason is that they will be caught and punished. The successful autocrat is beyond fear of punishment, and Polus appears to be surprised that Socrates will not admire and envy such men, however unjust their methods. Like Thrasymachus, he grants that it is "shameful" to commit injustice, but he will not grant that it is "bad." And though Socrates convicts him of verbal inconsistency, he is not really convinced that his opinion is wrong. The idealism of the Funeral Oration represents politicians as conferring benefits and winning good repute. Cleon denies that they can afford the luxury of conferring benefits and winning good will. Polus does not mind if they also abandon the effort to achieve good repute; he expects them to commit "shameful" acts if they are to succeed.

The *Gorgias,* like the *Republic,* starts out with the assumption that popular ethical standards deserve consideration, and gradually moves away from this attitude. Once Callicles, who is more sophisticated than Polus, enters into the discussion, the popular ethical approach is discarded altogether. Callicles is not concerned with the rules of conduct for the ordinary man; he wants to explain and justify the behaviour of the autocratic ruler, who can afford to ignore ordinary "bourgeois" notions of ethics; his crude theory of sovereignty maintains that the stronger or better man is entitled to have his own way by the law of nature. Socrates, in his attempts to show how illogical and inexact such thinking is, pays equally little attention to the rules of popular ethics; he is concerned, rather, with describing the end of justice and happiness (which Plato constantly seeks to identify). With a man like Callicles, who regards the old morality as totally irrelevant, it would be waste of time to invoke traditional rules and standards that were thought to be applicable to weaker and stronger alike. Just as the rule of charis was found inadequate to meet every emergency, so now the ideal of arete is so grossly perverted, by Callicles and others like him, that appeals to the old definition would be useless.

Callicles, as part of his argument (484b), quotes Pindar's lines about "*nomos,* king of all." But he quotes them in support of his own theory, and not in order to explain or praise the Pindaric ideal of arete; he interprets Pindar's "law" as meaning "the law of the jungle," in accordance with which the strong man comes to the top and stays there. Pindar's lines appear to mean:

> Law, the king of all,
> Of mortals and immortals alike,
> Leads with sovereign hand the act of violence
> And makes it just. I call to witness
> The acts of Heracles. . . .

The acts of Heracles that Pindar means are indeed acts of violence, like the theft of the oxen of Geryones; and Callicles claims that, according to Pindar, the "lawless theft" is "made just" by the law of success which justifies the means—like the man behind the manager's desk in a *New Yorker* cartoon who says to the humble employee: "I didn't get where I am by begging for raises, Mason; I *took* what I wanted."

As Dodds points out in his commentary on *Gorgias* 484b, "we can hardly credit the pious Pindar with this shocking opinion." Pindar's famous lines are more often quoted than understood, as indeed they were misunderstood by Herodotus (iii.38), who assumed that by *nomos* Pindar meant not "law" but "custom," since customs approved in one country could be considered abominable in another. And it is for this reason that they have been kept back until the end of this chapter. Since Pindar's own context is lost (the lines are a fragment from a poem that has not survived), the context must be supplied from the sentiments about law and justice that are known to have prevailed in the fifth century. Heracles, in the fifth and fourth centuries alike, is an instrument of law and civilization who crushes barbarism "justly" but by violent methods; his deeds, then, help us to understand that the law sometimes demands, and so justifies, violence; that wars may be "just," as the Romans stoutly said their wars always were. Such a view is far less extreme than that of Creon in the *Antigone*.

Whoever thinks in terms of ends, as Plato does, or judges individual acts by reference to a universal ideal or an absolute standard of truth and justice, will suppose Pindar to mean that even violence can serve the end of justice. But this is not the language of popular ethics, and the ordinary citizen, compelled by the law of his city to commit acts of violence as a soldier, would not defend the rightness of his conduct in such terms. He would be more likely to say that sometimes justice demands violence, and so the illegal becomes lawful and praiseworthy. Law or even custom, under special circumstances like war, that "violent teacher" as Thucydides (iii.82.2) calls it, can teach us to regard actions differently or even actually change their ethical quality temporarily or permanently; the famous chapter of Thucydides about the change in ethical vocabulary in times of revolution is the best text here. This is how popular ethics presents its own inadequacy, the impermanence and uncertainty of its rules and maxims which particular circumstances may threaten, and the equal impermanence of the lessons which special circumstances appear to enforce. Philosophy is not content to accept such an attitude; it seeks more general definitions which will be absolute and unshakeable in all situations, which neither feeling for charis nor regard for expediency nor the force of law and circumstance can alter.

NOTES

The following abbreviations have been used in the Notes:

AJP	*American Journal of Philology*
CP	*Classical Philology*
CQ	*Classical Quarterly*
CR	*Classical Review*
CW	*Classical Weekly*
HSCP	*Harvard Studies in Classical Philology*
JHI	*Journal of the History of Ideas*
JHS	*Journal of Hellenic Studies*
RE	*Realencyclopaedie der klassischen Altertumswissenschaft*
Rh. Mus.	*Rheinisches Museum für Philologie*
SIG[3]	*Sylloge Inscriptionum Graecarum*, 3d ed.
TAPA	*Transactions and Proceedings of the American Philological Association*

INTRODUCTION

1. The far stronger emphasis in Spartan tradition on training and obedience to rule is emphasized by Pericles in the Funeral Oration (Thuc. ii.39); and a certain distrust for intellectual independence and argument is voiced by two Spartan speakers, king Archidamus and the ephor Sthenelaidas (i.80–86). In a speech at the Congress of Sparta, the Corinthian representative warns the Spartans that they do not understand the dangers of the restless and energetic Athenian character, so different from their own, which is more cautious and less disposed to novelty (i.68–71). And the Spartan preference for "laconic" brevity of speech is illustrated by numerous anecdotes.

Apart from the violent attack on Spartan morals and manners in the *Heraclidae* (which is to be explained by the bitter feelings in Athens during wartime), Euripides tries to show the uniqueness of Athenian character by his portrayal of Theseus in several plays. One might also compare the beautiful choral ode in praise of Athens in the *Oedipus at Colonus* of Sophocles. The emphasis on military virtues, which is so strong in all praise of Sparta (for example, in the warning that the exiled Spartan king Demaratus offers to Xerxes in Herodotus vii.102–4), never appears in panegyrics of Athens, where freedom is more likely to be the theme than steadfastness. A character like the Spartan Clearchus, whom Xenophon admires so much (*Anabasis* ii.6.1–15), might not meet with much approval in Athens. In general, the Spartan character lacks the many-sidedness on which the Athenians prided themselves.

2. The most famous holy wars of classical times centred around the sanctuary of Apollo at Delphi and the fertile Sacred Plain below. The state of Phocis was always anxious to control Delphi; when the Phocians gained control in the fifth century, the Spartans sent a special expedition to dislodge them in 448 B.C., but they were soon afterwards reinstated by the Athenians (Thuc. i.112.5). In the fourth century the Phocians again seized Delphi and, helped by support from both Athens and Sparta, used the temple treasures to finance a ten years' war (356–46 B.C.) against Thebes and its allies. The full story is told in Diodorus xvi.23–64. It was as champion of Delphi and its protectors, the Amphictyonic League, that Philip of Macedon was invited into central Greece in 346 and 339 B.C.

3. This point of view is stated dogmatically by Bruno Snell in *The Discovery of the Mind* (Eng. trans.; Oxford, 1953). It was first presented by him in an essay entitled "Aischylos und das Handeln im Drama," *Philologus,* Supp. 20 (1928), and in reply to the criticisms of his reviewer, Erwin Wolff in *Gnomon,* 5 (1929), 386–400, he re-stated it with greater insistence in "Das Bewusstsein von eigenen Entscheidungen im frühen Griechentum," *Philologus,* 85 (1930), 141–58. The position taken by Snell and his followers is that Homeric man has not yet discovered himself; that his decisions, in the *Iliad* and the *Odyssey,* are represented as made for him either by a god or by force of circumstances; and that Aeschylus "was the first to show clearly that when a man acted some mental process is involved" (*The Discovery of the Mind,* p. 106). Snell writes as follows (p. 103):

"The Homeric scenes in which a man deliberates what he ought to do are deficient in one distinctive feature, which makes the decision of Pelasgus (in the *Suppliants* of Aeschylus) what it is: a wholly independent and private act. In Aeschylus, the hero's choice becomes a problem whose solution is contingent on nothing but his own insight, but which is nevertheless regarded as a matter of compelling necessity. Homer's scenes of reflection and resolution are usually cast in a stereotype form. A man speculates whether he ought to do this or that; finally, when he decides, the resolution may be described in one of two ways: either Homer says that it seemed better to the man to choose such and such a course, or we learn that a god intervened and directed the hero's decision. This is what usually happens in the *Iliad.* Sometimes—and this we find occasionally in the *Odyssey*—somebody else enters the scene and helps to bring about the choice. The formula: 'it seemed better to him' means literally: 'it seemed more profitable, more remunerative to him.' The decision is made on the grounds that one alternative is recognized as the more advantageous procedure. Evidently this has little to do with subjective choice, not to speak of an internal struggle. And where the final voice is given to a deity the decision is of course wholly determined from without."

If this thesis is accepted, it means that no judgment of man's moral worth is possible in the language of Homer, that no Homeric character is better than another, but only luckier or more cunning. The basis on which Homeric characters judge one another will be discussed in a later chapter. For the present it will be enough to show how incorrect the statements of this paragraph are (indeed, every sentence contains an element of untruth) by recalling one famous scene from the *Odyssey* in which Odysseus is faced with a difficult decision—the scene in the cave of the Cyclops.

When the Cyclops falls asleep the first time, Odysseus thinks of stabbing him as he lies there; but "a second thought restrains him" (ἕτερος δέ με θυμὸς ἔρυκεν, ix.302), and he changes his mind, remembering that he and his men could never move the boulder that blocked the entrance of the cave. This "second thought" bears the signs of being some mental process; and his deliberations all next day, when he is imprisoned in the cave and devising plans, "if some way I might take vengeance, and Athena grant me the glory," are equally independent and private:

αὐτὰρ ἐγὼ λιπόμην κακὰ βυσσοδομεύων
εἴ πως τισαίμην, δοίη δέ μοι εὖχος 'Αθήνη.
ἥδε δέ μοι κατὰ θυμὸν ἀρίστη φαίνετο βουλή.
(316–18)

The sentence that follows begins with γάρ, and one might expect it to explain why the plan which he adopts seemed best (not "more profitable," which would be κέρδιον, a common alternative word, though φέρτερον and κάρτιστον also occur. Cf., for example, *Od.* xii.109, 120). In fact it explains a mental process, how Odysseus reached his decision. It was the sight of the Cyclops' club that put the idea into his head; but the rest of his plan—the offer of wine to make Polyphemus drunk and the *Outis* trick—is not revealed in advance. The fact is that Odysseus can save himself and others of his company only by sacrificing two lives (it is the same as when his ship passes between Scylla and Charybdis); this is the decision he has to make.

Next morning he describes a mental process clearly enough by comparing the different plans to trial pieces of weaving:

πάντας δὲ δόλους καὶ μῆτιν ὕφαινον,
ὥς τε περὶ ψυχῆς· μέγα γὰρ κακὸν ἐγγύθεν ἦεν.
(422–23)

The problem is how to save the lives of all who now survive, and it is the sight of the ram with its thick fleece that gives the answer. Finally, when they are on board ship and he insists on calling to the Cyclops a second time, despite the entreaties of his companions, it is very clear why he is not overruled by them: ὣς φάσαν· ἀλλ' οὐ πεῖθον ἐμὸν μεγαλήτορα θυμόν (500). He cannot leave without letting the Cyclops know who he is; the desire to win fame, even in a land of savages, is stronger than his sense of obligation towards his men. As he remembers what he did, he does not regret it. He does not say: "I was sure that we were out of range of any rock the Cyclops might throw." But he lets us know that he has measured the distance, that they were twice as far away as before.

On this occasion Odysseus decides to take the risk of provoking anger. On another occasion he decides differently, and says so clearly; before addressing Nausicaa he ponders whether or not to grasp her by the knees, and decides not to do so, for fear that it might make her angry (vi. 145–47).

On all these occasions the motives for Odysseus's decision are clearly given; the hero knows what he is doing and why, and his decision is certainly made "independently and privately."

Christian Voigt, *Überlegung und Entscheidung* (Berlin, 1934), argues in a manner similar to Snell. Cf. the objections to his point of view raised by L. A. Post, "The Moral Pattern in Homer," *TAPA*, 70 (1939), esp. p. 166 n., and likewise the protests of C. del Grande, "La Grecia antichissima, i moniti e i concetti etici," *Convivium*, n.s. 6 (1954), 641–65, in reply to a lecture of Giorgio Pasquali.

CHAPTER ONE

1. There was a temple of "armed Aphrodite" at the summit of Acrocorinth (Pausanias ii.5.1), a warrior goddess like Athena who protected Corinth from her enemies (see E. Will, *Korinthiaka* [Paris, 1955], pp. 225–27). It was to her that prayers were made for the safety of the city at the time of the Persian invasion, as in the epigram quoted by Plutarch, *De malig. Herodoti*, 871B (see Diehl, *Anthologia Lyrica Graeca* [Leipzig, 1925], II, 101).

2. Texts of treaties, whether preserved on stone or by ancient writers, often give the names of the gods and goddesses whom all the signatories must invoke in their oath to maintain the treaty. See, for example, M. N. Tod, *Greek Historical Inscriptions* (Oxford, 1948), II, no. 127, which names Zeus, Apollo, Demeter; in no. 142, we find Zeus, Athena, Poseidon, Demeter; and in no. 157 (an alliance between Athens and some semi-Greek kings in Thrace, Paeonia, and Illyria) Zeus, Earth, Sun, Poseidon, Athena, Ares. The same list is restored, probably rightly, in the text of the oath sworn by the various Greek states to maintain the treaty of peace arranged by Philip of Macedon after his victory at Chaeronea in 338 B.C. (no. 177).

3. A few quotations from books that attempt to describe Greek ethical thought for the general reader may be in place here.

G. Lowes Dickinson, *The Greek View of Life* (7th ed.; London, 1909), opens his section on Greek ethics as follows:

"And as with the excellence of the body, so with that of the soul, the conception that dominated the mind of the Greek was primarily aesthetic. In speaking of their religion we have already remarked that they had no sense of sin; and we may now add that they had not what we are apt to mean by a sense of duty. Moral virtue they conceived not as obedience to an external law, a sacrifice of the natural man to a power that in a sense is alien to himself, but rather as the tempering into due proportion of the elements of which human nature is composed. The good man was the man who was beautiful—beautiful in soul. 'Virtue,' says Plato, 'will be a kind of health and beauty and good habit of the soul; and vice will be a disease and deformity and sickness of it.' It follows that it is as natural to seek virtue and to avoid vice as to seek health and to avoid disease. There is no question of a struggle between opposite principles; the distinction of good and evil is one of order or confusion, among elements which in themselves are neither good nor bad.

"This conception of virtue we find expressed in many forms, but always with the same underlying idea. A favourite watchword with the Greeks is the 'middle' or 'mean,' the exact point of rightness between two extremes. 'Nothing in excess' was a motto inscribed over the temple of Delphi; and none could be more characteristic of the ideal of these lovers of proportion" (pp. 142–43).

The author is writing as though Greek ethics were epitomized in Plato and Aristotle; as an exposition of the general Greek view of life in ethical matters his remarks are completely misleading, as will, I hope, become clear in the pages that follow.

Hilda Oakeley, in her Introduction to *Greek Ethical Thought from Homer to the Stoics* (London, 1925), which is a collection of extracts from Greek authors in translation, writes of "the idea of the good life as a harmony" as one of the principles—"the most characteristic and probably the best known"—that "pervade Greek thought upon ethics generally" (p. xiv). Earlier, in speaking of the development of Greek ethical thought as illustrated in literature, she writes: "Pursuing our way from the Epic Poets through the Tragic drama to the philosophers, we seem to pass through the whole scale of ideas revolving round the central thought of conduct as a thing commanded. We begin with man as under compulsion of destiny driving him to complete the dread unfinished deed from generation to generation. We rise to the thought of man as attaining the vision of the Good, and thereafter necessarily obedient to that vision. Or we may prefer to describe the passage as one from bondage to the idea of a blind force to which man is enslaved, to service to the idea which gives freedom" (pp. viii–ix).

Here, then, we find two principles emphasized—harmony and obedience. If we turn to Léon Robin, *La Morale antique* (Paris, 1938), we find that he has concentrated his discussion, which is generally confined to the thought of philosophic writers, upon three themes: the notion of moral good, virtue and happiness, and the psychological conditions of the moral act.

Sir Richard Livingstone, *The Greek Genius and Its Meaning to Us* (2d ed.; Oxford, 1915), who concentrates his discussion upon what he calls "the notes of Hellenism," writes in his first chapter with some scepticism about "a view of the Greek genius which seems to be gaining ground at the present":

"Today our attention is being called to the moral genius of the Greeks, to their deliberate, laborious, and triumphant battle for virtue. We are asked to see in them a race of men who, emerging, like other nations, from their primitive state with a conventional code of morality and clinging shreds of barbarism became conscious of these, and quietly corrected or put them aside, and, using no art but what every one possesses, confessing no standard but what every one admits, felt after, found, and securely possessed themselves of, the rational principles of justice, mercy, humanity, and truth. . . . There is much to support this theory. The severest critic of Hellenism can hardly deny that a nation which produced the Aristotelian doctrine of the Mean and the Stoic ideal of virtue, which gave to the Roman Empire a philosophy of life, and to the Christian religion a framework of ethics, stands among the moral benefactors of mankind; nor is it surprising that some persons are inclined to see the greatest achievement of Greece in its struggle out of barbarism to a rational virtue. Certainly it was a great achievement. Yet before it dazzles us into believing that the central quality in the Greek spirit was its moral genius, let us reflect. Is moral genius really the essential, exceptional, unique gift of the race?" (pp. 24–25).

It would be easy to multiply these quotations. They emphasize progress from non-philosophical, tribal, or semibarbaric ethics to philosophy; and until the progress is complete or nearly complete one can hardly expect to find coherent systems or strict logical principles. The germs of Platonism, Aristotelianism, and Stoicism may doubtless be found in some degree in popular Greek thought, inherited by their founders from earlier generations; but the achievements of the great philosophers should not be confused with the heritage of popular thought and tradition.

4. For some good comments on the value of proverbs as a source of Greek ethical thought, see F. R. Earp, *The Way of the Greeks* (Oxford, 1929), pp. 26–29.

5. M. L. Clarke, *The Roman Mind* (London, 1956), is prepared to deduce what were "the virtues which the Romans particularly admired" by picking out the qualities which Cicero praises in his speeches (p. 16); but he also recognizes that Cicero's private philosophic views find little expression in his speeches and that "the maxims of the speeches derive not so much from Cicero's studies in philosophy as from the conventional copybook morality of the rhetorical schools" (p. 17). Elsewhere he speaks of "the academic classifications and trite morality which the rhetorician contributed to the Roman's training in public life" (p. 11). For two admirable pages on the traditional Roman virtues—virtues that boys and girls were expected to learn within the family circle—see Hugh Last, *The Legacy of Rome* (Oxford, 1923), pp. 210–12. Cf. also the remarks of R. H. Barrow, *The Romans* (Penguin Books, 1949), in his Epilogue about the Roman "sense of self-subordination."

6. Isocrates insists that it is Athenian *paideia* and Athenian influence that was responsible for this development: "Our city has so far surpassed other men in its wisdom and its power of expression that its pupils have become the teachers of the world; it has caused the name of Greek to be regarded no longer as a mark of racial origin but of intelligence, so that men are called Greeks because they have shared our education rather than because they share in our common natural origin" (*Paneg.* 50). For commentary on this famous passage, see E. Buchner, *Der Panegyrikos des Isokrates, Historia,* Einzelschriften, Heft 2 (1958), 53–65.

Isocrates is not thinking primarily of ethical tradition when he speaks of upbringing and education; but in so far as there is any unity to Greek ethical tradition, it must be connected with the widespread uniformity of Greek literary education. The case is well stated in the opening paragraph of Leopold Schmidt, *Die Ethik der alten Griechen* (Berlin, 1882). See also the first two chapters of F. R. Earp, *The Way of the Greeks,* in which he discusses the necessary precautions that must be taken in treating Greek literature as a source in a search for the ideas of the ordinary man.

7. According to Aristotle, *Poetics,* 1460b, the remark was made by Sophocles; and as the *Frogs* of Aristophanes seems to show, some contemporaries thought Euripides went too far in his realism, thereby diminishing the dignity of the tragic stage.

8. It makes very little difference to the value of Thucydides as a source of popular ethics whether he reports the words or even the actual opinions of the speakers accurately; what he is doing is making them say what they very well might have said, making them use arguments which they might well have thought cogent and acceptable to their audience. Nonetheless, he maintains that he has tried to keep as close as possible to "the general purport of what was actually said" and has made them say "what seemed to me was demanded by the particular situation" (i.22.1). The actual historical accuracy of the speeches of Thucydides has been discussed many times; it should be sufficient to refer the reader to A. W. Gomme's discussion in his note on Thuc. i.22, in *A Historical Commentary on Thucydides,* I (Oxford, 1945), 140–48, and his earlier discussion, "The Speeches in Thucydides," in his *Essays in Greek History and Literature* (Oxford, 1937). For the ethical or even universal quality of the speeches, cf. Jacqueline de Romilly, "L'Utilité de l'histoire selon Thucydide," in *Histoire et historiens dans l'antiquité, Fondation Hardt, Entretiens,* IV (Geneva, 1958).

9. Nonetheless, the analogy between moral character and technical skill must inevitably have seemed natural to any Greek who was accustomed to think in terms of arete—a word which denoted both excellence of character and pre-eminent ability or skill in some occupation or art. Furthermore, in all arts or specialized activities for which the Greeks felt any respect—statesmanship, oratory, poetry, medicine, athletics—eminence was thought to indicate some degree of moral excellence in addition to mere technical expertness; the point is admirably made by H. D. F. Kitto, *The Greeks* (Penguin Books, 1951), pp. 171–76. For example, that anyone should be a good poet or sculptor or soldier but a bad citizen was a disturbing thought; the charge against Phidias that he misappropriated the gold provided for his great statue of Athena (Plutarch, *Pericles* 31) was the more shocking to popular sentiment because he was admittedly a magnificent artist. The fear that sophists should use their superior ability for unworthy or even personal advantage was highly disturbing. And this new fear had serious consequences; one of the worst was the prosecution of Socrates on the charge of corrupting the young by misusing his talents as a teacher. Polemarchus never suspects that a man could misuse his arete.

10. If obligations exist only when there is a recognized relationship of friendship or enmity, it might appear to follow that a just or unjust act

cannot be committed by one stranger to another. It might be thought possible to rationalize such a conclusion by calling it a survival from tribal morality, which is supposed to regard all outsiders as enemies, legitimate victims of aggression, protected by no law; and one might be inclined to add that, unlike the Romans, the Greeks were generally inarticulate about any *ius gentium* or formal code that regulated behaviour towards non-Greek peoples. In actual fact, however, such a conclusion would be quite unjustified historically, and one should not postulate survivals of prehistoric barbarism unless they are properly attested. The same charge of injustice (*adikia*) could be made against any aggressor state or any state practising piracy that could not show good cause for its behaviour (cf. below, Chap. Five). Even though no precise theory of natural or international law had been formulated, its existence was implicit; the first association of city with city established a moral relationship. So far as individuals go, the case is even clearer; strangers who meet are bound by the law of host and guest, which is strict and is religiously observed.

In the narrative of Thucydides, when the Corcyraeans, who have hitherto held aloof from alliances, approach the Athenians with a request for alliance, it is noteworthy that they begin at once with a statement of what is "just" for them to do—they must make their request an attractive one, since the Athenians are under no obligation to grant it (i.32). Any other type of approach, it is implied, would be not merely foolish, but shameless; the Corinthians, who urge the Athenians to refuse the Corcyraeans' plea, argue that their request is in fact as shameless and dishonest as their previous policy of isolation (i.37–43).

11. The discussion of friendship by Aristotle in the *Nicomachean Ethics,* Books viii–ix, is the classic source for the Greek view of friendship. Friendship has no meaning without the recognition of obligations and the ability to observe them; hence the need for a special discussion of "friendship between unequals," in which adequate return of favours will be difficult if not impossible.

In the Funeral Oration, Thucydides makes Pericles say that the Athenians generally make friends by conferring benefits rather than by receiving them (ii.40.4); their foreign policy consists in putting other states under an obligation to them, so that any act by a friendly state which is not an outright benefaction runs the risk of being an injustice. Their position, therefore, is very strong and the exact opposite of the one in which the Corcyraeans found themselves (see n. 10).

12. Thrasymachus denies the validity and the importance of any so-called obligation which is not actually enforceable; he denies the importance of friendship as an influence on behaviour, making fear and desire the only factors that exercise control. In modern language, he is denying morality altogether; but the interesting point is that he does this by denying the importance of friendship.

13. In describing the lawlessness that began to prevail in Athens at the time of the plague, Thucydides (ii.53) makes it clear that one of the main factors was the lessened respect for what people would think. They looked

to the immediate pleasures rather than the ultimate results of what they might do, since the future was so uncertain; "no one was eager to toil for the sake of what might appear honourable or good." He adds, as he must, that "neither fear of god nor law of man acted as a deterrent." The usual attitude—that honesty is the best compromise that promises the best returns—did not stand up in the face of such difficulties. He does not neglect to point out that people who were unselfish in looking after their sick friends and relatives ("especially those who laid some claim to arete," those who insisted on meeting their obligations) were the ones most likely to be attacked by the plague themselves (ii.51.5). Every incentive to justice seemed to have disappeared. This would have been a good passage for Glaucon to quote as an illustration of the general attitude.

14. It would be equally absurd to regard the *phrontisterion* in the *Clouds* of Aristophanes as a faithful representation of sophistic or Socratic teaching. It appears nonetheless that harm was done to the reputation of Socrates (and presumably of the sophists also) by this kind of comic parody, if the complaint of Socrates in Plato's *Apology* is to be taken seriously (18b–19c). Socrates says that the prejudice against him, the mistaken notion of his methods and opinions, is of long standing, something that his judges could have acquired when they were boys. Whatever its true origin or justification, the prejudice seems to have been real enough.

The evidence relating to the real Thrasymachus is collected by H. Diels in *Die Fragmente der Vorsokratiker*, 6th ed., revised by W. Kranz (Berlin, 1951), II, 319–26. In a fragment (A4) from Aristophanes' lost play *The Banqueters* (produced in 427 B.C.), he is mentioned apparently as a rhetorician who might be considered capable of ridiculing conventional virtue. Naturally this condemnation has no higher claim to be taken seriously than anything in the *Clouds*. And a commentator on Plato (B8) quotes from a speech of Thrasymachus in which he appears to have said that "the gods do not have regard for human affairs, because if they did they would not disregard the greatest of human goods, justice; we see that men do not observe justice." Taken out of context, such a text should not be regarded as evidence of the speaker's cynicism; any advocate might use such language in complaining that his client had been unfairly treated. Cf. K. Oppenheimer, *RE*, s.v. "Thrasymachos" (1), 586.

15. Cf. Ernest Barker, *Greek Political Theory: Plato and His Predecessors* (4th ed.; London, 1951), Appendix to chap. iv. Antiphon's distinction between appearance and reality or law and nature (*nomos* and *physis*) is not a purely ethical matter, any more than it is for Plato. Nonetheless, he recognizes that the kind of justice which consists in obeying the laws is only a superficial sort of justice, though it may be adequate and advantageous for the ordinary man, as the opening words of one of the fragments show: "It is justice not to disobey the laws of the city in which one is a citizen; but a man would use justice most advantageously to himself if, when witnesses are present, he had high regard for the laws, but if, when no witnesses are present, he had regard for the demands of nature." Obedience to the laws is not the ultimate kind of justice, and the demands of

the law often oppose the demands of nature. The motivation for obedience to the laws, however, comes from regard for "appearance." The distinction between the law and nature comes out more clearly when disobedience is considered: disobedience to law brings shame when it is discovered, but not when it remains hidden; but to go against nature is equally damaging whether others observe it or not. It is easy to see how such views could be twisted so as to bear an immoralist meaning, especially if the first half of the sentence were quoted out of context. In the conversations between Socrates and Antiphon recorded by Xenophon (*Memorabilia* 1.6), Antiphon is represented as thinking Socrates "unhappy" because of his poverty, and "just but not wise" because he fails to take advantage of his talents by taking fees for his teaching. This is certainly an over-simplification of the actual views of Antiphon, but the fragments definitely suggest that he thought of justice in terms of "advantage"—whether one's own advantage or that of another party—in a manner which to some extent recalls the Thrasymachus of the *Republic*.

16. The precise meaning of the Greek in this last statement (iii.82.7) is uncertain. It is possible that Thucydides means stupid men were called good and were ashamed of the title. See the discussion in Gomme and in *CQ*, 42 (1948), 14. There are many difficulties in this chapter of Thucydides, and no translator would be prepared to say that he was certain of his interpretation in every detail. The following translation, by Rex Warner (Penguin Books, 1954), is offered without guarantee that it is correct at all points:

"In the various cities these revolutions were the cause of many calamities—as happens and always will happen while human nature is what it is, though there may be different degrees of savagery, and, as different circumstances arise, the general rules will admit of some variety. In times of peace and prosperity cities and individuals alike follow higher standards, because they are not forced into a situation where they have to do what they do not want to do. But war is a stern teacher; in depriving them of the power of easily satisfying their daily wants, it brings most people's minds down to the level of their actual circumstances.

"So revolutions broke out in city after city, and in places where the revolutions occurred late the knowledge of what had happened previously in other places caused still new extravagances of revolutionary zeal, expressed by an elaboration in the methods of seizing power and by unheard-of atrocities in revenge. To fit in with the change of events, words, too, had to change their usual meanings. What used to be described as a thoughtless act of aggression was now regarded as the courage one would expect to find in a party member; to think of the future and wait was merely another way of saying one was a coward; any idea of moderation was just an attempt to disguise one's unmanly character; ability to understand a question from all sides meant that one was totally unfitted for action. Fanatical enthusiasm was the mark of a real man, and to plot against an enemy behind his back was perfectly legitimate self-defence. Anyone who held violent opinions could always be trusted, and anyone who objected to them became a suspect. To plot successfully was a sign of intelligence, but it was still cleverer to see that a plot was hatching. If one attempted to provide against having to do either, one was disrupting the unity of the party and acting out of fear of the opposition. In short, it was equally praiseworthy to get one's blow in first against someone who was going to do wrong, and to denounce someone who had no intention of doing any wrong at all. Family relations were a weaker tie than party membership, since party members were more ready to go to any extreme for any reason whatever. These parties were not formed to enjoy the benefits of the established laws, but to acquire power by overthrowing the existing regime; and the members of these parties felt confidence in each other not because of any fellowship in a religious communion, but because they were partners in crime. If an opponent made a reasonable speech, the party in power, so far from giving it a generous reception, took every precaution to see that it had no practical effect.

"Revenge was more important than self-preservation. And if pacts of mutual security were made, they were entered into by the two parties only in order to meet some temporary difficulty, and remained in force only so long as there was no other weapon available. When the chance came, the one who first seized it boldly, catching his enemy off his guard, enjoyed a revenge that was all the sweeter from having been taken, not openly, but because of a breach of faith. It was safer that way, it was considered, and at the same time a victory won by treachery gave one a title for superior intelligence. And indeed most people are more ready to call villainy cleverness than simple-mindedness honesty. They are proud of the first quality and ashamed of the second.

"Love of power, operating through greed and through personal ambition, was the cause of all these evils. To this must be added the violent fanaticism which came into play once the struggle had broken out. Leaders of parties in the cities had programmes which appeared admirable—on one side political equality for the masses, on the other the safe and sound government of the aristocracy—but in professing to serve the public interest they were seeking to win the prizes for themselves. In their struggles for ascendancy nothing was barred; terrible indeed were the actions to which they committed themselves, and in taking revenge they went further still. Here they were deterred neither by the claims of justice nor by the interests of the state; their one standard was the pleasure of their own party at that particular moment, and so, either by means of condemning their enemies on an illegal vote or by violently usurping power over them, they were always ready to satisfy the hatreds of the hour. Thus neither side had any use for conscientious motives; more interest was shown in those who could produce attractive arguments to justify some disgraceful action. As for the citizens who held moderate views, they were destroyed by both the extreme parties, either for not taking part in the struggle or in envy at the possibility that they might survive.

"As the result of these revolutions, there was a general deterioration of character throughout the Greek world. The simple way of looking at things, which is so much the mark of a noble nature, was regarded as a ridiculous quality and soon ceased to exist."

For another good and careful translation of this passage see Gomme, *Commentary on Thucydides,* II, 383–85.

17. For a further discussion of these two arguments, see pp. 165–68.

18. *Knights* 985–91. Cf. Gomme's note on Thuc. iii.37.4. Part of Cleon's strength as a politician lay in the fact that many of his followers were conservative in sentiment.

19. So also the decision of the Athenians to send an expedition to Sicily, according to Thucydides (vi.24), is principally motivated by their hopes of enriching themselves; the moral and legal issues are of secondary importance. Compare the similar account given by Polybius (i.10–11) of the decision of the Romans to interfere in Sicily at the request of the Mamertines—the momentous step which brought on the First Punic War.

20. R. C. Jebb (Sophocles, *Antigone,* p. xvii) begins his discussion of the play by speaking of "the conflict of divine with human law"; but he recognizes that Antigone had no alternative, that it was as impossible for her to obey Creon's edict "as it was impossible for the Christian maiden to avoid the torments of the arena by laying a grain of incense on the altar of Diana" (p. xxv).

21. Strict piety, of course, cannot recognize the existence of such conflicts. An eclipse of the moon, as interpreted by the soothsayers, prevented Nicias from ordering his forces to leave Syracuse when there was still a good chance of escape (Thuc. vii.50.4). Nicias was a pious man and therefore could not believe that it would be useful to leave against the will of the gods; a journey begun in the face of such a warning was doomed to failure, he would suppose. To argue publicly that the will of the gods should be disregarded was quite out of the question; the only alternative (if Nicias or his colleague Demosthenes had been a man more like Themistocles) would have been to bribe the soothsayers to revise their interpretation. During the Persian Wars, the Spartans on three separate occasions found religious reasons for delaying the start of their army from Sparta, although their allies needed them in a hurry (Hdt. vi.106; vii.206; ix.6). It was the sincerity of their scruples that the allies were inclined to doubt; they could not question or complain of their piety. And if the Athenian jury which tried Socrates believed his claim that he was obeying the voice of a god (Plato, *Apology* 28e, 31d), they could not have condemned him, even if they did believe he was corrupting the youth; but it was hardly likely that they would believe such a claim.

CHAPTER TWO

1. Sections entitled "Homer, the Educator of Greece" and "The Homeric Ethic" will be found in H. L. Marrou, *Histoire de l'éducation dans l'antiquité* (Paris, 1948), pp. 34–38, and in the English edition, *A History of Education in Antiquity* (London, 1956), pp. 9–12. But Marrou's treatment is much too brief and not very satisfactory.

2. Max Wundt, *Geschichte der griechischen Ethik* (Leipzig, 1908), in his chapter on Homer, claims to distinguish between a more primitive type of Homeric individual, the warrior, who has no scruples about homicide and even sees nothing wrong in harming others (p. 24), and a man of peace, whose sensibilities are more refined, who is a later development, i.e., to be found only in parts of the *Iliad* and the *Odyssey* that were composed at a later date. This belief, which implies that the *Iliad* has its roots in barbarism, is hardly acceptable; a distinction between a world of war and a world of peace can be maintained without postulating such a drastic change as Wundt imagines. Instead of recognizing two stages in social or moral development, we will find it more convenient and probably more accurate to recognize a distinction between circumstances that call for different virtues and cause different activities to be commended. Cf. A. W. H. Adkins, *Merit and Responsibility: A Study in Greek Values* (Oxford, 1960), pp. 6–7, who makes a distinction between "two complexes of values," the "competitive" and the "co-operative" or "quiet" values or excellences.

3. If the epic tradition has a long history of development before Homer—i.e., before the *Iliad* and the *Odyssey* took on the final form in which we know them—it is easy to understand how it could have absorbed and yet not quite assimilated elements that had their origin in various social and political settings. The variation in such things as the use of iron or bronze and different types of weapons is readily explained by a long tradition of oral poetry, which many critics now accept as an almost proven fact. The archaeologists have shown that material objects which appear in the Homeric poems must be assigned to a number of different periods. See, for example, H. Lorimer, *Homer and the Monuments* (London, 1950).

4. For the view that inconsistencies and contradictions, as conventional criticism would call them, are to be expected as part of the Homeric style, see B. E. Perry, "The Early Greek Capacity for Viewing Things Separately," *TAPA,* 68 (1937), 403–27, and A. Notopoulos, "Parataxis in Homer: A New Approach to Homeric Literary Criticism," *ibid.,* 80 (1949), 1–23, where further literature on the subject is indicated.

Herodotus is not always strictly consistent in characterizing historical personages, but this shortcoming can be explained by his unwillingness to eliminate contradictory evidence and his refusal to arrive at a decision or a compromise. Cf. L. Pearson, "Real and Conventional Personalities in Greek History," *JHI,* 15 (1954), 136–45.

5. From the historian's point of view, the existence of a consistent mode of thought and a consistent scale of ethical values throughout the *Iliad* and the *Odyssey* would have a very special value as historical evidence if it could be proved that each poem was the work of several different authors who lived in different epochs; in that case it would be evidence of a generally accepted system of popular ethics prevailing over a long period. It is likely, however, that many critics who believe in a multiplicity of authors will deny the existence of this consistent mode of thought. They may even appeal for support to the statement of Aristotle that the *Odyssey* is more "ethical" than the *Iliad* (*Poetics* 1459b).

The proper reply to such objections is that the ethical difference between the poems lies not in the moral attitude of the poet or poets, but in the themes and the setting, since the *Iliad* depicts a world of war and the *Odyssey* a world of comparative peace. And if consistency is denied within the *Odyssey* itself, here again the inconsistency is in themes, not in ethical attitudes. This is easy to understand if the themes have a long history, and are not themselves the invention of the poet who was responsible for the final form of these poems. It appears that some incidents and legends were not originally conceived in ethical terms at all, and it is doubtful if a poet would have accomplished much by attempting to present them in ethical terms. On this and similar matters, see F. Jacoby, "Die geistige Physiognomie der Odyssee," *Die Antike,* 9 (1933), especially the closing section, pp. 182–94. Jacoby points out the difference between the anger of Poseidon with Odysseus, which is a selfish and personal anger (we are not expected to think Odysseus guilty because he kills the Cyclops), and the anger of Zeus and Athena at the behaviour of Aegisthus, which is moral indignation. He refuses to accept the contention that the anger of Poseidon, an "amoral" god, represents the work of a poet who thinks more archaically than the poet who describes the anger of Zeus and Athena. He insists that such an apparent contradiction does not destroy the unity of the poem: "Hier müssen wir uns mit der Feststellung des 'Widerspruchs' begnügen, dass der Held 'schuldlos' leidet, dass aber der Gesamthergang unserer Odyssee (die in der Rache an den Freiern nicht nur kulminiert sondern von vornherein auf sie zuläuft und die Heimkehr nur als Vorgeschichte, die mit diesem vermutlich auch ursprungsmässig nicht verbundenen Abenteuer sogar nur als Einlage in den Nostos behandelt) wirklich unter den Gesichtspunkt 'Rache folgt der Freveltat' gestellt ist, so dass die abschliessende Götterszene mit der einleitenden Zeusrede auch innerlich teils kontrastiert teils mit ihr sich zusammenschliesst zu einer einheitlichen Betrachtung menschlichen Geschehens."

Werner Jaeger goes much further than this, maintaining that the Zeus who presides over the heavenly council in the *Odyssey* personifies a high philosophical conception of the world-conscience, that the entire poem is filled with the same purpose (to justify the ways of God to man), and that the poem in its present state conforms to a rigid ethical plan. (See his *Paideia* [Eng. trans.; Oxford, 1939].) This so-called ethical plan, he thinks, "belongs to the last stage in the development of the *Odyssey,*" though Homeric critics have not yet worked out the process by which the plan was imposed on the earlier versions of the traditional saga of Odysseus (pp. 52–53). Jaeger also insists on a "single ethical plan" in the *Iliad* (p. 46). I am not convinced by his attempt to find a deliberately didactic element in Homer; the idea that a poet should preach to an audience of courtiers on festive occasions is hardly tenable.

6. Cf. *Od.* iv.195–98, where Peisistratus tells Menelaus that he feels no nemesis for anyone who weeps and mourns for the dead, "for this is an honour that we show unlucky mortals, cutting off our hair and letting tears roll down our cheeks." Display of grief in this manner is not "beyond one's due."

7. The conception of hybris is not lacking in Homer; and though the word actually occurs more frequently in the *Odyssey* than in the *Iliad,* there is no occasion to insist that the conception is different in the two poems, as C. del Grande does (*Hybris* [Naples, 1947], p. 16). Like other critics, Del Grande is disposed to present hybris and its punishment as the theme of the *Odyssey* (cf. p. 12). But an examination seems to show that any persons accused of hybris in Homer are guilty on other more specific counts as well; although Del Grande maintains that Odysseus is more immune from the taint of hybris than any other hero (p. 19), it would seem an almost absurd weakness to define the crime of the suitors as hybris. All offences against the gods can be summed up in the term; it is the appropriate word to describe the wickedness for which men are punished in the next world. But for offences against men, it is not by any means the strongest term that can be used. The language of Hesiod and Theognis makes this clear (see Chap. Three).

8. Cf., for example, *Il.* vi.111; *Od.* iv.784 (ὑπέρθυμος).

9. Cf. xvii.578, κακὸς δ' αἰδοῖος ἀλήτης, and Hesiod, *Works and Days,* 317–19.

10. The Cyclops has no incentive to behave in a civilized way or to respect justice. In that respect he is like the Athenians at the time of the plague, as described by Thucydides, ii.53.

11. This word, ὄπις, generally means the "wrath of the gods," which almost all men, unlike the Cyclops, fear and respect, even when they are beyond the reach of human dike, as they are if they are safely started on the voyage home. Even though they have no need to fear human dike, they know that they have exceeded their "due portion"; but fear of the gods is the only thing that disturbs them.

12. The limitations of Homeric legal vocabulary should not lead us to believe that Homeric man is so primitive ethically as to be unaware that there is a distinction between a judgment and true justice; his way of making the distinction is to distinguish between straight and crooked judgments, even though he cannot explain in legal or philosophical terms how the straight differs from the crooked.

Kurt Latte, in his admirable article "Der Rechtsgedanke im archaischen Griechentum," *Antike und Abendland,* 2 (1946), 63–76, says that the judge's verdict is accepted "only because of the respect which he commands as a person and its correspondence with normal custom" (p. 65). But there is not a precedent for every decision, and respect for precedent will not settle a dispute over facts. An unpopular decision can be enforced only by an appeal to the sceptre that kings are said to receive from Zeus himself. The authority of a king or judge is therefore supported by the authority of the gods, but it will be hard for him to maintain authority if he disregards precedent, like those who "make one man an enemy and another a friend," which Penelope says is unfortunately the way of kings (*Od.* iv.691). Gods, however, unlike kings and judges, cannot pass crooked judgments—the mere thought of such a thing seems not to arise until Aeschylus. Hence Latte is surely wrong in taking the offer of Amphinomus seriously and considering it as evidence for the "unreflective" character of archaic thought (p. 64).

An oracle that sanctioned an attack on Telemachus would soon lack serious customers and lose the respect of law-abiding people, who would be unable to accept it as the voice of a god.

13. Rather than connect themis with "laying down" or "setting," some scholars have attributed the meaning of "counsel" to it, and have laid emphasis on the association of the goddess Themis with Greek oracles, the means by which the gods communicated their counsel to men. And attempts have been made to force the meaning of "way" on to dike, since a fair verdict is often called straight and an unfair one crooked; or else to connect it with the rare verb δικεῖν, "to throw," on the principle that judges "threw down" their staffs of office between the litigants. For etymological discussion cf. Rudolf Hirzel, *Themis, Dike, und Verwandtes* (Leipzig, 1907); V. Ehrenberg, *Die Rechtsidee in frühen Griechentum* (Leipzig, 1921), pp. 42–52; Ernst Fränkel, "Graeca-Latina," *Glotta,* 4 (1913), 22–31; L. R. Palmer, "The Indo-European Origins of Greek Justice," *Trans. Philological Society,* 1950, pp. 149–68; H. Vos, ΘΕΜΙΣ (Assen, 1956), pp. 35–38.

14. Cf. V. Ehrenberg, *Die Rechtsidee in frühen Griechentum,* pp. 36–41. He notes the close connexion of Themis with Zeus in the *Cypria,* as well as in the *Iliad* and the *Odyssey,* since Themis is supposed to urge Zeus to start the Trojan War. He also discusses the evidence from Greek art and the genealogy which makes Themis a chthonic goddess, daughter of Uranus and Gaia (Hesiod, *Theogony* 135), as the Delphic tradition maintained. And when we find Dike, Eirene, and Eunomia given to her as daughters (Hesiod, *Theogony* 901), we can note a considerable change from the Homeric tradition.

15. For an attempt to make the distinction see Hartvig Frisch, *Might and Right in Antiquity* (Eng. trans.; Copenhagen, 1949), pp. 37–49, who cites earlier literature. He maintains that themis is "traditional right" and may be defined as what is "right and lawful"; that dike has to do with concrete cases and may be defined as "right and suitable." But the table of Homeric passages that he gives on pp. 46–47 does not support his conclusions.

J. W. Jones, *The Law and Legal Theory of the Greeks* (Oxford, 1956), recognizes that "attempts to draw a clear line between *dike* and *themis* are to be treated with caution," but thinks that possibly dike was originally more suggestive than themis "of some quality attributable not only to human society and its members but also to the physical world." Such a distinction cannot be valid if the physical world is conceived as controlled by gods; nor is it a useful distinction if the words are descriptive of behaviour rather than of rules or standards. If we cannot go back beyond the stage when the words are practically synonymous, attempts to distinguish their original connotation are no better than conjectures. Cf. H. Vos, ΘΕΜΙΣ, esp. pp. 29–32.

16. This particular passage in the *Iliad* has been interpreted as a late addition "inspired by Hesiod." Cf. M. Gigante, Νόμος Βασιλεύς (Naples, 1956), p. 19.

17. I cannot accept the interpretation of *Od.* xxiv.194–202 offered by

L. A. Post, "The Moral Pattern in Homer," *TAPA*, 70 (1939), 186–87. He thinks that common sense urged Penelope to forget Odysseus, and that "her sentimental refusal to forget her husband and save the property could be justified only by his actual return, which duly happens in accordance with poetic justice. . . . Penelope has, like Achilles, made the great decision to sacrifice common sense and aim at glory by following a noble ideal regardless of consequences." Strangest of all, he thinks Homer depicts her "like Achilles, as noble by instinct, not by calculation." These contrasts have no meaning in Homeric ethical vocabulary; phrenes cannot be interpreted as instinct, and there is never any doubt that Penelope's behaviour is right. "Sentimental" behaviour is not a Homeric idea at all, and one cannot say that a woman disregards the consequences when her decision wins her arete and *kleos*. It is her good phrenes (her intelligence, not her instinct) which enable her to see values in the proper light; of this the suitors, in their witlessness, are incapable.

18. For a good statement, see A. Heuss, "Die archaische Zeit Griechenlands als geschichtliche Epoche," *Antike und Abendland*, 2 (1946), 38. See also the valuable discussion of "Nobility and Arete" in Jaeger, *Paideia*, Bk. I, chap. i. Jaeger goes too far, however, in insisting on the "highly social character of all human values in early times" (p. 3, n. 3), when he argues that "the Homeric man estimated his own worth exclusively by the standards of the society to which he belonged," and that "he measured his own *arete* by the opinion which others held of him" (p. 7). Nevertheless, he thinks that "the element of social recognition" in arete, which gives the word the meaning of "esteem" or "respect," is secondary, and that "the word must originally have been an objective description of the worth of its possessor" (p. 2, n. 3). He therefore rejects the etymology from ἀρέσκω, "to please," suggested by M. Hoffmann, *Die ethische Terminologie bei Homer, Hesiod, und den ersten Elegikern und Iambographen* (Tübingen, 1914), p. 92. It is difficult to see how any society could have started by using an "inner standard" (as Jaeger calls it in speaking of later philosophers) to measure moral worth and later have abandoned it in favour of the standard of public opinion. Jaeger's view does not seem altogether logical, though he maintains that "the Greek conception of man and his *arete* developed along an unbroken line throughout Greek history" (p. 10). Later on he declares triumphantly that "for Homer and the Greeks in general the ultimate ethical boundaries are not mere rules of moral obligation, but fundamental laws of Being" (p. 49).

The proper answer seems to be that Homeric man combines a social standard ("what the world thinks") with a personal or inner standard ("what I think") in judging his own conduct. It would be hard for man to do otherwise in any human society, though naturally the power of convention is greater in some societies than others. There would have been no need to raise this point if Jaeger had not spoken with such conviction.

19. One might compare the famous remark of Pericles in the Funeral Oration (Thuc. ii.42.2) that the end of a man's life "first reveals and finally confirms his arete" and that the heroic dead "obliterated evil by good."

It is not strictly accurate to say that in heroic thought the idea of morality and the idea of arete are the same, though this is often said, as for example by M. Gigante, Νόμος Βασιλεύς, p. 18. Does the Cyclops, who lacks justice, also lack arete? I am not clear what Gigante means by "the right of *arete*": "Il diritto dell' ἀρετή non è il diritto della βία; è il diritto che fonda la sua giustizia su un predominio di qualità morali che non infrangono le leggi della società e il diritto degli altri" (p. 19).

20. But despite her intelligence Clytaemnestra agreed to do what Aegisthus proposed, an action that is roundly condemned by the gods. She agreed to do it because she was "persuaded"—she changed her mind, lost her intelligence, abandoned prudence for folly. This does not mean that she can be forgiven, any more than Odysseus's men can be forgiven for slaughtering the oxen of the Sun god when they were desperately hungry.

21. M. Wundt, *Der Intellektualismus in der griechischen Ethik* (Leipzig, 1907), pp. 1–18, claims that Homer constantly contrasts the intelligent man with the man who is swayed by passions. But Homer does not represent man as torn between two conflicting forces, one good and the other evil; and the notion that passions are evil will not be found in Homer. There is, indeed, no general word in Homer for "passions," nothing corresponding to the "appetitive element" in the soul which, in Plato, is in conflict with the element of reason. *Thymos* ("anger," "spirit," "impulse") is not a bad thing in Homer; excess or strength of *thymos* is not so dangerous as weakness of the intelligence; and intellectual weakness does not necessarily result in outbursts of passion.

If the distinction between intellect and will is not clearly made in early Greek thought, it might also be asked whether a distinction between knowledge and ability should be pressed—the distinction between "knowing that" and "knowing how," as it is called in recent studies of Plato. See, for example, J. Gould, *The Development of Plato's Ethics* (Cambridge, 1955), Bk. I, chap. i, who adopts the terminology of Gilbert Ryle, *Concept of Mind* (London, 1949). Gould points out, quite rightly, that the verb ἐπίστασθαι, in earlier Greek usage at least, often seems to mean practical knowledge and ability, rather than theoretical knowledge of facts. Gould wants to understand the Socratic theory that "virtue is knowledge" "in the light of earlier usage going back to Homer and beyond" (p. 7). He thinks that "the ἐπίστήμη which Socrates envisaged was a form of knowing *how*, that is, *how to be moral*." And he claims to find support for his view in early Greek usage.

If Homeric thought recognizes a difference between "knowing that" and "knowing how," it must be admitted that Homeric language is inadequate to define the difference. But there certainly is a recognized difference between kinds of arete; and each arete is acquired by knowing how to do something, whether to fight or sing or behave like a faithful wife. The necessary ability in each case may be valued more or less highly according to the importance of the arete itself. Euryalus, for example, in the scene between him and Odysseus in *Od.* viii.158–85, taunts Odysseus because he does not look like a man capable of athletic prowess, but like a man who could sit back giving orders to others or keeping his accounts straight; and in his judgment the latter abilities are relatively unimportant. When Odysseus in reply tells Euryalus that he lacks *noos* (a term that will be discussed later in this chapter), he might mean either that Euryalus lacks judgment ("knowing that") or that he does not know how to behave, that he has certain abilities but lacks others. So also in *Od.* vi.258, when Nausicaa tells Odysseus that he looks like an intelligent man, she means both that Odysseus knows the dangers of gossip and that he knows how to behave.

Noos, unlike arete, is a gift of the gods which, according to Odysseus, they denied to Euryalus though they gave him personal beauty. This ought to mean that he cannot be blamed for his lack of noos, just as he could not be blamed if he were ugly; but he can be blamed because he does not know how to behave. One can imagine into what difficulties a Homeric character would fall if Socrates were to question him on his favorite topic: Is arete teachable?

22. Cf. P. T. Justesen, *Les Principes psychologiques d'Homère* (Copenhagen, 1928), pp. 4–16; R. B. Onians, *The Origins of European Thought* (Cambridge, 1951), pp. 23–43. For the purpose of the present argument it matters little which organ is meant by phrenes; the precise identification is important only to students of Homeric anatomy and physiology and to those who are anxious to locate the organs traditionally connected with the different emotions.

23. Cf. *Il.* xiii.431–32 and the remarks of A. M. Frenkian, *Le Monde homérique* (Paris, 1934), pp. 89–92, on the contrast of phrenes with *erga*.

24. See the analysis in J. Boehme, *Die Seele und das Ich im homerischen Epos* (Berlin, 1929), pp. 37–50.

25. τέων αὖτε βροτῶν ἐς γαῖαν ἱκάνω;
ἦ ῥ' οἵ γ' ὑβρισταί τε καὶ ἄγριοι οὐδὲ δίκαιοι,
ἦε φιλόξεινοι, καί σφιν νόος ἐστὶ θεουδής;.
(*Od.* vi.119–21; ix.174–76; xiii.200–202)

26. πολλῶν δ' ἀνθρώπων ἴδεν ἄστεα καὶ νόον ἔγνω. νόμον, the reading of Zenodotus, has recently been defended as preferable to νόον. Cf., for example, R. Merkelbach, *Untersuchungen zur Odyssee* (Munich, 1951), p. 158; Gigante, Νόμος Βασιλεύς, p. 44 n. But νόμος never occurs elsewhere in Homer, and the verses from the *Odyssey* quoted in the previous note certainly support the reading νόον. M. Pohlenz, "Nomos," *Philologus*, 97 (1948), 139, is quite right in saying that only νόμους, not νόμον, would be defensible. The notion of an abstract *nomos* is scarcely conceivable in Homer, as it is unlikely in Solon, though here, too, Gigante (p. 32) is vigorous in defending νόμου against ὁμοῦ in Frag. 24 (Diehl):

ταῦτα μὲν κράτει
ὁμοῦ βίην τε καὶ δίκην συναρμόσας
ἔρεξα.
(15–17)

27. On the historical development of the meaning of noos, see R. Schottländer, "Nus als Terminus," *Hermes*, 64 (1929), 228–42. He shows

how in earliest usage noos is a "neutral" word, in the sense that it must be qualified by some positive or negative attribute before its value in a man is established; it is not necessarily "good sense" until Semonides (Diehl, Frags. 1, 7) and Theognis (35–36).

28. Cf. Frenkian, *Le Monde homérique,* pp. 93–94.

29. The Herodotean usage of noos is generally in conformity with the Homeric. It often means purpose, as in iii.122, when Oroetes learns the noos of Polycrates, his intention of establishing a maritime empire (cf. the νόος τῆς θυσίης in i.216). The contrast between outward appearance and real intention (νόῳ δὲ ἄλλα μηχανᾶσθαι) is made in ii.100. Cf. δολερῷ νόῳ, ii.151; ἀπ' οὐδενὸς δολεροῦ νόου, iii.135; and also i.71, 117.

Likewise in Sophocles, *Electra* 913–14, when Chrysothemis argues that the offerings at Agamemnon's tomb cannot have been made by Clytaemnestra, she says:

> ἀλλ' οὐδὲ μὲν δὴ μητρὸς οὔθ' ὁ νοῦς φιλεῖ
> τοιαῦτα πράσσειν οὔτε δρῶσ' ἐλάνθανεν

(ἐλάνθαν' ἄν, Heath's reading, may be right).

The meaning is that such procedure is not in conformity with her feelings, her attitude towards Agamemnon; and she cannot have concealed her noos in this matter, because if she had made such an offering before we should have known about it.

30. This passage is discussed by Hermann Fränkel, *Dichtung und Philosophie des frühen Griechentums,* American Philological Monographs, XIII (1951), 184–85 (cf. also "Man's 'Ephemeros' Nature According to Pindar and Others," *TAPA,* 77 [1946], 131–45). He goes too far in saying that a man's whole being is thought to be changed with circumstances ("mit seiner Lage hat sich sein Wesen ausgewechselt"). And I cannot agree with him when he maintains that this insistence on the power of circumstance ("the Day") over man is characteristic of post-Homeric thought, and that it first appears in the *Odyssey.* The passages from the *Iliad* quoted in the next paragraph show that similar ideas are current throughout Homer.

31. On the meaning of noos in these passages, see the valuable article of K. von Fritz, "ΝΟΟΣ and ΝΟΕΙΝ in the Homeric Poems," *CP,* 38 (1943), 79–93. His criticism of earlier writers is well founded. He rightly finds fault with the view of J. Boehme, *Die Seele und das Ich im homerischen Epos* (Berlin, 1929, pp. 52–63), who thinks that noos always means something "purely intellectual" and that it is "put in contrast with emotion." One may properly ask whether the distinction between "intellectual" and "emotional" is really applicable to Homer, unless one speaks simply in terms of individual emotions at particular moments, like greed, anger, or pity, which can certainly turn the purpose of a man—although as semipermanent characteristics, they might also be considered part of a man's noos or attitude. The insistence of Odysseus in taunting the Cyclops from his ship, despite the urging of his companions (ix.500), may be recalled again (see above, pp. 209–10). Odysseus says his companions could not persuade

him: ἀλλ' οὐ πεῖθον ἐμὸν μεγαλήτορα θυμόν. It would have been equally possible to say that they could not turn his noos. His insistence on winning kleos, his inborn desire for arete, are part of his heroic character; he cannot accept anonymity without a change of noos; the issue means nothing to his companions, who have far less to gain and just as much to lose by his rashness. His behaviour, moreover, is not irrational and is not presented as such; he has measured the distance they have come from shore and is confident that they are out of range of the Cyclops' rock.

32. No verb from this root (*σνεύω or *σνέϝω) is known in Greek, but the possibility of such a verb, cognate with Middle High German *snôuwen* (English "sniff"), has been considered by E. Schwyzer (*Festschrift für Paul Kretschmer* [Leipzig, 1926], pp. 247 *et seq.*), with the meaning "to smell" or "perceive by the sense of smell" or even "perceive by *any* of the senses." This etymology has therefore been suggested for noos, from **snowos* with the original meaning of "perception." Cf. V. Larock, "Les Premières Conceptions psychologiques des Grecs," *Revue belge de philologie et histoire,* 9 (1930), 388, who thinks that noos must originally have meant "le regard, mais non pas le regard purement physique uniquement." Cf. also von Fritz, *CP,* 38 (1943), 92–93.

The verb νοεῖν certainly means "to perceive" (generally by sight) and it is used also of the aged dog Argus, who is perhaps blind, recognizing his master (*Od.* xvii.301). Hence, this etymology might be thought satisfactory as an explanation of the verb νοεῖν and the meaning of "understanding" which noos bears in later Greek. But an original meaning of "perception" does not explain the meaning of noos suggested by the Homeric passages discussed in the preceding paragraphs.

33. J. Boehme, *Die Seele und das Ich im homerischen Epos,* seeks to minimize this distinction by saying it was not recognized in primitive thinking, which did not distingush between "Träger einer Handlung" and "Fähigkeit." He is therefore prepared to recognize three distinct meanings for noos: Soul, Understanding, and Plan. Like Bruno Snell, Boehme is concerned with the lack in Homeric language of words to express man's entire psychic being, and he is trying to establish the relation of words like noos, phrenes, and thymos to his *Ich.* This preoccupation makes it almost inevitable that they should regard noos as an organ or a part of the psychic structure of a man. Cf. also H. Fränkel, *Dichtung und Philosophie des frühen Griechentums,* pp. 110–11.

Snell, *The Discovery of the Mind,* pp. 9–16 (cf. his review of Boehme's book in *Gnomon,* 7 [1931], 74–86), even goes so far as to say that noos in Homer is "the cause of ideas and images" or "the recipient" or "the organ of clear images." But there is no warrant for crediting Homeric man with a theory of perception such as this language suggests. Indeed, there is nothing anywhere in Homer to suggest that noos was ever considered an organ "on analogy with the physical organs"; although the phrenes may have been located in a specific part of the body, the same cannot be said of noos.

It is very difficult to explain Homeric usage on the assumption that the original meaning of noos is "soul," "mind," or "intelligence." The etymology that connects it with νεύω is better suited to the meaning which it bears in Homer. It is favoured by W. Prellwitz, *Etymologisches Wörterbuch der griechischen Sprache* (Göttingen, 1905); the matter is left in doubt by E. Boisacq, *Dictionnaire étymologique de la langue grecque*. The connection with νέω, "swim," is also possible linguistically; it is less attractive, but might be defended on the principle that νέω may originally have meant simply "move" or "flow."

The form of a noun like νόος must also be taken into account in any discussion of its history and original meaning. There are in Greek only a limited number of dissyllabic nouns ending in -οος or feminine -οη (older -oϝος, -oϝη), and the most familiar of them are nouns denoting action or movement: ῥόος (flowing), πλόος (sailing), χόος (pouring), πνοή (breathing), βοή (shouting), γόος (weeping), θρόος (speaking). The first four of these nouns have corresponding verbs in -εω (εϝω), and three of them have neuter nouns in -μα formed directly from the root:

ῥόος	(flowing)	ῥέω	(flow)	ῥεῦμα	(stream)
πλόος	(sailing)	πλέω	(sail)		
χόος	(pouring)	χέω	(pour)	χεῦμα	(pouring)
πνοή	(breathing)	πνέω	(breathe)	πνεῦμα	(breath, wind)

It is extremely tempting to complete the pattern by adding:

νόος	(?)	νεύω	(nod, incline)	νεῦμα	(nod)
		or νέω	(swim)		

γόος, βοή, and θρόος have no corresponding verbs formed directly from the root, but only γοάω, βοάω, θροέω, formed from the nouns like νοέω from νόος. γόος and βοή are probably derived from the same root, *g^uow-*. χνόος, "froth" or "scum" (in *Od.* vi.226, it means the salt scum left on the skin of Odysseus after his long immersion), is tentatively connected by Boisacq with the verb χναύω, "gnaw," and στοά with στεῦμαι, "stand firm." χλόη has no corresponding verb, and the adjectives like θόος and those ending in -σοος, -ξοος are not relevant. Nor should πόη be taken into account, since no digamma has been lost here. Where the link between the two vowels is a consonantal *i*, the pair κλοῖος, κλείω is worth noting.

If the parallel between νόος and other nouns in -οος is of any value, and the relation of νόος to νεῦμα is the same as that of ῥόος to ῥεῦμα, the presumption must be that the original meaning of νόος is not an agent or organ (mind, intelligence) but a movement or activity (thinking, intending, purposing, inclining, directing). Perhaps νεῦμα may have meant originally simply "inclination" and have acquired later the more limited meaning of "nod"; and when both νεύω and νεῦμα have acquired this limited meaning, the language then requires forms like νοέω and νόημα to take their place in the meaning of "think," and "thought." If the foregoing argument is accepted, then noos might be described as meaning originally "a mental movement or inclination towards or away from a person or thing." "Richtung auf einen Gegenstand" is suggested by R. Schottländer, *Hermes,* 64 (1929), 239, and "a function rather than an organ" is the conclusion of von Fritz, *CP,* 38 (1943), 83.

A word like the Greek ῥόος or English "stream" can denote equally well the movement of water or its force or the actual body of water; when it is called "swift" the movement is in question, when it is called "deep," "cold," or "muddy" the material of the stream is meant. The different adjectives applied to noos can easily be understood on the same principle—"swift," "god-fearing," "evil." If the parallel between noos and ῥόος is kept in mind (perhaps πλόος is an even better example), the combination of meanings like "inclination," "thought," "purpose," and "plan" is readily understandable. A voyage can equally well be a movement or a plan or purpose.

The proper names ending in -noos that occur in Homer are worth noticing. Autonoos (*Il.* xi.301; xvi.694) appears to mean "thinking (or purposing) for himself." Pronoos (*Il.* xvi.399) evidently means "moving forward," that is, "kindly" or even "assenting," "nodding assent," almost a synonym of *prophron*; and the feminine name Eunoe means "with kindly noos." On the other hand, Antinoos, the disagreeable leader of the suitors, seems to be deliberately named as an "unsympathetic," hostile person. Naturally enough, the name is not normally given to children. Rather curiously, it is the name of the young man on whom the emperor Hadrian lavished his affections; it seems that at this late date its unpleasant etymology was forgotten (it is easy enough to find equally uncomplimentary names in any telephone directory—Coward, Maldonado, Unruh). Alcinoos perhaps means "with strength in his noos," just as Horace's Leuconoe means "with clear and crystal mind" (*anima candida*); but Hipponoos cannot mean "with the mind of a horse" but "with his mind on horses." In Euripides, *Helena* 821–2, Theonoe is hailed as a suitable name for a prophetess, presumably one who "knows the will of the gods" not "with the mind of a god."

34. A final caution may be given against supposing that the noos is located in the phrenes or anywhere else in the body. When Agamemnon is said to "rejoice in his noos" (*Od.* viii.78), this does not mean that he felt joy in any particular part of him, as one might say he rejoiced in his heart, but rather "he rejoiced as he thought about it."

CHAPTER THREE

1. A. Heuss, "Die archaische Zeit Griechenlands als geschichtliche Epoche," *Antike und Abendland,* 2 (1946), 26–62, tries to show that the archaic age, from the migrations to the Persian Wars, is dominated by and centred upon a great task—the building of a Greek society—and that the basis of this society is the common heritage of morals, customs, religious beliefs, and the common language. Where literature is concerned and intellectual tradition, and to a great extent also moral tradition, this heritage means

simply the Homeric poems. In comparison with the influence of Homer, new developments mean little.

2. Jaeger, "Tyrtaios über die wahre ἀρετή," *SB. der Akad. Berlin,* 1932, *phil. hist. Kl.,* pp. 537–68 and esp. p. 540. He is following F. Jacoby, "Studien zu den älteren griechischen Elegikern," *Hermes,* 53 (1918), 1–14. His criticism of the attitude taken by earlier scholars towards Tyrtaeus is well founded. It is a mistake to think that the poems of Tyrtaeus were not written until the fifth century simply because their tendency and tone is appropriate at that time, when we are not in a position to say that they would have been less appropriate at an earlier date in Sparta—even though the more elaborate story of the Messenian Wars may not have been worked out until the fourth century. E. Schwartz, "Tyrtaios," *Hermes,* 34 (1899), 428–68, argued that the poems of Tyrtaeus were in fact written by an Athenian in the fifth century, but subsequently abandoned this view (*Philologus,* 92 [1937], 19–46).

3. For the fragments of Solon, see Diehl, *Anthologia lyrica graeca* (henceforth cited as Diehl).

4. The treatment of hybris and koros in the poetry of the sixth and seventh centuries is discussed by C. del Grande, *Hybris,* pp. 37–53. He makes the point that between Hesiod and Theognis the concept of hybris is developed more *sub specie pietatis* than *sub specie iuris.*

Herodotus shows particular interest in the cause of Polycrates' downfall (iii.120–22). According to one story he insulted Oroetes by ignoring his messenger, but according to another he gave Oroetes no cause for offence at all. In any case, he is entrapped by his greed for more wealth, by koros, and by his desire for more and more power, which Oroetes exploits. It is likely that some versions explained his downfall without emphasizing his violence and criminal behaviour at all. The same is certainly true of Croesus, whom Herodotus clearly admires; his fate is supposed to prove that complete prosperity is not only dangerous but in fact impossible. Herodotus knows the story that he tortured and murdered his half-brother Pantaleon and that many of his offerings to Delphi were the fruits of this criminal act (i.92); but it is the belief that he is the most successful man in the world which brings down nemesis on Croesus (i.34). The gods are supposed to be punishing him for his hybristic thought, not his hybristic actions.

5. Cf. Chap. Two above.

6. The two versions are as follows:

Μηδὲν ἄγαν σπεύδειν· πάντων μέσ' ἄριστα· καὶ οὕτως,
Κύρν', ἕξεις ἀρετήν, ἥντε λαβεῖν χαλεπόν.
(335–36)

Μηδὲν ἄγαν σπεύδειν· καιρὸς δ' ἐπὶ πᾶσιν ἄριστος
ἔργμασιν ἀνθρώπων· πολλάκι δ' εἰς ἀρετὴν
σπεύδει ἀνὴρ κέρδος διζήμενος, ὅντινα δαίμων
πρόφρων εἰς μεγάλην ἀμπλακίην παράγει.
(401–4)

True arete, it seems, the kind of arete that is hard to win, is a kind of mean. The second version defines it as dependent on *kairos,* the right touch or timing (as though there were times to strive and not to strive), because there are times when success will mean disaster, when good fortune or "a favouring god" (δαίμων πρόφρων) may destroy you (like the good fortune that brought back to Polycrates the ring he had cast into the sea). The famous conversation of Solon with Croesus, as described by Herodotus (i.30–33), fits in with this argument: Tellus and Cleobis and Bito enjoyed *kairos* in their death as well as their life; they died after their particular act of striving was successful and when their honour was at its height.

7. Cf. the discussion of arete in E. Schwartz, *Ethik der Griechen,* pp. 19–25, and Jaeger, *Paideia,* I, 68, where he translates arete by "success" and comments: "The full meaning of the words κακότης and ἀρετή is not given in 'misery' and 'success'; but these translations show that the Greek words do not signify the moral qualities of vice and virtue, as the later Greeks and Romans believed." Jaeger stresses the difference between the arete of the warrior noble and the "working-class ideal." But he neglects to point out that each is the same kind of ideal, the winning of respect and distinction within the community or section of the community to which one belongs. It is scarcely necessary to say that one must be a successful farmer in order to establish oneself as a respected member of a farming community. Hesiod grants that it is not easy, and proceeds to give practical advice on methods.

8. Here I find myself in sharp disagreement with C. M. Bowra, *Early Greek Elegists* (Harvard University Press, 1938), pp. 39–70, and Jaeger, *Paideia,* I, 74–95, whose views are repeated in summarized form by Marrou, *History of Education in Antiquity,* pp. 15–16. Bowra apparently regards Tyrtaeus, Frag. 9, as the first attempt to define arete and the ἀνὴρ ἀγαθός, on the principle that Tyrtaeus uses these words in a different sense from the Homeric. He says (rightly) that arete in Homer does not cover the whole duty of man, and concludes (arbitrarily) that for Tyrtaeus it does. Arete and duty are two completely different conceptions; they are two different ways of judging human behaviour, according as one word or the other is used. Tyrtaeus is offering his views on the best kind of arete, not saying anything about duties. He is not, as Jaeger thinks, "transvaluing" the idea of arete (p. 87) or declaring that "whatever helps the state is good, whatever injures it is bad" (p. 89). It is not as though every man can do what Tyrtaeus asks; and Tyrtaeus must know as well as anyone else that the state cannot survive by the spear alone, that others besides the soldier benefit the state.

In his earlier discussion of Tyrtaeus (see n. 2 above), Jaeger has a fuller discussion of this passage. He is anxious to prove that it is an attempt to define arete. In Frag. 8 the appeal for steadfastness reaches its climax with the line: τρεσσάντων δ' ἀνδρῶν πᾶσ' ἀπόλωλ' ἀρετή (14). What, Jaeger asks, is this "entire arete" that can be ruined if a man turns tail in battle? He asks what relation it bears to the "end" of arete of which we hear in Frag. 11: πρὶν ἀρετῆς πελάσαι τέρμασιν ἢ θανάτου. His reply is that Frag. 9 is devoted to answering the question, that it defines arete by exalting the virtues of the fighting man and insisting that other aretai cannot provide what the warrior needs. It would seem that Jaeger is at fault in neglecting the Homeric passage which Tyrtaeus' readers might be expected to remember: "Zeus takes away half a man's arete when the day of slavery seizes him" (*Od.* xvii.322–23, cf. Chap. Two above, p. 49). To anyone recalling this passage, the meaning of "all arete" in Frag. 8 would be perfectly clear. A slave has some self-respect left, he can still hold up his head and win recognition in small ways, but a coward loses all hope of winning respect or recognition, in whatever walk of life he might have hoped to gain or retain it, πᾶσ' ἀρετή must mean "all arete" or "all his arete" not "entire arete." Jaeger, who seems to have missed the Homeric clue, is led far astray in search of something quite new. He concludes that this new "entire arete" or true arete is "working for the common good of the city" and Tyrtaeus must therefore be credited with "Politisierung der Ruhmesidee" (pp. 547–52).

What does Tyrtaeus in fact say in Frag. 9? He lists the kinds of arete that are not to be compared with the warrior's, namely athletic prowess, strength, beauty, wealth, the arete of the king and the orator (or politician); he cannot value any of them very highly unless they are combined with the arete of the warrior:

οὐ γὰρ ἀνὴρ ἀγαθὸς γίγνεται ἐν πολέμῳ,
εἰ μὴ τετλαίη μὲν ὁρῶν φόνον αἱματοέντα
καὶ δήων ὀρέγοιτ' ἐγγύθεν ἱστάμενος.
ἥδ' ἀρετή, τόδ' ἄεθλον ἐν ἀνθρώποισιν ἄριστον,
κάλλιστόν τε φέρειν γίγνεται ἀνδρὶ νέῳ.
ξυνὸν δ' ἐσθλὸν τοῦτο πόληΐ τε παντί τε δήμῳ,
ὅστις ἀνὴρ διαβὰς ἐν προμάχοισι μένῃ
νωλεμέως, αἰσχρῆς δὲ φυγῆς ἐπὶ πάγχυ λάθηται
ψυχὴν καὶ θυμὸν τλήμονα παρθέμενος,
θαρσύνῃ δ' ἔπεσιν τὸν πλησίον ἄνδρα παρεστώς.
οὗτος ἀνὴρ ἀγαθὸς γίγνεται ἐν πολέμῳ.

(9.10–20)

The form of the argument is very simple: a man does not achieve arete (become an ἀνὴρ ἀγαθός) in war unless he stands steadfast in the front ranks, forgetting all thought of flight, and so on. Only the man who does this achieves the kind of arete which the poet prizes. And why does he prize it? Because it benefits the whole city, which an athlete can hardly be said to do. Jaeger thinks that ἥδ' ἀρετή means "this is *arete*," but the alternative possibility, "This arete, this feat is the noblest," as given by J. M. Edmonds, *Elegy and Iambus* (Loeb Class. Lib.), should be considered. At the end of the poem, after the warrior's arete is fully described, we have the conclusion:

ταύτης νῦν τις ἀνὴρ ἀρετῆς εἰς ἄκρον ἱκέσθαι
πειράσθω θυμῷ, μὴ μεθιεὶς πολέμου.

(43–44)

There is no new definition here, only a description of what a man must do to win "this arete" which the poet prizes, and what rewards follow even if a man dies in winning it. Nothing is said of duty or obligation, and of "transvaluing" arete there is no trace. The chorus in Euripides, *Helena* 1151–57, gives the lie to Tyrtaeus in no uncertain terms:

ἄφρονες ὅσοι τὰς ἀρετὰς πολέμῳ
λόγχαισί τ' ἀλκαίου δορὸς
κτᾶσθε, πόνους ἀμαθῶς θνα-
τῶν καταπαυόμενοι.
εἰ γὰρ ἅμιλλα κρινεῖ μιν
αἵματος, οὔποτ' ἔρις
λείψει κατ' ἀνθρώπων πόλεις.

9. ὅθεν φαμὶ καὶ σὲ τὰν ἀ-
πείρονα δόξαν εὑρεῖν,
τὰ μὲν ἐν ἱπποσύναισιν ἀνδρέσσι μαρνάμενον,
τὰ δ' ἐν πεζομάχαισι· βουλαὶ δὲ πρεσβύτεραι
ἀκίνδυνον ἐμοὶ ἔπος
<σε> ποτὶ πάντα λόγον
ἐπαινεῖν παρέχοντι.

(*Pyth.* 2.63–67)

10. The different meanings can be identified as follows in various passages: Meaning (1) in 29–30, 129–30, 401–4, 699–700, and 867; Meaning (2) in 149–50, 335–36, 971, and 1003 (which is borrowed from Tyrtaeus); Meaning (3) in 147–48, 319, 623–24, 789–96, and 1062. Lines 933–36 suggest a combination of meanings (1) and (2), while lines 316–18 and 465 suggest a wavering between (2) and (3).

J. Gerlach, 'Ανὴρ ἀγαθός (Diss. Munich, 1932), pp. 19–21, maintains that in all the poetry attributed to Theognis, ἀγαθός has the meaning "distinguished," *angesehen* (not "noble" or "brave"), but he does not notice the variations in meaning of arete.

11. The inevitable decline of the golden age is not simply a proof that human prosperity is short-lived; it must be intended to show that human life cannot be maintained without certain elements which are lacking in the golden age. Among these elements justice and arete must be included, and likewise toil and sweat, since arete is unattainable without them. Hesiod should mean, then, that dreams of a golden age, without hardship or organization, are purely illusory. Cf. Eduard Meyer, "Hesiods *Erga* und das Gedicht von den fünf Menschengeschlechtern," in his *Kleine Schriften,* II (Halle, 1924), 17–66 (originally published in a Festschrift for Carl Robert, *Genethliakon,* Berlin, 1910). He thinks that Hesiod presents the golden and silver ages as a "Phantasiebild," a picture of man's impracticable dreams, but that the succession of the next three ages, from the bronze through the age of heroes to the iron age, is supposed to represent what actually happened. See also T. G. Rosenmeyer, "Hesiod and Historiography," *Hermes,* 85 (1957), 257–85.

12. *Dike* is sometimes interpreted as "the way of the universe," as though its eventual triumph were considered part of the scheme of nature. This is going some way beyond the Greek texts, which can in fact be interpreted more simply. Any kind of religious faith (even superstition) includes the belief that gods can punish (fear of the gods), and popular ethics always insists that crime does not pay (fear of the consequences). But it is important to recognize that neither Greek religion nor Greek popular ethics makes fear of the gods or the consequences the reason for disapproval of injustice; the order of the argument is, first, crime is undesirable, second, it is generally punished in the long run, directly or indirectly, by gods if not by men. An action is not right because the gods will it so; rather, a given act is right and the gods will reward it. This order of argument does not make the gods a law unto themselves. They, too, can be punished if they break certain rules; divine Moira stands over them, a power whose logical system is beyond man's understanding. But for practical purposes it is of course useless for man to argue with the gods, as Theognis does not neglect to say.

13. Jaeger, however, is determined to represent Hesiod as a sort of religious prophet: "When Hesiod identifies the will of Zeus with the concept of justice, when he creates a new divinity, the goddess Dike, and sets her close beside Zeus the highest of all gods, he is inspired by the burning religious and moral enthusiasm with which the rising class of peasants and townsfolk hailed the new ideal of Justice the saviour" (*Paideia,* I, 67). He also says that Hesiod "borrows from Homer the content of his ideal of justice." But Hesiod's justice is not an ideal; it is simply the foundation of civilized life, and as such cannot be called the invention of either Homer or Hesiod. Nor is it a new religious idea that a high god enforces justice and punishes *hybris*; the idea is as old as religious thought itself. Jaeger's fundamental mistake is in apparently taking for granted that ethical and religious thought did not begin until Homer, which is an astonishing assumption.

Compare, for a contrast with Jaeger, the discussion of Hesiod by J. Defradas, *Les Thèmes de la propagande delphique* (Paris, 1954), pp. 45–52. He shows that Hesiod's moral attitude is not really founded on religious belief at all; that he always regards justice "d'une façon que nous pourrions dire paysanne; comme le respect du bien d'autrui" (p. 49). Defradas rejects entirely the view that Hesiod's poetry reflects Delphic influence.

14. T. G. Rosenmeyer in *Hermes,* 85 (1957), argues that "as far as it is possible to recover the original intentions of an author, it appears that Hesiod's mind was past-directed when he wrote the passage, that he was listing past events in their true colours to the extent that the past was accessible to him and his poetry" (p. 265). Or again: "Hesiod, we have seen, tries to account for the social and moral situation of his own world. To do this he collects a certain class of data and arranges them to fit the aetiological and moral purposes of his design. The data with which he is concerned are what Herodotus calls τὰ λεγόμενα" (p. 268). Nonetheless, Rosenmeyer does not mean that Hesiod was writing or attempting to write accurate history, but rather that he had "an approach to man's actions

in time which deserves the epithet historical because it has freed itself from the shackles of the mythological and theological perspective" (p. 277). I regret that this argument is not intelligible to me.

Much time has been spent in arguing whether or not the succession of changes, as told by Hesiod, is logical. Certainly it is not a tale of continuous decline; and why should it be? But if Hesiod wishes to imply that the good things, justice and arete, are to be found in the future, with some regard for the achievement of the past, his scheme is well-constructed. It is not only the increased difficulty of life in the world that matters; it is the development of man in facing his difficulties. Herein lies the meaning of the age of heroes.

15. Cf. Chap. Two above, pp. 55–58.

16. The drunkard is "master neither of noos nor of tongue" (480). Cf. also lines 1185–86:

> Noos is good and tongue likewise; but how few men
> Know how to be good stewards of these.

17. Cf., for example, what Pericles says in the Funeral Oration, Thuc. ii.40.4: "We make friends not by receiving but by conferring benefits." This is an example of Athenian arete ("in matters of arete we differ from most people"); so we see that by this time friendship is a part of arete.

18. In the discussion of different forms of government which is supposed to be held between Otanes, Megabyzus, and Darius, in Herodotus iii.80–82, Darius stresses the part played by "powerful friendships" in a democracy.

19. *Nic. Eth.* viii.1163a.

20. *Paideia,* I, 199.

CHAPTER FOUR

1. Athenaeus, viii.347e.

2. Aristophanes misleads us, presumably deliberately, in the scene in the *Frogs* in which it is argued that Aeschylus teaches us the traditional lessons and Euripides does not. Indeed, the inept criticism in the *Frogs* may be designed to show that some of the Athenians who claimed to like Aeschylus were incapable of comprehending him. There is no more reason to expect consistently genuine criticism here than to look for accuracy in the presentation of Socrates in the *Clouds.*

3. For a recent attempt to reach a decision, see D. Kaufmann-Bühler, *Begriff und Funktion der Dike in den Tragödien des Aischylos* (Bonn, 1955), who lists earlier literature. A distinction must be made between the imperfect ideas of justice which Aeschylean characters uphold and any ideal of justice in which Aeschylus himself may believe.

4. H. G. Robertson, "Legal Expressions and Ideas of Justice in Aeschylus," *CP,* 34 (1939), 218, writes: "We may conclude that the *Suppliants* and the *Oresteia* are chiefly concerned with problems of justice, while the

Persians and the *Prometheus* reveal slight interest in them. The *Seven against Thebes* occupies an intermediate position; while assertions are made about justice, no real problems are stated." The existence and recognition of a problem does not necessarily need a statement. The dramatic situation may be enough in itself, without a specific statement by a character. Hence it is quite untrue to say that the *Persians* and the *Prometheus* reveal slight interest in the problems of justice; both plays show characters in search of what they believe to be justice.

5. Even the famous fragment in which Dike herself appears as a character (*Oxyrhynchus Papyri,* XX, 2256, Frag. 9a; H. J. Mette, *Die Fragmente der Tragödien des Aischylos,* Frag. 530) offers hardly anything that is strictly relevant to the present discussion.

6. See especially i.158–60.

7. It is strange that some critics have written about the *Suppliants* as though it were a play complete in itself, and not the first play of a trilogy in which the way is prepared for tragic happenings. F. Stoessl, "Aeschylus as a Political Thinker," *AJP,* 73 (1952), 121–26, writes as though the reception of the Danaids at Argos were to have no tragic consequences, and speaks of Pelasgus as "the poetic incarnation of the ideal of the democratic ruler of the state" (p. 123). Is it only an ideal ruler who has any sense of responsibility? H. N. Couch, "The Problem of Pelasgus in Aeschylus' *Suppliants,*" *CW,* 35 (1941–42), 279–80, is careful to point out that the *Suppliants* does not contain the whole story; but he also ranks Pelasgus much too highly, as one who has "attained the moral stature to choose the way of justice" and "has taken unto himself the high moral purpose of the finest of Greek tragic heroes." In fact, the choice of Pelasgus was almost inevitable, since the religious law that protected suppliants was imperative in its demands; and the Danaids' threat of suicide, which would bring the curse of blood on the country as well if he rejected them, was one more pressure that served to force his hand. The issue of the play is well set forth by H. D. F. Kitto, *Greek Tragedy* (2d ed.; London, 1950), who reminds us that "the simple story of the protection of injured innocence is no dramatic material for such as Aeschylus" (p. 14). "Through no Aristotelian flaw of character, through no deficiency of sense, intellect, or morality, has the king fallen suddenly into this awful dilemma. A disharmony in the make-up of things, and a perfectly innocent man is broken" (p. 9).

A useful, though hardly complete, parallel to the story is offered by the story of Croesus and Adrastus told by Herodotus, i.35–45. Adrastus is received as a refugee suppliant by Croesus, and he unintentionally kills Croesus's son.

8. The distinction is not between religious and ethical obligation, as M. Pohlenz thinks, *Die griechische Tragödie* (Leipzig-Berlin, 1930), p. 34, but between the claim of the gods and the claim of the state. There ought not to be any difficulty in deciding the conflict; it is apparently not a real conflict at all, since the god's claim is higher. But a suppliant may in fact be unworthy of the protection of Zeus Hikesios, his plea being based on a false pretence. A mere fugitive does not have the rights of a suppliant, though he is often granted them.

Since the chorus of Danaids insists so strongly on the justice of their cause, some critics have been led to think that Aeschylus is merely upholding justice against hybris. The issue of the play is greatly oversimplified by H. G. Robertson, "Δίκη and Ὕβρις in Aeschylus' *Suppliants*," *CR*, 50 (1936), 104–9.

9. A papyrus fragment (*P. Oxy.*, XX, 2256, Frag. 3) appears to record that the Danaid trilogy of Aeschylus won the first prize in competition with Sophocles. Sophocles' first production cannot be, at the earliest, before 470, so that a later date, possibly 463, should now be recognized for the *Suppliants*. For discussion see E. C. Yorke, "The Date of the *Supplices* of Aeschylus," *CR*, n.s. 4 (1954), 10–11; A. Lesky, "Die Datierung der *Hiketiden* und der Tragiker Mesatos," *Hermes*, 82 (1954), 1–13; P. Orgels, "Une Révolution dans la chronologie d'Eschyle," *Bull. acad. royale Belg., classe des lettres*, Ser. 5, No. 41 (1955), 528–36. F. R. Earp, "The Date of the *Supplices* of Aeschylus," *Greece and Rome*, 22 (1953), 118–23, refuses to accept the evidence of the papyrus and still believes that the *Suppliants* must be an early play.

This new date for the *Suppliants* has stimulated historians to find a new political meaning for the play. Themistocles, when he fled from Athens, took refuge in Argos in or about 470 (but was subsequently obliged to leave). Are we to believe, then, that the Athenian audience would in some way identify Danaus and his daughters with Themistocles? And that applause for the hospitable behaviour of Pelasgus was a means of showing loyalty to Themistocles? That the play was a condemnation of Cimon's policy, which caused Athens to abandon friendship with Argos and give her support to Sparta? That it was not only a condemnation of this policy, but a piece of propaganda in favour of the new Periclean party which continued the policies of Themistocles, and that the play's success was a victory for this new party? W. G. Forrest, "Themistokles and Argos," *CQ*, n.s. 10 (1960), 235–41, would have us believe some, if not all of this. But such an interpretation is hard to accept unless one also believes that the pro-Themistoclean members of the audience, including the judges, slept solidly through the second and third plays of the trilogy, in which the disastrous consequences of sheltering the suppliants were revealed (cf. n. 7 above). I am not ready to believe that the Danaid trilogy carried any such simple or direct political message.

10. The present discussion is concerned only with the ethical aspects of the *Prometheus*, not with its theological implications.

Modern critics have been disturbed by the difficulty of defending Zeus's conduct, which seems to be more appropriate to a cruel tyrant than to the father of the gods, and have also been unwilling to admit that Prometheus is at fault at all. Some cannot believe that he is serious in acknowledging his guilt—ἑκὼν ἑκὼν ἥμαρτον, 266. The favourite solution is to suppose that Aeschylus represents a development in the character of Zeus, from a young, "tyrannical" god (as cruel and brutal to Prometheus as he was to his predecessor Cronos) into a more mature "father of gods and men." See, for example, L. R. Farnell, "The Paradox of the *Prometheus Vinctus*," *JHS*, 53 (1933), 40–50, and H. D. F. Kitto, "The *Prometheus*," *JHS*, 54 (1934), 14–

20. I am not convinced that this is the correct solution or that the theological problem is as serious as it is supposed to be; strictly speaking, the play is about Prometheus, not about Zeus, just as the *Oresteia* is about Orestes, not Apollo; and if there is any "development" in the Prometheus trilogy, it should be a development of human civilization and man's understanding of justice and law.

It is no solution of the problem to say that Aeschylus did not write the *Prometheus*.

11. For a statement of this view and a brief summary of earlier criticism, see H. D. Broadhead, *The Persae of Aeschylus* (Cambridge, 1960), pp. xv–xvi, xxxiii, and H. D. F. Kitto, *Greek Tragedy*, pp. 36–41.

12. Previous to this the Chorus actually blames Xerxes only in these lines:

> Ξέρξης μὲν ἄγαγεν, ποποῖ,
> Ξέρξης δ' ἀπώλεσεν, τοτοῖ,
> Ξέρξης δὲ πάντ' ἐπέσπε δυσφρόνως
> βάριδές τε πόντιαι.
>
> (550–53)

δυσφρόνως must mean "in his folly," though some critics have tried to give the word a gentler meaning (cf. Broadhead's note on these lines). There may be room for some difference of opinion over the tone which the members of the Chorus adopt towards Xerxes, when he appears, in the lyric exchanges of the closing scene; is it a tone of reproach or sympathy? Even if they address him once as μεγάλατε (1016, though the text is doubtful), they do not correct him when he excuses himself, and they neither accept nor deny his words of self-accusation. But there is no hint that he is guilty of hybris or impiety; he is not told what Darius had said about him.

13. Cf. K. Deichgräber, "Die Perser des Aischylos," *Nachr. der Akad., Göttingen, phil.-hist. Klasse*, 1941, pp. 169–78.

14. Cf. J. Bidez, "À propos des Perses d'Eschyle," *Bull. acad. royale Belg., Classe des lettres*, Ser. 5, No. 23 (1937), 213.

15. Just as an assailant in war or any other quarrel does not, as a rule, open hostilities without some justification or excuse (*prophasis*), some insult or injury which gives him an opening, and just as disease often takes advantage of some opportunity that a man offers (fatigue, weakness, an accidental fall, or exposure to rain and cold), so the gods, however angry they may be, usually wait for men to give them the occasion to strike, to offer them a *prophasis* and so preserve the illusion that it is man who is to blame for his own downfall. Cf. L. Pearson, "Prophasis and Aitia," *TAPA*, 83 (1952), 209–10.

16. Except when the members of the Chorus beg the gods "to hear them in all justice" (πανδίκως, 171), a prayer which sounds like an echo of the opening chorus in the *Suppliants*:

> ἀλλὰ θεοὶ γενέται κλύετ'
> εὖ τὸ δίκαιον ἰδόντες.
>
> (77–78)

17. And against Amphiaraus also, who is a just man but doomed by the company that he keeps; his loyalty is in part to blame, no doubt. Eteocles explains that a pious man who joins with others in an impious enterprise has no special privilege; his fate is part of dike no less than theirs:

> ἢ γὰρ ξυνεισβὰς πλοῖον εὐσεβὴς ἀνὴρ
> ναύτῃσι θερμοῖς ἐν πανουργίᾳ τινὶ
> ὄλωλεν ἀνδρῶν ξὺν θεοπτύστῳ γένει·
> ἢ ξὺν πολίταις ἀνδράσιν δίκαιος ὢν
> ἐχθροξένοις τε καὶ θεῶν ἀμνήμοσιν
> ταὐτοῦ κυρήσας ἐνδίκως ἀγρεύματος
> πληγεὶς θεοῦ μάστιγι παγκοίνῳ 'δάμη.
> (602–8)

ἐνδίκως is certainly the right reading, not ἐκδίκως.

These lines offer a good commentary on the misfortune of Pelasgus in the *Suppliants*. Either he must link himself with the Danaids, "whom the gods hate," or else he must support those of his fellow citizens who are "unmindful of the gods and hostile to strangers." He is doomed no matter which course he takes—the common scourge of the gods strikes him along with the rest.

Atossa in the *Persians* tries to excuse Xerxes by putting the blame on the company he keeps:

> ταῦτα τοῖς κακοῖς ὁμιλῶν ἀνδράσιν διδάσκεται
> θούριος Ξέρξης.
> (753–54)

The ghost of Darius ignores her remark completely. And though her explanation may be true historically, as the Herodotean account implies, the play requires the exact opposite; it does not represent a "just" Xerxes misled by dishonest advisers, but loyal advisers involved in the fate of a hybristic king. It is the Persian chorus, not Xerxes, that must be compared with Amphiaraus.

18. Cf. F. Solmsen, "The Erinys in Aischylos' *Septem*," *TAPA*, 68 (1937), 197–211.

19. J. Finley, *Pindar and Aeschylus* (Cambridge, Mass., 1955), p. 255, emphasizes the part played by contradiction in the "complex and deeply troubled outpourings" of the chorus. The war may be just because it is punishing Paris, but every act of justice mentioned in the *Agamemnon* is at the same time a guilty act, and every ostensibly just avenger is also guilty. The alternation between the themes of justice, guilt, and suffering is discussed by A. Maddalena, *Interpretazioni Eschilee* (Turin, 1953), pp. 1–6.

20. Any victory is a favour granted by the gods; so at least a victor should believe, unless he is arrogant enough to take all the credit himself. Pindar is a valuable guide here, since it was part of his professional task to praise victors without arousing the envy of their fellow countrymen or making them appear unduly arrogant themselves. In his language it is Charis or the Charites who grant the victory (for example, *Ol.* 2.55; *Nem.*

5, fin.), and Hiero's victory at Olympia is called the charis of Pisa and his horse Pherenikos (*Ol.* 1.18). The envy of others for success is always to be guarded against, even by those winners of whom it can be said that "modest Charis sheds beauty on them" (*Ol.* 6.75–76). One can imagine the consequences if Pindar were to speak of victory in the games as a dike, a judgment given by the gods that reflected discredit on the loser. Such tactlessness would quickly give him a reputation as "quarrelsome and too great a lover of victory," the reputation which he was so anxious to avoid (*Ol.* 6.19). If a victory is a judgment and not a favour of the gods, this must mean that the less fortunate competitors are judged unworthy and should be filled with shame—and it seems they did feel ashamed to meet their fellow countrymen, if we are to take seriously the harsh description of the unsuccessful athlete's return to his home in the eighth Pythian, how he lurked in alleys and found no charis in his mother's welcome. See also *Ol.* 8.67–69. Yet curiously enough, though the result is not a dike, it can be called a *krisis,* a decision by the gods: κρίνεται δ' ἀλκὰ διὰ δαίμονας ἀνδρῶν (*Isth.* 5.11).

21. Clytaemnestra also betrays her trust, denying him pistis, and it is dramatically appropriate that she is the first to introduce the motif of trust, in the message that she sends to Agamemnon by the Messenger: γυναῖκα πιστὴν δ' ἐν δόμοις εὕροι μολών (606). This cold-hearted message, filled with false praise of herself, with a specific denial that she has pilfered or enjoyed the favours of a lover, by its elaborate claim of pistis serves to underline her lack of that quality:

> So may he find at home on his return
> A loyal wife, a watchdog of the house
> To him devoted, fierce against his foes,
> The same good wife as ever otherwise.
> I broke no storeroom seal in that long time,
> I knew no joy (and none could think I did)
> From another man.
>
> (606–12)

22. Cf. the two verses known only from Aristophanes' *Frogs* and usually printed as the opening lines of his speech:

> Ἑρμῆ χθόνιε, πατρῷ' ἐποπτεύων κράτη,
> σωτὴρ γενοῦ μοι σύμμαχός τ' αἰτουμένῳ.

See also the discussion by H. D. F. Kitto, *Form and Meaning in Drama* (London, 1956), pp. 39–47. Kitto is concerned with the dramatic structure of the *Choephoroe,* and attacks vigorously and successfully the view that Orestes is shown struggling against his destiny in the first part of the play: "If we would construct, out of these scenes, an Orestes who is tragically torn between the necessity and the horror of matricide, we do it with singularly little help from the dramatist" (44). "The old bloody and hopeless conception of Dike remains unabated, and is set before us time after time, both in plain statement and in imagery. Blood for blood, slay in return, a blow for a blow, the law is proclaimed throughout by the chorus; Apollo enforces it; Orestes and Electra fully accept it, except when, at the beginning, Electra asks her question 'Is this a lawful thing to ask of the gods?' " (46).

23. I have followed Mazon in adopting Canter's emendation λαβάς for the βλαβάς of the MSS:

ἤτοι δίκην ἴαλλε σύμμαχον φίλοις,
ἢ τὰς ὁμοίας ἀντίδος λαβὰς λαβεῖν,
εἴπερ κρατηθείς γ' ἀντινικῆσαι θέλεις.

According to this reading, Orestes asks Agamemnon to help him by means of his defeat. Agamemnon, by his faults, gave Clytaemnestra an excuse for killing him, so he can justify their killing of a mother; since Clytaemnestra pointed to Cassandra, they can point to Aegisthus as their justification.

24. In the *Eumenides* (598), Orestes is still confident that his father will help him from the tomb. Is he not thinking there of the same sort of help?

25. In that case οὐκ ἄνευ δίκης means ἀπὸ δικαίας αἰτίας. Orestes claims, then, to have "a fair complaint," "a genuine grievance." In my discussion of aitia and prophasis (*TAPA*, 83, 205–23), I tried to show that *aitia* really means "complaint," that is, cause in the legal, not the scientific, sense, *due* cause not *real* cause; that it is, as it were, a weapon of offence, while *prophasis* is "explanation" or "excuse," a weapon of defence that will be useful after the deed is done (as Pindar calls *prophasis* "child of afterthought," *Pyth.* 5.28). Neither "grievances" nor "excuses" can make murder or treachery a good or just deed; they can only palliate it or explain why a man with moral scruples might commit it. They may even secure acquittal in the courts and win the sympathy of the jury and the public. Orestes seems capable of understanding the distinction between legal justification and moral right, as Athena certainly is, while the Furies and the chorus in the *Choephoroe* are both unable to grasp it.

26. καὶ τοὺς κτανόντας ἀντικατθανεῖν δίκῃ.
ταῦτ' ἐν μέσῳ τίθημι †τῆς κακῆς ἄρας†
κείνοις λέγουσα τήνδε τὴν κακὴν ἄραν.
(144–46)

The corruption in line 145 seems beyond cure. The last three words are clearly added by mistake from τὴν κακὴν ἄραν in the next line, but no really convincing supplement has been found. It may be that these two lines are not intended as part of the prayer, but as an aside to the chorus, an apology for modifying the prayer suggested by the leader of the chorus and not keeping to his instructions.

27. δακρυτὸς ἐλπὶς σπέρματος σωτηρίου. For Orestes as the hope of the house, cf. 699, 776.

28. Both Orestes and Electra are desperately in need of *kratos*—power, success, lawful authority. The word has all these implications. Orestes begs

Agamemnon to grant him "*kratos* in thy house," αἰτουμένῳ μοι δὸς κράτος τῶν σῶν δόμων (480). This is a prayer to the dead Agamemnon to give Orestes his blessing as a legitimate successor. But when Electra asks Persephone for "fair-faced *kratos*," ὦ Περσέφασσα, δὸς δέ γ' εὔμορφον κράτος (490), she means success or victory, and her language recalls Pindar, *Ol.* 1.19–21, when he tells how the horse Pherenikos won victory for Hiero, κράτει δὲ προσέμειξε δεσπόταν. A competitor at the games and the author of a triumphal ode would want a victory to be fair-faced, not marred by ill-feeling or suspicion of foul play. It is too much for Electra to expect such a victory.

29. In Sophocles' *Electra* Electra has few doubts, if any at all, and neither she nor Orestes is concerned about any distinction between justice and vengeance. But Euripides seems to have made up his mind that either brother or sister should be more scrupulous—technically scrupulous, that is—about dike (scrupulous is hardly a word that one would apply lightly to his Electra). Following the Aeschylean model, he makes Electra and Orestes pray together, asking divine help, before Orestes departs in search of Aegisthus. Unluckily it is impossible to be quite certain how the speeches in the stichomythia should be distributed among the three characters, Orestes, Electra, and the Old Man. It depends whether the order of speakers is constant or not. In Murray's Oxford text, lines 671–76 are printed as follows:

ΟΡ. ὦ Ζεῦ Πατρῷε, καὶ Τροπαῖ' ἐχθρῶν γενοῦ . . .
ΗΛ. οἴκτιρε θ' ἡμᾶς· οἰκτρὰ γὰρ πεπόνθαμεν . . .
ΠΡ. οἴκτιρε δῆτα σοὺς γε φύντας ἐκγόνους.
ΗΛ. Ἥρα τε, βωμῶν ἣ Μυκηναίων κρατεῖς . . .
ΟΡ. νίκην δὸς ἡμῖν, εἰ δίκαι' αἰτούμεθα.
ΠΡ. δὸς δῆτα πατρὸς τοῖσδε τιμωρὸν δίκην.

Murray argues that the prayer to Hera comes more appropriately from Electra than Orestes (see the note in Denniston's edition). And Zürcher, *Die Darstellung des Menschen im Drama des Euripides* (Basle, 1947), p. 110 and n. 7, is anxious that Orestes should represent the "traditional factor" of dike. Parmentier, in the Budé text, keeps the order of speakers constant, so that Orestes prays to Hera and Electra qualifies his prayer by saying "if what we ask is just." In lines 583–84 Murray follows manuscript tradition, which gives them to Orestes:

πέποιθα δ'· ἢ χρὴ μηκέθ' ἡγεῖσθαι θεούς,
εἰ τἄδικ' ἔσται τῆς δίκης ὑπέρτερα.

Zürcher agrees with him, but Parmentier follows Victorius in assigning them to Electra. My own preference would be to follow Parmentier. It is certainly Electra who greets the announcement of Aegisthus's death with the cry: ὦ θεοὶ Δίκη τε πάνθ' ὁρῶσ', ἦλθές ποτε (771), and it would be in keeping with the Aeschylean model if Electra were more preoccupied with dike than Orestes, except in the closing scenes of the play.

If the lines that involve dike are both given to Electra, the attitude of Orestes is then found remarkably similar to his attitude in the *Choephoroe*. He has little to say of dike, but more about *timoria*, "requital." He says in his opening speech that he has come to Argos φόνον φονεῦσι πατρὸς ἀλλάξων ἐμοῦ (89), and to the servants of the house whom he faces after he has killed Aegisthus he makes no plea of justice but only of *timoria*: φονέα δὲ πατρὸς ἀντετιμωρησάμην (849). It is Electra who, at the end of her outburst against the dead Aegisthus, speaks of Justice winning the victory (955). The thought of dike occurs to Orestes only when he begins to flinch at the prospect of killing Clytaemnestra—and it occurs as something that might overtake *himself*: ἐγὼ δὲ μητρός—τῷ φόνου δώσω δίκας; (977). Electra replies with the reminder that *timoria* is an obligation: τῷ δ' ἢν πατρῴαν διαμεθῇς τιμωρίαν; (978). In her *agon* with Clytaemnestra she claims to reject the principle of *timoria*, but the audience will remember that in fact she believes in it:

εἰ δ' ἀμείψεται
φόνον δικάζων φόνος, ἀποκτενῶ σ' ἐγὼ
καὶ παῖς 'Ορέστης πατρὶ τιμωρούμενοι·
εἰ γὰρ δίκαι' ἐκεῖνα καὶ τάδ' ἔνδικα.
(1093–96)

Comparison with Aeschylus is no longer possible here, since Electra is no longer on the stage at this point in the *Choephoroe*. But cf. Sophocles, *Electra* 577–83.

30. τί τῶνδ' εὖ, τί δ' ἄτερ κακῶν;
οὐκ ἀτρίακτος ἄτα;

Her words are an echo of those that the chorus puts in Agamemnon's mouth:

τί τῶνδ' ἄνευ κακῶν;
πῶς λιπόναυς γένωμαι
ξυμμαχίας ἁμαρτών;
παυσανέμου γὰρ θυσίας
παρθενίου θ' αἵματος ὀρ-
γᾷ περιοργῶς ἐπιθυ-
μεῖν θέμις. εὖ γὰρ εἴη.
(*Ag*. 211–17)

31. Unluckily the text of the final strophe (639–45), in which their comments begin, is badly corrupted, and no complete translation is possible, though the last two lines seem to make it clear that they who wield the sword cast aside all respect for Zeus:

τὸ πᾶν Διὸς
σέβας παρεκβάντες οὐ θεμίστως.
(644–45)

The following translation of the whole stanza is offered by Lattimore, *Aeschylus, Oresteia* (Chicago, 1953):

> The sword edges near the lungs.
> It stabs deep, bittersharp,
> And right drives it. For that which had no right
> Lies not yet stamped into the ground, although
> One in sin transgressed Zeus' majesty.

This version can scarcely be justified as a fair translation, and it must not be used as a basis for argument. Unfortunately, it has led the translator himself to render ἐπίμομφον ἄταν (830) as "innocent murder."

32. With grim irony, Clytaemnestra's offer of hospitality to the presumed stranger, who is Orestes in disguise, includes:

> Warm baths, a couch to charm away the ache
> Of weariness, a welcome of just eyes.
>
> (670–71)

These are exactly what she did not offer to Agamemnon. The welcome of "just eyes" (δικαίων ὀμμάτων παρουσία) for Agamemnon meant the stern glance of revenge—which will be turned back on her. She is, as it were, justifying her own death.

33.
> νῦν γὰρ ἀκμάζει Πειθὼ δολίαν
> ξυγκαταβῆναι, χθόνιον δ' Ἑρμῆν
> καὶ τὸν Νύχιον τοῖσδ' ἐφοδεῦσαι
> ξιφοδηλήτοισιν ἀγῶσιν.

This is an echo of *Ag.* 385–86:

> βιᾶται δ' ἁ τάλαινα Πειθῶ,
> προβούλου παῖς ἄφερτος ἄτας.

34. They claim to be εὐμήχανοί τε καὶ τέλειοι (383), and they call their verdict final:

> τίς οὖν τάδ' οὐχ ἅζεταί
> τε καὶ δέδοικεν βροτῶν,
> ἐμοῦ κλύων θεσμὸν
> τὸν μοιρόκραντον ἐκ θεῶν
> δοθέντα τέλεον;
>
> (388–92)

35. Athena and Apollo, therefore, cannot of themselves solve the problem, though Athena (representing Athenian law) can set up the machinery and Apollo can lay down the religious prerequisites of purification. The issue of the *Oresteia* goes beyond the legal issue of the crime of matricide and the religious issue of bloodguilt; but it is hard to believe that Delphic influence or teaching goes beyond the religious issue into the more theo-

retical realm of ethics. The supposed Delphic origin of the Orestes legend is another matter altogether. Cf. J. Defradas, *Les Thèmes de la propagande delphique* (Paris, 1954), pp. 160–204, who cites earlier literature.

36. The same verdict appears again in the *Orestes*: "Justly, yes, but an ugly deed" (δίκᾳ μέν, καλῶς δ' οὔ, 149). Plato, in the *Gorgias,* shows his disagreement with this type of reasoning when he insists that what the patient suffers must be similar in kind to what the agent does, and that nothing just can be ugly (476a–d). This is part of his proof that to suffer just punishment is better than to go unpunished. He knows that the world thinks otherwise, that most people will refuse to regard just punishment as a benefit. His idea of justice is different from the popular view; but it is noteworthy that he does not take time to make any distinction between justice and just revenge. The issue which seems so vital to the *Oresteia,* but can be dismissed in a few words by Euripides, is not even noticed by Plato.

CHAPTER FIVE

1. The classic discussion of friendship is in Books viii and ix of the *Nicomachean Ethics.* One hesitates to criticize Aristotle for neglecting the obvious, but it would have been helpful if he had said: "Friendship is a relationship of mutual respect and obligation" (it is doubtful if any other Greek writer could have found the language in which to express such an idea). In addition to Aristotle and his commentators (especially G. Percival, *Aristotle on Friendship* [Cambridge, 1940]), the Greek idea of friendship has been discussed by L. Dugas, *L'Amitié antique* (2d ed.; Paris, 1914), and most recently by J. Ferguson, *Moral Values in the Ancient World* (New York, 1959), esp. pp. 74–75. The insistence of the Epicureans on friendship is well known and calls for no special discussion here.

2. The hope that an act of kindness will somehow be rewarded need not lead us to believe that the Greek attitude was as selfish as some modern interpreters maintain. A generous Christian does not, to most people at least, seem the less unselfish because he believes that God will reward his act of charity; nor is it a serious weakness in modern morality if it preaches that "Crime does not pay," or if a man who helps his neighbour tells him "You may do the same for me some day." Snell, *Discovery of the Mind,* p. 168, overstates the case when he writes: "The Athenian *bouzygeioi arai,* for instance, decree that a traveller must be shown the right way, that a neighbour be given fire if he asks for it, that a newly-found corpse should be buried, and so forth. On the whole the Greeks were comparatively chary of proposing that people should shoulder inconveniences for the purpose of helping others. The commandments which we have mentioned specify assistance in particular emergencies only. They are plausible enough, because anyone might find himself in a similar situation; it is pure self-interest, therefore, to support such rulings. The principle: *do ut des* applies to all of them in equal force. Certainly the Greeks did not admit to a universal law which required them to love their neighbour, or to feeling any great responsibility towards their fellow-humans."

Cf. J. Ferguson, *Moral Values,* p. 64: "Aristotle is unusual among Greek theorists in laying some stress upon the other-regarding, altruistic aspect of friendship. In fact it is rare elsewhere in his own writings or indeed elsewhere in the *Ethics* to find this mentioned. Here (*Nic. Eth.* viii. 1159a) he says explicitly that friendship consists rather in giving than receiving affection, and in benefiting the friend for his own sake, though if there is not reciprocity it is goodwill rather than friendship."

Perhaps the point can be made by saying that the Greeks used the word *philia* to describe a relationship, not an emotion or a virtue. Though Aristotle does reckon friendship as an arete, it is arguable that he means something more like a "blessing" than a "virtue" (cf. the opening sentence of Bk. viii, quoted in n. 3 below).

3. The strongest remarks on this subject are to be found in the opening paragraph of Aristotle, *Nic. Eth.* viii: "No man would choose to live without friends, even if he had no other advantages; and friends are especially necessary to rich men and those who hold office or positions of power."

4. The exaggerated idealism of the *Cyropaedia* is perhaps not in keeping with practical politics, and the constant emphasis on Cyrus's attempts to win friends and please his subjects is at times almost nauseating. Latin writers, who are less sentimental and more realistic where exercise of authority is concerned, show little respect for military commanders who try too hard to win the popularity of their men. Tacitus, for example, shows no surprise at the dismal failure of Trebellius Maximus in Britain when he tries to rule his province by kindness—"comitate quadam curandi" (*Agricola* 16).

5. I have discussed this inability of Herodotus to give consistent characterization in "Real and Conventional Personalities in Greek History," *JHI,* 15 (1954), 136–45. Herodotus gives one example of rather barbaric cruelty on Darius's part. A Persian, Oeobazus, who had three sons in the army that was setting out for the Scythian expedition, asked that one might be left behind; instead of merely refusing him, Darius said that all three sons should be left behind—and ordered all three to be killed before the expedition started (iv. 84). Herodotus neither doubts nor attempts to explain this gruesome humour, which would need no explanation if it were told of Cambyses, who is said (v. 25) to have killed a judge whom he found guilty of giving corrupt judgments and to have used his tanned skin as leather to make a judge's chair—and then to have appointed the dead man's son to sit on the chair as judge and remember what had happened to his father.

6. The point appears not to have been noticed by critics, who have been more interested in the political than the ethical theory of the speeches; and the question has been raised whether Herodotus was borrowing ideas from some political pamphlet. See P. Legrand, *Hérodote, Histoires,* III (Budé ed.), 106–8; W. Nestle, *Herodots Verhältnis zur Philosophie und Sophistik* (Schöntal, 1908), and "Gab es eine ionische Sophistik?" *Philologus,* 70 (1911), 252–57.

The speech of Darius might well be matched with Haemon's speech in reply to Creon in the *Antigone,* 683–723, when he finds fault with his father for insisting exclusively on a single political or ethical principle (obedience to authority), excellent and theoretically irrefutable though the theory is in itself:

> ἐγὼ δ' ὅπως σὺ μὴ λέγεις ὀρθῶς τάδε
> οὔτ' ἂν δυναίμην μήτ' ἐπισταίμην λέγειν.
> γένοιτο μέντ' ἂν χἀτέρῳ καλῶς ἔχον
> (685–87)

> (I cannot—I would rather lack the wit—
> I cannot tell thee how thy thoughts are wrong;
> And yet some other's thoughts might well be right).

He is more explicit in 705–6:

> μὴ νῦν ἓν ἦθος μοῦνον ἐν σαυτῷ φόρει,
> ὡς φῂς σύ, κοὐδὲν ἄλλο, τοῦτ' ὀρθῶς ἔχειν

> (Thou must not keep one rule alone in sight—
> The rule that "What I say is always right").

Perhaps a paraphrase would be safer than a translation. E. Schwartz, *Ethik der Griechen* (Stuttgart, 1951), p. 15, notes the "very peculiar" use of the word *ethos* here, remarking that Sophocles is the most individual of the dramatists in his use of language. Haemon asks his father not to carry only one *ethos* in his mind, not to be guided exclusively by the principle that "Right is what the king says," but to remember that there may be circumstances when this rule of conduct will not apply.

7. So also it is a Persian, Mardonius, who finds fault with the "foolish way in which the Greeks wage war"—how they assemble in the largest and most level plain, with the result that at the end of the battle even the victors are in a bad way (Hdt. vii.9).

8. Cf., for example, H. D. F. Kitto, *Greek Tragedy*, pp. 215–21; G. Norwood, *Greek Tragedy* (2d ed.; London, 1928); J. A. Spranger, "The Problem of the *Hecuba*," *CQ*, 21 (1927), 155–58. For some replies to these criticisms, see G. M. Grube, *The Drama of Euripides* (London, 1941), pp. 82–84, 93–97, 214–28.

9. Cf. the scornful description of a politician in a democratic city by the Theban herald in the *Suppliant Women*:

> τὸ δ' αὐτίχ' ἡδὺς καὶ διδοὺς πολλὴν χάριν,
> ἐσαῦθις ἔβλαψ', εἶτα διαβολαῖς νέαις
> κλέψας τὰ πρόσθε σφάλματ' ἐξέδυ δίκης.
> (414–16)

10. Louise Matthaei, *Studies in Greek Tragedy* (Cambridge, 1918), chap. iv, has argued that the play is concerned with a conflict between the society and the individual, the justice of the community and the justice of the individual. This might be possible if an Athenian audience had been prepared to take a sort of anthropologist's view of the Homeric age, as a time when human sacrifice was a normal demand for the state to make of

an individual. She is technically correct in saying that there was no controversy about human sacrifice in Athens, no Anti-Human-Sacrifice Society (p. 129); but this does not alter the fact that it was something that inspired horror, which no one would seriously attempt to justify. Cf. E. L. Abrahamson, "Euripides' Tragedy of Hecuba," *TAPA,* 83 (1952), 120–29, esp. n. 10.

G. M. Kirkwood, "Hecuba and Nomos," *TAPA,* 78 (1947), 61–68, thinks that the play shows the transformation from a Hecuba who recognizes Nomos (law) and submits to it—a character of restraint and stability—to a "vengeful Hecuba, the fiend incarnate," who in her plea to Agamemnon throws aside the restraint of Nomos entirely. What seems curious, to me at least, is that Kirkwood regards the sacrifice of Polyxena by the Greeks as made "in obedience to the demands of Nomos" (p. 64), and he is not quite sure whether Euripides condemns this obedience or not. He adds, in a note: "The unfeeling smugness of Odysseus' manner seems to me to suggest Euripides' condemnation." But Odysseus is not merely smug. His manner of argument is patently false; it is indeed a good Nomos to honour the heroic dead, but not by human sacrifice; there is nothing wrong with the Nomos, but the application of it is unacceptable. Cleon was not successful in arguing that Nomos demanded the massacre of the Mytilenians; at Melos the Athenians never attempted to use any such argument.

11. Kirkwood distinguishes the two sides of Hecuba's plea as made in the name of Nomos and of Peitho (as though her plea started by being legitimate and she lost all scruples when her appeal to Nomos failed). He does not distinguish between dike and charis, though Agamemnon makes the distinction very clearly (850–56). Agamemnon admits that her plea is just (it is unreasonable to say he is unmoved), but he can see no practical way of granting it; it seems he had taken a similar attitude to Achilles' request (120–22), but had been overruled. In a recent article, D. J. Conacher, "Euripides' *Hecuba,*" *AJP,* 82 (1961), 1–26, has some good answers to earlier critics and recognizes the contrast between charis and dike.

12. The interpretation of the *Hecuba* by J. H. Oliver, *Demokratia, the Gods, and the Free World* (Baltimore, 1960), chap. iii, did not come to my notice until this chapter was in the final stages of revision. Both Oliver and Conacher recognize that the theme of charis plays an important part (though neither shows how it creates the whole pattern of the play); but they are not content to take it in the sense of "favour" or "gratitude," and claim to find "a kind of dialectic" on the word, which Oliver (p. 102) interprets as "a contrast between the base *charis* of an *achariston* race and the noble *charis* of the true *charientes.*" Oliver also cites the constant allusions to charis in the *Agamemnon* (see above, pp. 112–16) and finds some connexion with the cult of the Graces. This is unnecessarily complex, since the issue in the play does not concern different kinds of charis, but rather the occasion or manner in which charis should be shown or withheld.

By way of final comment, it may be worth while to mention two Attic inscriptions (3d century B.C.), which follow one another at the beginning of Vol. III of Dittenberger, *SIG*³ (911, 912). The first records a vote of thanks to Antisthenes because he has kept a careful eye on the properties of the

Erechtheid tribe, "not thinking charis towards anyone more important than the interest of the tribe and not accepting gifts from anyone." In the second a crown is conferred upon Callidamas for his services to the community of Piraeus, and the purpose of the resolution is stated: "So that all may recognize that the people of Piraeus knows how to return due *charites*." Charis is inappropriate in a public official who has to make judicial decisions; it is appropriate in encouraging public spirit and generosity.

13. See R. C. Jebb, *Attic Orators,* I, 58–59; F. Blass, *Die attische Beredsamkeit,* I, 166.

14. A fragment from a lost play, quoted in Aristophanes, *Frogs* 1392.

15. Cf., for example, Plutarch's essay, "How to Distinguish a Flatterer from a Friend."

16. Cf., for example, Dem. iii.21, iv.51.

17. 108.3–4: "The cities subject to the Athenians, when they heard of the fall of Amphipolis and the offers that were being made and the friendly attitude of Brasidas, were more than ever stimulated to take the initiative in deserting Athens; they sent messengers to him secretly, inviting him to come to them, each city anxious to anticipate the other in the act of secession. The fact is that they thought they had nothing to fear; but they were mistaken about the extent of Athenian power, as it was subsequently revealed, and for the most part their judgment was based on vague wishful thinking rather than sound foresight; it is the habit of men, when they want something, to let rash hopes take control and to thrust aside details that they do not like with imperious argument" (εἰωθότες οἱ ἄνθρωποι οὗ μὲν ἐπιθυμοῦσιν ἐλπίδι ἀπερισκέπτῳ διδόναι, ὃ δὲ μὴ προσίενται λογισμῷ αὐτοκράτορι διωθεῖσθαι).

The language is difficult and compressed. Thucydides appears to mean that when men are faced with an offer that is superficially attractive, their hopes rather than their fears decide their choice—they ignore the possible dangers and disadvantages, and develop irrefutable arguments to show that they do not exist.

18. G. A. Kennedy, "Focusing of Arguments in Greek Deliberative Oratory," *TAPA,* 90 (1959), 131–38, points out that speakers in Thucydides usually appeal either to the just and honourable or to the expedient, but do not commonly combine both arguments; and he adds that "in successful speeches most frequently the center of attention is the expedient" (131). The speeches of Brasidas, which he does not discuss, offer a notable exception to his general rule, and it seems to me that he has underestimated the degree of "moral sensitivity," as he calls it (133), which Thucydidean speakers expect from their audiences.

CHAPTER SIX

1. In a speech of Lysias (7.20), the defendant speculates on the possible motives of the prosecutor—the wish to harm an enemy, help the city, or enrich himself—and points out how he missed his opportunity, no matter what his motive was: "You ought to have summoned the persons present

as witnesses, and made the matter clear at the time. You would have left me no means of defence, and (if I were an enemy of yours) you would have taken vengeance on me in this way; if you were acting in the interests of the city, you would have proved my guilt and not won the reputation of a dishonest accuser; and if profit was your object, then was the time when you would have obtained the most, because, with the matter plainly revealed, I would think I had no hope of saving myself except by paying you off."

2. See L. Pearson, "Three Notes on the Funeral Oration of Pericles," *AJP*, 64 (1943), 399–404, for a defence of this interpretation. Others would prefer "thinking fit even to die in the act of resistance rather than to save themselves by surrender," as a version of ἐν αὐτῷ τῷ ἀμύνεσθαι καὶ παθεῖν μᾶλλον ἡγησάμενοι ἢ ἐνδόντες σῴζεσθαι (Thuc. ii.42.4). For a less heroic defence of self-sacrifice compare the final argument of Diodotus in his reply to Cleon: he claims that it is more expedient to submit willingly to injustice than to claim one's right by killing men whom one should not kill: ξυμφορώτερον ἡγοῦμαι . . . ἑκόντας ἡμᾶς ἀδικηθῆναι ἢ δικαίως οὓς μὴ δεῖ διαφθεῖραι (Thuc. iii.47.5).

3. A contemporary epitaph on men killed in the war says that "they exchanged their lives in return for arete,"

ψυχὰς δ' ἀντίρροπα θέντες
ἤλλαξαντ' ἀρετήν.
(Tod, *Greek Historical Inscriptions*, I, 59)

The suggestion that their death was a kind of deliberate transaction, with an eye to their subsequent fame, is not intended to diminish its merit. It is useful to remember that formal praise of what we should call self-sacrifice can be so expressed, whenever we are disposed to think that Greeks who helped others were really motivated in the main by self-interest (see above, p. 136, and n. 1).

Taken out of context, the argument of Pericles might strike some modern readers as an artificial paradox, or the suggestion that death is better than life might be taken as an indication of "pessimism in Greek thought." Schwartz, *Ethik der Griechen*, pp. 58–65, shows convincingly that both these conclusions are unjustified. A man does not *wish* to die unless life has lost its savour for him; but under certain circumstances he is *willing* to die, knowing that death must come sooner or later, and that like any misfortune, it will be less bitter if it comes at the right time (cf. above, p. 70). To think that he can escape misfortune in life altogether is pure "witlessness"; the only way to escape is never to be born at all (and so, logically, this is the greatest blessing man can have) or else to die quickly before any suffering falls to his lot, as the chorus of Athenian old men proclaim in the *Oedipus at Colonus* (1225–28) to show what folly it is to wish for a long life. Schwartz comments (p. 64): "Solche Bekenntnisse soll man nicht als Pessimismus werten; die sie geäussert haben, waren allem Menschlichen sehr zugeneigt; sie haben das Leben ergriffen, wo es sich bot.

Viel mehr als einem faulen Pessimismus und mönchischen Lästern über die sonnige Welt entspringen sie dem Bestreben, dieses Leben nicht über sich Herr werden zu lassen, es zügeln zu können." A more "pessimistic" interpretation will be found in J. C. Opstelten, *Sophocles and Greek Pessimism* (Eng. trans.; Amsterdam, 1952), chap. vi.

4. Pericles does not neglect the element of charis that there is in real patriotism; he goes on to tell his hearers that they must look upon the splendour of Athens and become "passionate lovers" (*erastai*) of their city (Thuc. ii.43.1). This should remind them that the glorious gift which the dead offered Athens in dying for her (κάλλιστον ἔρανον αὐτῇ προιέμενοι) was not given in a spirit of pure calculation.

5. Just as the argument from justice can be misused, so also can the argument from sophrosyne—the most prudent, sensible course may, on occasion, be morally reprehensible, as Sthenelaidas maintained. The result is that sophron, as an adjective, sometimes takes on the meaning of an undesirable quality; it means something like selfish, self-seeking, morally obtuse. But Helen North, "A Period of Opposition to *Sophrosyne* in Greek Thought," *TAPA,* 78 (1947), 1–17, is not justified, it seems to me, in concluding that the meaning of the word suffered any real change in connotation during the Peloponnesian War; it would be equally wrong to draw any serious conclusions from current expressions like "Don't be so damned sensible!" Particular circumstances could even induce a speaker to argue that sophrosyne was the last refuge of a scoundrel, and a cowardly scoundrel at that; and there are certainly times when one cannot be strictly just without also being imprudent.

6. Cf. E. Delebecque, *Euripide et la guerre du Péloponnèse* (Paris, 1951), Part II, chap. i, esp. pp. 65–66.

7. δίκαια μὲν ἐν τῷ ἀνθρωπείῳ λόγῳ ἀπὸ τῆς ἴσης ἀνάγκης κρίνεται, δυνατὰ δὲ οἱ προὔχοντες πράσσουσι καὶ οἱ ἀσθενεῖς συγχωροῦσιν.

An accurate translation that keeps the form of the Greek is not easily made. An alternative version might be: "Justice is an issue only when external pressure is equally strong on both parties; it is only possibility that matters when the strong want to impose their will and the weak submit." For further comment on this passage, see G. Méautis, "Le Dialogue des Athéniens et des Méliens," *Revue des études grecques,* 48 (1935), 250–78.

8. An Athenian who disliked democratic institutions or a foreigner who found himself pleading a case in an Athenian court might be tempted to say, in exasperation, that Athenian juries always took this attitude, that they were only interested in getting money for the Athenian treasury. This in fact is exactly what the Old Oligarch says, [Ps. Xen.] *Resp. Ath.* 1.13: "In the law courts they are not so much concerned with justice as with their own interest." He does not say that juries did not know the difference between justice and the interest of the democratic majority. One might think that Aristophanes was accusing them of this sort of moral obtuseness, if the *Wasps* was a political tract; but it is, after all, a comedy, supposed to amuse the *demos,* not to make them angry.

9. Theognis (401–4) could have provided Neoptolemus with a ready-made reply, warning him that it was a mistake to seek arete at any price. See above, pp. 73–74.

CHAPTER SEVEN

1. G. H. Sabine, *A History of Political Theory* (New York, 1937), is content to say that since analysis of Greek political life "runs necessarily in terms of services and not of powers," "the notion of authority or sovereign power, such as the Roman attached to his magistrates, has practically no part in Plato's political theory, nor indeed in that of any Greek philosopher" (p. 55). And W. W. Willoughby, *The Political Theories of the Ancient World* (New York, 1903), is satisfied that once Greeks accepted the *polis* as necessary for man's well-being, "it did not and, in fact, until the rise of sophistic scepticism, it could not, occur to the Greeks to seek further for a justification of the state's right to be" (pp. 55–60).

2. A notable example is the resolution honouring Bulagoras of Samos, in the middle of the third century (*Supp. Epig. Graec.* I, 366). After enumerating his many acts of generosity and public service, the formal resolution runs: "In order to make it clear that we also respect good men and invite large numbers of our fellow citizens to follow his example, be it resolved to crown Bulagoras with a golden crown, etc."

3. Demosthenes, in a famous passage in the speech "On the Crown" (47–49), insists that the gold which traitors receive for their services does not really benefit them, and that when they escape the fate that they deserve, it is because worthy citizens prevent their treacherous designs from being completed.

4. But cf. Sophocles, *Phil.* 386–88, when Neoptolemus is still acting the part that Odysseus made up for him:

> πόλις γάρ ἐστι πᾶσα τῶν ἡγουμένων
> στρατός τε σύμπας· οἱ δ' ἀκοσμοῦντες βροτῶν
> διδασκάλων λόγοισι γίγνονται κακοί.

5. Many years later Euripides, in the *Orestes,* represents Tyndareus as holding this same view; he thinks Menelaus must have become barbarized if he has forgotten the great principle of Greek civilization, "not to wish to set oneself above the law" (καὶ τῶν νόμων γε μὴ πρότερον εἶναι θέλειν, *Or.* 487). Tyndareus does not understand how Menelaus or any intelligent man can defend the violent action of Orestes: all that Orestes had to do was bring Clytaemnestra into court! (491–503.) But Tyndareus is a Spartan and unusually stupid even by Spartan standards, and it is hardly fair to compare him with men like king Archidamus; Menelaus, in Sophocles' *Ajax* (see p. 194), offers a better parallel. Cf. J. H. Finley, "Euripides and Thucydides," *HSCP,* 49 (1938), 34–35.

6. Cf. V. Ehrenberg, *Sophocles and Pericles* (Oxford, 1954), pp. 105–10.

7. One might expect that the need for considering "the interest of the

stronger" and combining this with good will towards the weaker (and Athens' failure in this respect) would be particularly keenly appreciated in Delos. It is interesting that a Delian inscription (*Orientis Graeci Insc. Sel.* *40*) from the time of Ptolemy II commends a certain Theon because "he furthers the interest of the king and shows constant good will towards the islanders." Cf. also *OGIS* 41, 42 (arete and pistis commended in Cos), and 44 (arete and eunoia in Thera).

8. v.89. For Greek text and suggested translations, see p. 251, n. 7.

9. Cf. *Ajax* 666–70:

> τοιγὰρ τὸ λοιπὸν εἰσόμεσθα μὲν θεοῖς
> εἴκειν, μαθησόμεσθα δ' Ἀτρείδας σέβειν.
> ἄρχοντές εἰσιν, ὥσθ' ὑπεικτέον. τί μήν;
> καὶ γὰρ τὰ δεινὰ καὶ τὰ καρτερώτατα
> τιμαῖς ὑπείκει.

10. Cf. the comment of E. Schwartz, *Das Geschichtswerk des Thukydides* (2d ed.; Bonn, 1929), pp. 351–56.

11. Ajax is a serious character, and though we may think his attitude exaggerated he still deserves our respect. In contrast to him, Helen, in the *Helena* of Euripides, makes herself somewhat ridiculous by her declaration that, since her reputation is ruined, it would be better for her to die, and to die καλῶς (298). Lines 299–302, in which she compares the different forms of suicide, deciding that hanging is unseemly and fit for a slave, but death by the knife is worthier, have been deleted as spurious by some critics. They are, however, quite appropriate if Helen is intended as a sort of caricature of Ajax. Menelaus, in his vanity, cuts an equally ridiculous figure, ashamed to speak to anyone because he has no decent clothes to wear.

12. Cf. K. von Fritz, "Zur Interpretation des Aias," *Rh. Mus.* 83 (1934), pp. 113–28, who shows, in reply to W. Schadewaldt, *Aias und Antigone* (Berlin, 1929), that though Ajax is disillusioned about the world, in Sophocles' play he does not suffer a change of character; he learns not that he was or is in the wrong, but that it is impossible for him, being what he is, to remain in the world. He has lived hitherto by "clear and simple rules," and is quite incapable of adapting to any incident for which they make no provision. A less stubborn character might simply throw all rules overboard and live henceforth by the rule of expediency.

13. An interesting parallel is suggested by the story in Herodotus (iii.120) of Oroetes, the Persian satrap who determined to destroy Polycrates and conquer Samos himself, because Mitradates questioned his arete if he let Polycrates survive. The issue of charis did not concern him at all. Polycrates had done him no harm such as might justify his attack; according to the prevalent version, therefore, his attack was "an unholy thing" (cf. Chap. Five, p. 142); an alternative version maintained that Polycrates had in fact insulted him by refusing to listen to his emissary (121). His undue desire for arete leads him to hybris (126–27).

14. Cf. C. H. Whitman, *Sophocles* (Harvard, 1951): "The heroic as-

sumption means precisely this: the possession of a standard which becomes a kind of fatal necessity that drives toward self-destruction. It is this which made Achilles 'godlike' to Homer and which prompted the *Ajax* of Sophocles. The long-continued Wrath of Achilles might by some be called hybris, but it is also a defense of arete. It seems excessive and culpable only if one's standard is life and common sense; if one's standard is arete, it is an inevitable course. The true Greek hero raises the standard of his own excellence so high that he is no longer appropriate to life" (p. 73). I cannot, however, accept Whitman's argument that the *Ajax* is "one long paean of triumphant individualism" (p. 79), or that "it represents the triumph not of unleashed and unguided individualism, but of the disciplined individual whose guide is inner law" (p. 80). Sophocles could not have written the *Ajax* without feeling sympathy for his hero, but that does not mean that he credited him with a particularly "clear vision" that brought him "near to the gods" and "near the center of the world order" (73–74).

15. The distinction is emphasized in various places in Greek literature. An interesting example is Hdt. iii.83. The seven Persian conspirators decide, by majority vote, to establish a monarchy rather than an aristocracy or democracy, but Otanes, who is opposed to monarchy, is granted the special privilege for himself and his descendants, that "they shall be free, submitting to authority only as much as they wish, but not violating the laws of the Persians"—thus they are subject to law, but not to authority.

16. "Die griechische Staatsethik im Zeitalter des Platon," (Festrede, Berlin, Jan. 18, 1924), p. 10.

INDEX

INDEX